Michael Reiss

Change Management

A Balanced and Blended Approach

Michael Reiss is Full Professor of Organizational Design and Behavior at the University of Stuttgart (http://www.bwi.uni-stuttgart.de/lfo). He is author of more than 350 publications on strategic organization, networks, change management, business relationship management, controlling and leadership.

Change Management

A Balanced and Blended Approach

Michael Reiss

The Deutsche Nationalbibliothek registers this publication in the Deutsche Nationalbibliografie; detailed biliographical data are available on the Internet under dnb.d-nb.de.

Production: Books on Demand GmbH, Norderstedt

ISBN 9783844804133

Brief contents

Contents

Acknowledgments

I want to thank the team of the department of Organizational Design and Behavior at the University of Stuttgart, Germany, for their assistance. Special thanks go to Frank Ehrenmann (Graduate School of advanced Manufacturing Engineering) for his well-grounded feedbacks to several drafts and to Armin Guenther for professionally organizing the production process.

The publication predominantly contains the author's ideas about blended and balanced approaches to change management. The book does not contain quotes or exhibits (figures) imported from other publications. The existing approaches to change management, both "blended" and "straight" ones, are characterized from the author's perspective rather than from the perspective of the respective sources. The author's views in this book consider numerous feedbacks from colleagues, students, and practitioners received over some twenty years in response to prior publications and to the teaching activities of the author. Across the board, none of these inputs originates from members of some community of followers (let alone soul mates) of the BxB-approaches or nearby approaches.

This book is conceived as an electronic publication (e-book) accompanied by a print version. The handling of the publication is facilitated by

– a glossary of fundamental terms (appendix F)

– a list of sources (print and electronic), and

– available standard search devices, to be applied both for browsing inside the e-book and for Internet access to sources outside of the book (e.g. search engines).

The author is exclusively responsible for the content of this book. Not being a native English writer, I apologize for all the harm that is done to the English language by this publication.

In case you have any comments, you are welcome to contact me by e-mail: michael.reiss@bwi.uni-stuttgart.de

Stuttgart, March 2012

Michael Reiss

Introduction

Googling "Changing the way we change" gets something like 1.680.000 hits, not to mention "Change Management" with 25.400.000, let alone "change" with 3.600.000.000hits. These (unquestionably superficial) results do not signal any real demand for another publication on change management. They also give everybody a hard time to imagine that there is any space for some "new approach". On the other hand, academic authors, being permanently exposed to the publish-or-perish-threat, are nonetheless willing to search for some niche – as tiny as it may be – even on some highly frequented and possibly exploited terrain.

The niche of this publication has been spotted by some pragmatic reasoning. It constitutes the conclusion derived from a specific way of handling the - well-known - fact that we are living in a second best world or beta world, which also holds for managing change. For want of "the" better world of change management, some *blending* of existing second best worlds is proposed. The blended approach is more than a multi-paradigmatic perspective that merely reflects the *coexistence* of several models. Moreover, blending is not about combining similar or homogenous approaches, but about coupling opposites, such as evolutionary and revolutionary changes. This operation creates *hybrid* approaches, composed of antithetic components such as "soft" and "hard" tools or "physical" and "virtual" environments. In addition, the approach outlined in this book intends to *balance* diverse, sometimes even polar performance criteria pursued in change management. First and foremost, this means managing both *opportunities and risks* in a balanced fashion. The existence of manifold risks for change projects (due to resistance, inertia or confusion) impacts the performance prospects of change management: excellence appears to be less realistic than *resilience*. In conjunction with a balanced approach of handling risks and opportunities, a framework of *balanced resilience* evolves. This *BR framework* is focused on managing two categories of barriers: the (dismantling of) barriers to success as a contribution to opportunity management and the (building-up of) barriers to failure as a contribution to risk management. The combination of blending tools and balancing objectives defines the *balanced and blended approach* or *BxB approach* to change management that is developed in this book. This framework does not explore a realm of managing change – quite often characterized as "Change Management 2.0" - that lies beyond the familiar approaches. Instead, it operates on a (slightly modified) tetra-lemma logic: together with some approach X, there is not only its opposite non-X, but also the conjunction (or blend) of the two. Moreover, it adopts the strategies of (organizational) bricolage by relying on already existing ingredients instead of searching for something completely novel.

No blending operations can automatically create a best-of-both-worlds constellation. Against this background, it is some piece of cake for critics to detect the weak points of the BxB-approach: the list of cons most likely entails arguments such as "uncreative middle of the road", "oxymoron", "wishy-washy", "garbage-in, garbage out" or "doomed to get stuck in the middle". The author, being aware of these (but most certainly not all) drawbacks of his model, has incorporated them by means of a *balanced evaluation* of the pros and cons of hybrid approaches to change management.

Blending activities are only interesting for people (e.g. readers) who are familiar with at least some of the existing beta worlds of change management as well as their standard challenges. Hence, this publication is not recommendable (as a textbook) for beginners in the field of change management, let alone of management in general.

The core content of the book is structured in six chapters: In chapter 1 ("The Nature of Change and Management of Change"), the basics in terms of explications, scope and relevance of change and managing change are provided. Chapter 2 ("Performance Measurement and Management in Change Management") introduces the fundamental building blocks of the balanced approach, i.e. performance dimensions and the determinants of performance in terms of factors and barriers. Chapter 3 ("Paradigms, Patterns, and Parameters of Change Management") is dedicated to the three-level analysis and design of change management, ranging from (comparatively) intangible principles and philosophies to tangible tools. Chapter 4 ("Domains of Change Management") deals with the characteristic operational constituents of change management: processes, roles, skills, and tools. Chapter 5 ("Blended Toolbox for Change Management") specifies the core of the blended approach in terms of coupling heterogeneous tools for communication, training, motivation, and organization (to obtain acceptance) as well as the management of cost and complexity (to obtain time- and cost- efficiency). Chapter 6 ("Management of Opportunities and Risks") outlines the core activities of balancing: the handling of opportunities and of risks (errors, pitfalls and misconduct).

As building blocks of the core BxB-approach, several models are developed in the six chapters, among them a four determinant approach to change management performance, an extended model of change leadership, models of designing and evaluating hybrid blends, and four-cluster toolboxes to support intelligence and intervention activities in change projects.

In the final chapter 7 ("Change Management Frameworks") five prevalent frameworks of change management (Virtual organizations and Organizational Networks; Entrepreneurship, Intrapreneurship, and Interpreneurship; Business Reengineering; Knowledge Management; Multi-Channel Business) are analyzed from a BxB-point of view. Owing to the heterogeneity of this compilation, a wide range of challenges is covered. Furthermore, five appendices (Servitization; Projectification; Mergers & Acquisitions; Implementing Hybrids; Errors in Change Management) deal with core challenges to change management. Here, the focus is on handling complexity which constitutes the touchstone of resilient change management.

X

List of Figures

XIV

XVIII

List of Abbreviations

AIDA	Attention, Interest, Desire, Action
B2B	Business-to-Business
B2C	Business-to-Consumer
BPR	Business Process Reengineering
BR Framework	Balanced Resilience Framework
BSC	Balanced Scorecard
CBT	Computer-Based Training
CEO	Chief Executive Officer
CIP	Continuous Improvement Process
CLVN	Change Leadership Value Net
CMBOK	Change Management Body of Knowledge
CMMI	Capability Maturity Model Integration
CRM	Customer Relationship Management
DSL	Digital Subscriber Line
ECLVN	Extended Change Leadership Value Net
ERP	Enterprise Resource Planning
HR	Human Resource
IFRS	International Financial Reporting Standards
IPMA	International Project Management Association
ISO	International Organization for Standardization
IT	Information Technology
M&A	Mergers and acquisitions
MbO	Management by Objectives
MC	Mass Customization

manifold more transitions. On the *organization* level change affects all sectors of an enterprise. The spectrum of organizational change (see fig. 2) ranges from a change

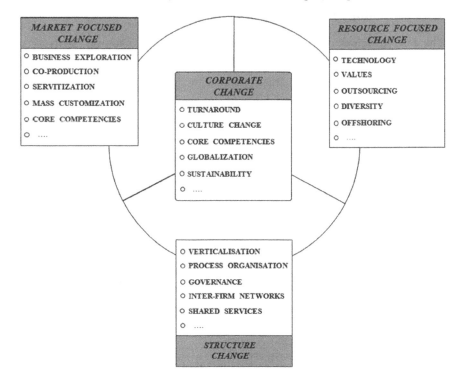

Figure 2:   Sectors of Organizational Change

in strategies (e.g. expansion via diversification), human resources (eg percentage of academics, freelancers, women and foreign executives), technologies and systems (Internet, Intranet, telework, ERP software, Business Intelligence, etc.), structures (e.g. holding structures, teamwork, business process orientation, empowerment), to cultures (servitization, visions of global players, compliance, going green, etc.). In addition to these varieties of *managed* change social entities and individuals are subject to emergent change, such as business cycles, global warming, natural disasters, seasons and lifecycles (youth, growth, and decline).

Three *formal* features capture the essence of change: Complexity, omnipresence, and prominence.

Complexity: Change goes along with specific features of complexity that differentiate this species of complexity from complexity as a generic feature of management (e.g. captured in Ashby's law of requisite variety). The specific *accumulation of complexity* represents a major challenge to both targets (recipients) and managers of change. The causes of complexity in change initiatives are obvious: the more *wide-ranging, far-reaching* and *quickly implemented* a change project, the more complex the work of leaders in the change process. The *overlapping* of old and new rules is another cause of complexity for those involved and affected: Within a transition period, old and new management principles, selection guidelines, salary systems etc. overlap. This makes sticking to the leadership principle of non-discrimination – e.g. of pre- and post merger employees - much more difficult if not totally impossible. For the transition itself, specific provisional regulations (for options, eligibility and deadlines etc) have to be drawn up. In established organizations, this leads to a segmentation of the workforce. On the one hand, we have the privileged employees, to whom - thanks to the protection of vested rights - favourable terms of the company apply. On the other hand, we have the newly recruited employees who get worse compensation and who have fewer rights to fringe benefits. Furthermore, the standard organization defined in the organization chart is overlain by a project organization for „change-focused tasks".

All exemplifications of complexity can be construed and explained by a combination of four archetypes of complexity (see fig. 3).

Complementary relationships between the four dimensions are typical. They result in an escalation (proliferation) or de-escalation of the overall complexity. In production processes for example, manufacturing variants (variety) also require flexibility: variety has an impact on fuzziness ("Which variant is scheduled next"?), and dynamics ("people and/or technical facilities switching from one variant to another"). Likewise, a multi-objective goal system (multiplicity) is likely to generate conflict between objectives (variety). Conflict can be the source of instability (dynamics) of the production system. Conversely, low uncertainty can keep instability down. Dynamics is usually specified according to its variety (marginal versus quantum change) or its velocity (continuous improvement versus abrupt or punctuated change, first order versus second order change).

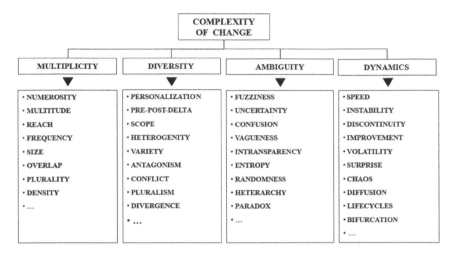

Figure 3:   Dimensions of Complexity in Change Management

Omnipresence: Change is a ubiquitous phenomenon (see fig. 2 for the organizational level). Patterns of sporadic change are more and more replaced by permanent change. Moreover, the change issue has also entered areas like promotion (slogans like "Drive the change" or "Change happenz") as well as the political area, e.g. as part of campaigns and revolutionary movements (e.g. place of change in Sanaa) that are focused on the idea of change.

Prominence: On the one hand, change represents a critical demand (for flexibility and agility). On the other hand, change management constitutes a key capability of managers. On the organizational level, it is usually considered as a meta-competence or so called dynamic capability.

1.2 Positioning of Change Management

The essence of change management, as the totality of all the activities dealing with far-reaching changes, is to create a change-friendly context for all change processes. Change Management, like other cross-functional management activities such as

Quality Management, Performance Measurement, or Integration Management, represents a mandatory building block of all kinds of mid and long term management activities. Hence, not only change but also the management of change are omnipresent: Whenever something new is about to be introduced – like new software releases, businesses, business models, products, processes, business relationships and other *"concepts"*, change management must support this implementation process.

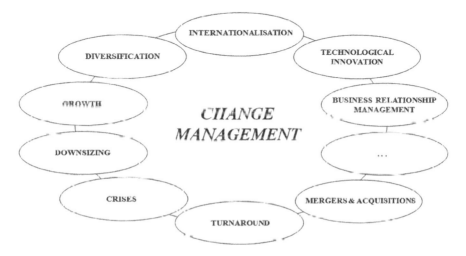

Figure 4:   Change Management in Standard Management Issues/Areas

Moreover, change management plays a major role in current management frameworks (see also chapter 7). Fig. 5 exemplifies these management frameworks that represent mainstreams since the 1990s.

Business Process Reengineering: In business process reengineering, the aim is to change from the isolated optimisation of specific value-adding activities (marketing, development, purchasing, recruiting, etc.) to the optimisation of cross-functional *core processes*. Product development, order fulfilment, business planning, customer acquisition, and other core processes are critical for competitive performance. Process reengineering transforms the company structure from a vertical functional structure into a horizontal process organization. Process owners responsible for these

Function Deployment (QFD) customer requirements are translated into technical features of products.

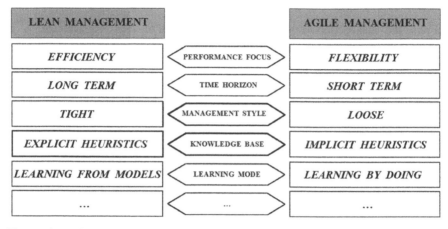

Figure 6:   Lean versus Agile Management

TQM implies that the responsibility for quality is *comprehensively integrated* in every organizational unit and assumed by everybody in a company. „Total" signals the holistic nature of the approach. Consequently, the introduction of TQM is frequently accompanied with a *culture change*. Quality orientation therefore also stands for enhanced communication, motivation and cooperation. This is particularly evident in a European variant of TQM, the European Foundation for Quality Management (EFQM) model. In this model of "business excellence", quality is not only measured in terms of financial performance but also in terms of customer and employee satisfaction, and social responsibility. These performance criteria are controlled by five „enablers": leadership, employee orientation, policies/strategy, resources and processes.

A typical feature of TQM is the use of "Oscars for quality" to boost motivation for quality improvement. These *awards* are part of reward systems based on a competition mechanism. Within a company, this means a competition for awards and titles (e.g. "Quality Team of the Year") among teams, departments or business units. The award concept has also been extended to awarding especially reliable suppliers (e.g. GM's Supplier of the Year Award, Ford's Q1).

Managers responsible for introducing TQM should always be aware of one *area of tension.* On the one hand voluntary participation in TQM initiatives is a guarantor for motivation. On the other hand comprehensive adoption of TQM can only be achieved by a company-wide top down approach. One way of surmounting this area of tension is the promotion of voluntary initiatives in decentralised areas by top management.

The outlined management frameworks form the background for company-specific projects since the majority of managers willingly adopt these mainstream trends, in other words "they go with the flow". On the one hand, the frameworks can be viewed as *paradigms.* However, from the critical perspective, they are just management *fashions* or *fads* based on herd behaviour. Since the 1990ies, these approaches have been reinforced by global consultancies and management gurus as trend setters. Fads are professionally created and marketed. Like all fashions they have a comparatively short life cycle and some approaches reappear after some time, i.e. they are re-launched. This cyclic pattern is captured in the metaphor of a pendulum of the critical success factors advocated and focused by the respective approaches (see fig. 7). It swings between a focus on hard factors (e.g. IT and control systems) and soft factors (e.g. corporate culture).

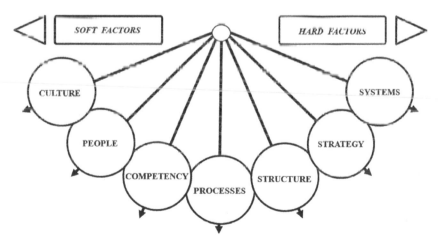

Figure 7:   Pendulum of Success Factors

The outlined frameworks of change management are part of a broader spectrum of approaches to dynamics and transition. A systemic taxonomy of frameworks from science as well as consultancies is based on two dimensions (see fig. 8): a (horizontal) dimension of *"intensity of intervention"* and a (vertical) dimension of *"reach"*.

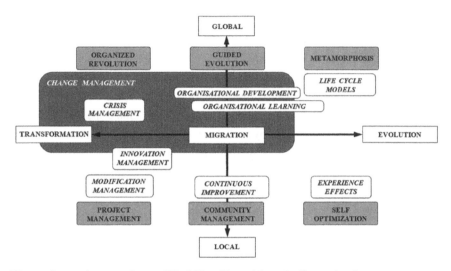

Figure 8:   Approaches to Modeling Transitions in Organizations

On the *horizontal* dimension, Business Transformation (e.g. Business Process Reengineering) is characterized by a high level of management intervention, migration (step-by-step replacement of old by new components, e.g. of IT systems) by a mediocre intensity and evolutionary models by a low intensity. On this dimension models based on emergent community work – such as Web 2.0 social communities or informal skunk works – go along with more self organization than models of traditional change management that rely on project organization. On the *reach* dimension, local transitions are restricted to departments, teams or business units whereas global transitions deal with the entire company, supply chain, region or industry. Several models of organizational transitions in fig. 9 do not belong to the domain of change management because the transitions in question are not complex (i.e. local or incremental) or not managed (but emergent or evolutionary).

So, modification management (e.g. product modifications or behaviour modifications) are not change management per se. However, change management projects may require modifications.

The taxonomy also allows the demarcation of change management, e.g. change versus innovation management. With innovation management, we are not dealing with a typical form of change management, though at first glance they would appear to be almost identical. Change management and innovation management cope with fundamentally different types of challenges (see fig. 9).

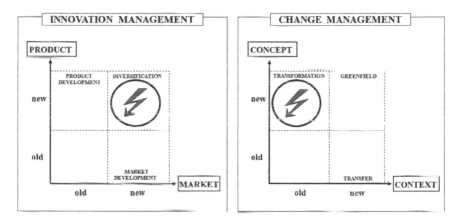

Figure 9:   Core Challenges to the Management of Innovation and of Change

Whereas the main challenge for innovation management is to generate a high degree of novelty (e.g. developing new products for new markets simultaneously), the art of change management lies primarily in introducing new "concepts" into an *existing* context and not into a totally new environment. This explains, for example, why the diffusion of e-business is not so much the job of innovation management but that of change management. In greenfields, e.g. new plants with new equipment, IT-systems, and young employees, there is less resistance to change than in brownfields.

1.3 Outline of the Balanced and Blended Approach to Change Management

The architecture of our approach relies on two mechanisms of *integrating* various approaches to change management: balancing and blending. *Balancing* combines diverse, sometimes even polar *objectives* and performance dimensions pursued in change management. The idea of balanced antithetic objectives is familiar from balanced scorecards (balancing financial and non-financial criteria), from work-life balance, rigor-relevance- balance or 360 degree feedbacks. *Blending* refers to the mix of diverse categories of *tools* instead of solely relying on "straight", non-hybrid toolboxes. This logic of combination is for example applied in blended learning. Balancing and blending characterize an eclectic and anti-dogmatic approach to change management as opposed to revolutionary approaches often characterized as "Changing the Way We Change Organizations". Consequently, this approach does not advocate paradigm shifts (such as "from hard factors to soft factors" or "from teaching to learning"). However, changes in the *proportions* of blended approaches are quite normal.

Both balancing and blending are ways of handling complexity, namely diversity and ambiguity (see fig. 3). Diversity as well as ambiguity are sometimes explicitly reflected in the labelling of the balanced or blended approaches, which is the case with "guided evolution", "organized anarchy", "logical incrementalism", "mass customization" or "leagile" (lean & agile). A high degree of diversity and ambiguity is typical of so called *hybrid approaches*. Within change management, the scope of hybrid models ranges from virtual world-real world combinations (e.g. electronic and face-to-face communication, brick & click) to hybrid systems, ambidexterity, dialectics or even schizophrenia. Their design is determined by a mix of different genes.

The philosophy of the balanced and blended approach or *BxB-approach* can be phrased as follows: We are, (always) have been and will be living in a beta world of change management. It contains only second best approaches. Instead of selecting a particular second best model, the BxB-approach advocates a mix of two (or more) second best solutions. This liberal or eclectic philosophy ("More than one church in town") contradicts all dogmatic approaches which prohibit diversity and favour straight approaches. In every beta world, only imperfect heuristics (not perfect algorithms) provide orientation, in terms of facilitators, enablers, catalysts, or promoters. From a heuristics point of view, it makes more sense to balance and blend existing frameworks than search for a new "(first) best way of change management", e.g. some "Change Management 2.0". Balancing and blending normally create hybrid frameworks. Unlike randomly emerging *patchwork* models or mixes of coexisting components, balancing and blending are based on a *professional design of these hybrid frameworks*.

Unfortunately there is also a dark side of balancing and blending. Some mixes may turn out to be compromises that only provide some vague "wishy-washy" orientation. Furthermore, opposite forces or beliefs may neutralise each other causing a state of confusion and disorientation that possibly leads to a standstill of change endeavours. This holds especially for hybrid mixes: mixing antithetic elements like water and fire may generate "steam" instead of "firewater". Via balancing and blending our approach to change management meets three generic performance criteria for management activities: feasibility, orientation, and balance.

Feasibility: All building blocks of a performance oriented change management approach should be realistic, all goals should be achievable in order to avoid mission impossible projects. Feasibility addresses for instance the time span for change projects and their costs. Project management has fostered an awareness for systematic misjudgments, for instance by Brooks's law ("Adding manpower to a late project makes it later"). Furthermore feasibility is related to the level of aspiration concerning the acceptance of a new concept by the change targets. The scope reaches from euphoria to forbearance. Corresponding to these two extremely different levels of performance there are two polar clusters of change management:

Excellence-focused approaches: The "excellence in change"-cluster contains models of transformational change, the management excellence-model of the European Foundation for Quality Management (EFQM), high performance systems-approaches, motivation via stretched or noble goals as well as models of fast learning companies. For at least two reasons the feasibility of these models appears questionable: Firstly, the high performance orientation does not fit to the 50 to 70% failure rates of change projects. Secondly, excellence-focused approaches overestimate the knowledge base of change managers ("Change Management Body of Knowledge") and underestimate the inherent risks in change processes. In change management, there is a gap between the wish for change on the one hand, and the actual extent to which the change has been realised on the other. Evidently, change plans deal with challenges that clearly go beyond the realm of daily management. Moreover, excellence approaches normally operate on "secrets" or "panaceas", i.e. guarantors of success which is not consistent with the insufficiencies of the available knowledge base that actually contains numerous highly conjectural elements.

Resilience-focused approaches: Models of migration or continuous improvement are less ambitious, but more realistic than excellence focused approaches. They pursue robustness of organizations and change endeavors with respect to obstacles and risks. "Resilience management" serves as the umbrella terms for these approaches, both on the organizational and the individual level. Whereas excellence-focused models are often related to transformational change (see fig. 8) with old patterns of behavior being radically replaced by new ones, resilience approaches often go along with *sedimented* change: new patterns co-exist as an overlay on old patterns. As far as performance determinants are concerned resilience models focus inhibitors of failure rather than guarantors of success.

Orientation: All approaches to change management should provide goal-path-data for a change initiative. Some mainstream approaches such as the learning organization or the agile organization (see fig. 6) offer plausible but rather vague, unspecific, an incomplete navigation data: this is usually accomplished by visions, guidelines, or manifestos (e.g. the Davos Manifesto or the Agile Manifesto), outlines of change friendly corporate cultures and mindsets as well as principles, like participation versus top-down-implementation or step-by-step-implementation as opposed to a big bang procedure. However these approaches do not contain specific roadmaps that would indicate the milestones to reaching the goal, like tips for selecting pilots in a stepwise procedure or recommendations for the optimal length of pilot periods. On the other hand, the pragmatic toolbox-approaches deliver procedural data, like cascading, milestones as well as tools, such as workshops, Open Space, survey feedback, change blogs or change radars, however without clarifying to what end they should be applied. Orientation is accomplished when all

Secondly, a *management* module informs about the determinants of change performance as well as ways to influence these determinants for a better outcome (*interventions*). *Dimensions*, *levels* and *determinants* of change performance as well as *interventions* to modify the determinants in order to enhance performance represent the four key elements of a balanced performance model.

Performance dimensions: Fig. 11 contains the core dimensions of effectiveness, i.e. *acceptance* by affected persons (targets), *innovativity* of the content of the change initiative (in comparison to existing solutions of the respective problem) and *alignment*, meaning compatibility with other areas of the context that are not subject to change. In addition to that traditional performance focus, efficiency dimensions complete the spectrum of relevant criteria for successful or (non-)successful change projects. They cover costs, time (first and foremost: speed) and flexibility, i.e. the easiness of substituting one path of implementation by another according to feed-forward or feedback information.

The relevance of efficiency for a balanced measurement of change performance can be illustrated by a classic soft control lever of change management: *participation*.

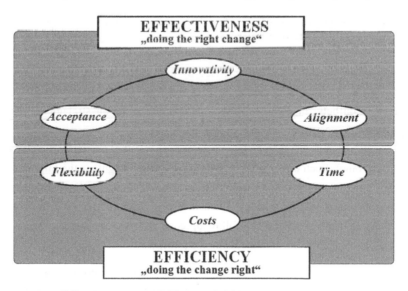

Figure 11:   Effectiveness and Efficiency of Change Management

By integrating cost and time criteria into the scope of performance criteria, the war of beliefs between „participation strategists" and „bomb-dropping strategists" is replaced by a model of life cycle costs (costs per period) of participative and hierarchical implementation (see fig. 12).

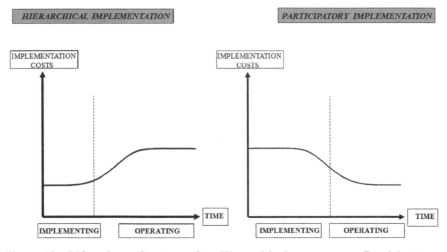

**Figure 12: Lifecycle   Costs   of   Hierarchical   versus   Participatory
         Implementation Patterns**

Participative procedures are characterised by high early implementation costs but make up for it with low operating costs as well as low follow-up costs, e.g. for managing conflicts. In contrast, *hierarchical* implementation strategies avoid the high ramp-up costs but are associated with the risk of expensive day-to-day implementation and with high follow-up costs (as a result of barriers which have not been overcome). Such consideration for life cycle costs heightens the importance of the time horizons of the involved actors. Some change managers (including external consultants and managers with a limited tenure) have a shorter time horizon and therefore personally view the late follow-up costs as irrelevant to their decisions, a fact that favours hierarchical implementation patterns.

Conflicting relationships between effectiveness and efficiency are widespread as we know from the classic "quick but dirty-dilemma". Moreover, time and cost efficiency of change projects may not be harmoniously, but disharmoniously related (see fig. 13)

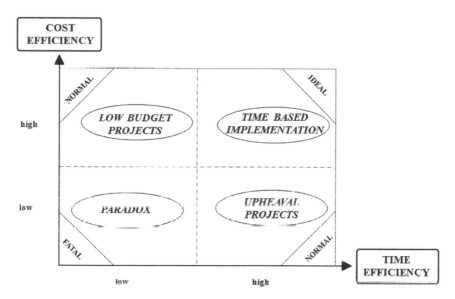

Figure 13:   Time and Cost Efficiency in Change Management

Conflict characterizes both transformational uphcaval projects ("quick but costly") and low budget projects ("cost-saving but never ending"). On the one hand, the hell of project efficiency, i.e. costly and longsome projects, is often provoked by paradoxes, such as Brooks's law. On the other hand, heaven is reached by time-based management where swift interventions avoid high costs because they avoid the risk of obsolete interventions due to a change in the turbulent context.

Performance levels: There are three critical levels on an ordinal performance scale: *existence* and *excellence* represent two levels of success of a change project, *exit* stands for its failure. The degree of differentiation in this 3E-measurement model is similar to some standard scales of IT-project performance (e.g. succeeded, challenged, failed), but less differentiated than scales to measure the maturity level of repetitive processes, such as *initial, managed, defined, quantitatively managed, and optimizing* within the Capability Maturity Model Integration. *Existence* serves as a level of reference determined either by modal values within a population (e.g. average duration of strikes triggered by cost-cutting projects in an industry), by ranking, by inter-project comparisons (e.g. manpower demand of prior change projects), or by goal attainment. The existence level signifies a down to earth-approach typical of the realistic resilience paradigm. *Excellence* marks an above average success, normally captured in success stories illustrating best practices in change management. Exit on the other end of the scale signals an extremely bad performance. Such flops in change management appear as informal fading out, official project cancellation as well as explicit articulations of dissatisfaction from project stakeholders.

Whenever a change initiative has positive or negative spillovers on neighboring projects both excellence and exit have to be re-defined in an even more extreme way: "super-excellence" characterizes projects that have a positive effect on the performance of an entire project-portfolio whereas "super-exit" means that one failed project also causes the exit of other projects.

Fig. 14 exemplifies the 3E-model of performance management with regard to one key dimension of effectiveness criterion, acceptance. Acceptance denominates not only an attitude but moreover a behavior that supports the change initiative. Excellent performance yields enthusiasm, commitment, and "buy-in". The existence level stands for forbearance whereas the exit level is correlated with obstruction and sabotage.

In between the existence level and the excellence level resides the opportunity impact zone of change management. In between the existence and the exit levels the risk impact zone. A realistic balanced resilience management of acceptance focuses a) the avoidance of rejection (risk management) and b) the promotion of accordance (opportunity management) in terms of forbearance and adjustment. It does not aspire buy-in nor enthusiasm.

Performance determinants: The force field-model developed in the Organizational Development approach provides a perfect framework to identify the key determinants that influence the performance of change initiatives. It operates on balancing „restraining forces" and „driving forces". Translated into a performance

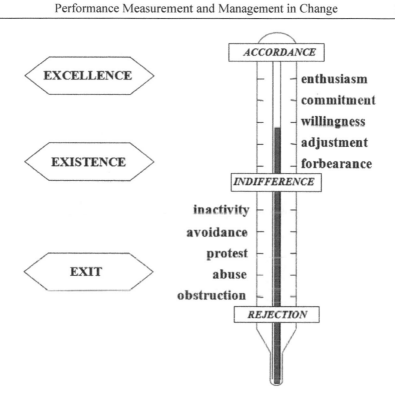

Figure 14: Levels of Acceptance

oriented change management framework, driving forces represent *performance enablers* whereas restraining forces stand for *performance disablers*(see fig.15).

For the sake of feasibility and balance, the framework operates not just on two, but on four categories of determinants ("forces"). They differ with respect to the direction and their quantitative impact on performance.

The two *performance enablers* in fig. 15 yield different levels of performance. Whereas *success factors* assure excellence (as guarantors), *barriers to failure* prevent the exit (as inhibitors). The list of inhibitors of failure contains slack resources in project manpower, buffers in the project scheduling, dynamic capabilities as well as trust as an element of corporate culture. On the side of the *performance disablers*, exit is provoked by *failure factures* whereas *barriers to success* inhibit excellence. This kind of restraining impact comes mainly from lack of acceptance (due to fears, ignorance, etc.) and restrictions in the available project manpower.

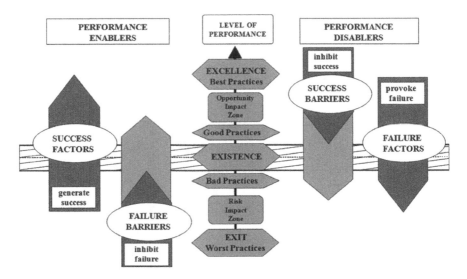

Figure 15:   Performance Framework for Change Management

In general, all four categories of determinants are clusters, with barriers to success for instance containing resistance of stockholders towards mergers and acquisitions, lack of leadership skills of project managers or top management involvement. In fact, resistance to change represents the traditional focus in this cluster of barriers to success. Resistance is the result of four deficits on the side of the change targets: „lack of information" „lack of competence", „lack of comfort" and „lack of control" (see fig. 16).

As a rule, this negative *attitude* will lead to oppositional *behaviour* (boycotts, sabotage, etc., see fig. 14). Resistance might be triggered categorically by any kind of change because change is regarded in principle as uncomfortable. Such a fundamentally negative attitude is aggravated by the tendency of change projects to be ephemeral fashions. This induces a certain amount of insensitivity towards and lack of attention for change initiatives in general.

In addition to these generic sources of resistance, some features of specific change projects can also be responsible for resistance. Think of the *fear of discrimination* through forced competition between young and old employees or between intra-corporate and external suppliers in lean management projects. Such real fears are subjectively and quickly generalised and extended to all, soft as well as hard change approaches. Hence, all change projects may acquire the image of a job killer. Indeed, there is objective evidence that even „soft" restructuring is accompanied by job cuts. In such situations, change managers sometimes have to use drastic arguments such as „job cuts or closure of the entire subsidiary". The coaching potential of the involved managers will most likely reach its limits when dealing with extensive manpower adjustments. In these cases, usually external consultants are involved to determine how to obtain the required manpower cuts.

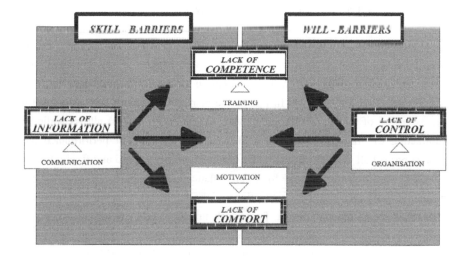

Figure 16:   Causes of Resistance to Change

In a balanced framework, barriers to efficiency have to be dealt with in addition to the barriers to acceptance (see fig. 17). *Time lags*, for instance due to (legal) *periods of notice* whenever contracts are subject to cancellations, impair both cost and time efficiency: they cause remanent costs and enforce a postponement of activities. Lags

are also a collateral phenomenon of inertia and processes of unlearning whenever
change requires that habits have to be abandoned.

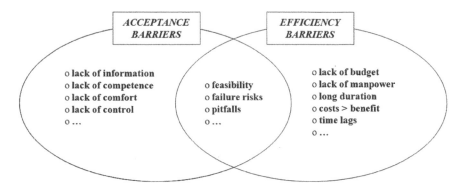

Figure 17:   Acceptance and Efficiency Barriers

In the performance framework (see fig. 15), the strengths of the performance
determinants – e.g. of corporate culture or of resistance – are measured on a
"primitive", but realistic scale with "1" signaling a weak, "2" a mediocre and "3" a
strong impact on performance. In fig. 15 the respective strengths are visualized by
the extension of the arrows. Utilizing the standard scores (1,2,3) allows adding or
subtracting of different determinants. To estimate the overall performance of a
change project all enablers as well as all disablers are aggregated and finally the two
bundles of positive and negative forces are balanced. The imperfect knowledge base
of change managers makes all estimations of the impact of determinants uncertain,
oftentimes even conjectural. The framework takes account of this uncertainty by
differentiating between a *basic impact* and an *add-on impact* (visualized in fig 16 by
the two extended arrows). So, some determinants are both verified *inhibitors* of
failure and potential *facilitators* of success. This additional effect is sometimes
accomplished by self-enforcing spiral processes, e.g. when success creates success
or trust generates trust. Inversely, success barriers basically inhibit success, but may
also turn out to be failure factors, for instance by inducing reactance in the behaviors
of change targets.

So called „anti-patterns" as negative lessons learned in project management (e.g.
paralysis by analysis) as well as archives of good or bad practices deliver ample

evidence of unexpected effects of determinants due to *overdosing* assumed performance enablers (see also chapter 6.3.2). So, long term success may trigger complacency and inertia. Moreover, according to the so called Icarus paradox an overdose of success may even represent a failure factor causing the decline of companies (e.g. new economy companies that became "dotgone"-victims of their skyrocketing prior performance during the shakeout in the new economy).

Interventions: All performance improving interventions intend to strengthen performance enablers and weaken performance disablers (see fig. 15). This is accomplished by applying tools from the voluminous toolboxes of change management (see chapter 5).

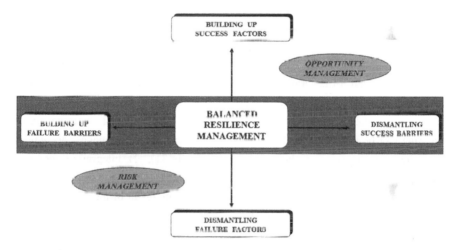

**Figure 18:   Management of Barriers as the Core Domain of the Balanced
Resilience Framework**

Strengthening is accomplished by *building up* success factors and barriers to failure. Weakening of disablers is accomplished by *dismantling* failure factors and barriers to success, e.g. inertia and resistance (see fig. 18). This mix of interventions is genuinely balanced since both opportunities (offensive interventions) and risks (defensive interventions) are covered. It is also realistic due to its focus on barriers.

The four areas of intervention differ considerably with respect to the *timing* of the interventions relative to the occurrence of a demand for change or to the start of a change project. This is reflected in the distinction between *reactive* change management (interventions after need for change) and *proactive* change management (interventions prior to need for change). As for the timing of change activities, reactive management is based on event pacing (ad hoc interventions) whereas proactive change management follows the pattern of time pacing (regular, continuous interventions).

If risk (i.e. failure, exit) is defined as the *probability times the severity of a negative outcome*, the building-up of barriers to failure does not only cover preventive measures to reduce the *probability* of damage, but also palliative interventions to reduce the *amount* of the damage. Consequently, the underlying notion of resilience does not focus the mere fact of being vulnerable or robust but differentiates different levels of robustness, e.g. depending on the amount of financial or reputational damage involved. In generic risk management a damage reduction is accomplished proactively by a) insurance (outsourcing of damages) and b) risk sharing. Whereas in change management the insurance option is only of secondary importance, risk sharing can be practiced in several ways: 1) making project managers accountable for the consequences of their activities (see fig.31), 2) integrating targets as multiplicators or members of a project team and 3) risk (and revenue) sharing contracts with consultants. Hence, exit may not be the result of incompetent change management, but of incompetent risk management whenever palliative activities such as risk sharing have not been appropriately applied.

The *traditional* arena of barrier management (see fig. 19) is reactive dismantling of barriers to success. This arena encompasses all activities to overcome resistance, in other words acceptance barriers. The extremely opposite way of handling barriers is to proactively build up failure barriers. As far as resources are concerned this is accomplished by fostering slack resources – just like 3 M's 15% rule in innovation management. Diversification or blending also supports proactive risk management. Risk sharing arrangements at least limit the damage.

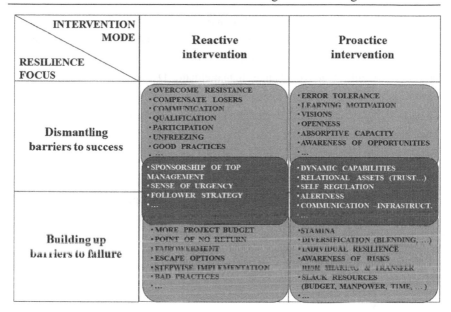

INTERVENTION MODE / RESILIENCE FOCUS	Reactive intervention	Proactice intervention
Dismantling barriers to success	• OVERCOME RESISTANCE • COMPENSATE LOSERS • COMMUNICATION • QUALIFICATION • PARTICIPATION • UNFREEZING • GOOD PRACTICES • ...	• ERROR TOLERANCE • LEARNING MOTIVATION • VISIONS • OPENNESS • ABSORPTIVE CAPACITY • AWARENESS OF OPPORTUNITIES • ...
	• SPONSORSHIP OF TOP MANAGEMENT • SENSE OF URGENCY • FOLLOWER STRATEGY • ...	• DYNAMIC CAPABILITIES • RELATIONAL ASSETS (TRUST...) • SELF REGULATION • ALERTNESS • COMMUNICATION –INFRASTRUCT. • ...
Building up barriers to failure	• MORE PROJECT BUDGET • POINT OF NO RETURN • FAIR INVOLVEMENT • ESCAPE OPTIONS • STEPWISE IMPLEMENTATION • BAD PRACTICES • ...	• STAMINA • DIVERSIFICATION (BLENDING, ...) • INDIVIDUAL RESILIENCE • AWARENESS OF RISKS • HIGH SHARING & TRANSFER • SLACK RESOURCES (BUDGET, MANPOWER, TIME, ..) • ...

Figure 19:   Proactice and Reactive Management of Barriers

One way of building up failure barriers is trying to reach a *point of no return*, i.e. a state that does not allow any atavistic behaviors. For top managers for instance this point is normally reached once they have committed themselves to the change project in public (in a kick-off or workshop, on a blog, etc.). *Step-by-step-implementation* is not only reducing the likelihood, but also the amount of damage. Escape options also help restrict the severity of damage. *(Early) follower-implementation* strategies avoid the errors that first movers usually commit. In addition, these strategies provide options to learn not only from good, but also from bad practices. Some change projects may not fail despite of their poor performance since they are considered as "too big to fail". This sometimes relates to the amount of budget already invested. However, when change managers become aware of this "sunk costs fallacy" they may have the courage to cancel even that category of mega-projects. Finally openness, awareness of standard opportunities for change, change intelligence skills as well as visions serve as infrastructures to overcome barriers to success, i.e. inertia or lack of entrepreneurial spirit.

Some ways of handling barriers are bi-functional in that they simultaneously affect both kinds of barriers. This holds especially for sponsorship from top management and for creating a sense of urgency (sometimes also characterized as a "burning platform") within reactive change management. Dynamic capabilities (agility, change readiness, absorptive capacity...) and relational resources (e.g. trust, empathy) have the same bi-functional potential within proactive change management.

Performance dynamics: The performance measures of change management are not stable over time. They follow generic patterns of devolution that are reflected in the variation of performance over different phases of a change project. This variation characterizes three phases in the lifecycle of a change project (see fig. 20).

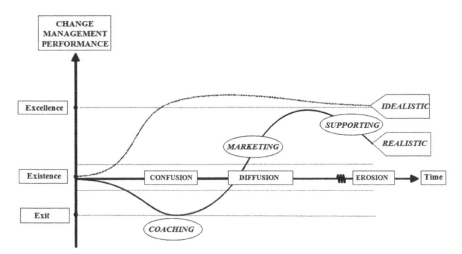

Figure 20:   Performance Dynamics in Change Management

The initial *confusion phase* is marked by mistakes, teething troubles, haste, fears, shocks, ignorance, unfreezing of routines, habits and attitudes as well as denial of relevance. In projects to speed product development (time to market) by concurrent instead of sequential engineering, confusion is caused by the fact that initial steps take more (not less) time than they would take in a sequential pattern. This triggers considerable doubt with respect to the overall acceleration benefit. A change manager is called upon first and foremost as a coach. His endeavors deal simultaneously with dismantling barriers to success, mainly resistance, and building-up barriers to failure. He has to see to it that the change process does not get stuck in a mere breakdown of the old structures, but that it develops into a new departure.

The *diffusion phase* corresponds to the penetration and dissemination of new products. Diffusion means the acquisition of new supporters, company-wide roll-out as well as implementation of more modules of the new concept (e.g. aligned reward system when profit centers have been implemented). In this phase, managers act primarily as sellers and multiplicators of a new idea. Their main concern is dismantling barriers to success. This is accomplished by turning undecided into supporters and compensating losers. Only by internal marketing the personal vision of some evangelists of change ("I have a dream") can be transformed into a collective vision ("We have a dream").

In the *erosion phase,* the impact of the new rules on behaviors (in other word: acceptance) is fading. With cost cutting projects eroding starts roughly one year after the start of the program. Some fads may even erode earlier than that. Managers have to prevent a relapse of change targets' behaviors into old habits and practices as well as nostalgic orientations (glorifying the good old pre-change times). Supporting means building up barriers to failure, for instance by stabilizers like refreshment workshops or by some updating of the original content of the change initiative. However, signs of erosion might signal the necessity for a new change process because the „new" concept is already showing signs of obsolescence.

The force fields vary over the lifecycle of a change project due to the occurrence of specific risks and opportunities in different phases of the lifecycle. In the confusion phase both risks of confusion and opportunities of overcoming resistance have to be taken care of. Risk management is accomplished by restricting the reach of change activities to a pilot area. Opportunity management is focused on opinion leaders (in terms of informal leaders or key accounts) and multiplicators. Unfortunately, there is a conflict between dismantling success barriers and building-up failure barriers: dismantling also means destabilizing opinions and attitudes which causes confusion which increases the risk of failure.

Realistic views of performance dynamics lead to unsteady "rollercoaster" models. Idealistic views (see fig. 20) ignore confusion and/ or erosion by focusing on a steady diffusion. An extreme version of diffusion is a hype model where targets are embracing change they can easily cope with and the losers of change represent only a minority. In times of permanent overdosed change the assumption of some euphoria in change is not only naive but dangerous. Likewise many models of sustainable change naively ignore the risk of erosion by referring to self reinforcing processes. This assumption ignores the fact that some mainstreams in change are fads with a comparatively short lifetime. They are marketed as offerings of consultancies, most likely implying planned obsolescence. So, business process management has been replaced by business process reengineering and business process reengineering modified by x- engineering. Despite processes of self reinforcement or habitualization the launch of a new version will most likely provoke the erosion of acceptance of an implemented concept.

3 Paradigms, Patterns, and Parameters of Change Management

3.1 Multi-level Architecture of Change Management

Just like in other areas of management, orientation is fostered by a multi-level design approach: building blocks of change management do not originate from one level of specification and extension but from different levels. A three level approach is quite common. So, hierarchical planning systems consist of a strategic, tactical and an operational level. Similarly the OGI model in the Organizational Development framework is based on *organization, group,* and *individual.* For change management, a 3P-model with a paradigm, a pattern, and a parameter level seems useful. Multi-level approaches balance extension (reach) and specification on each level: paradigms (e.g. guided evolution) have an ample extension (i.e. they affect all change activities) combined with a poor specification of items whereas parameters (e.g. tools) have a narrow extension coupled with high specification. In between, patterns (e.g. principles) are mediocre with respect to their range of application extension as well as their precision. As for numerosity, a multi-level architecture contains only few principles, but a plethora of tools.

Balance within a multi level architecture model is warranted by a two-way integration of the respective levels: a *top-down* design supports orientation, while a *bottom-up* design fosters feasibility. By a two-way *down-up* procedure both orientation and feasibility are obtained.

3.2 Paradigms of Change Management

Unfortunately the paradigm level of change management is not composed of universal axioms (such as the second law of thermodynamics) or of generally accepted codes of conduct (such as some "ten commandments" or a global charter or manifesto for change management). Instead, there is a scope of alternative paradigms.

Reactive versus proactive change management

There are two fundamentally different philosophies of intervention (see fig. 19). *Reactive* change management means implementing a new concept into an existing context, mainly by overcoming resistance. In contrast, *proactive* change management takes places before the need for a specific change arises. Apparently these two paradigms are not only a matter of the timing of interventions, but also of the content of activities. Reactive change management is primarily *interactional* (talking, negotiating, implementing, etc.), whereas proactive is *infrastructural* management: It means managing change by establishing change friendly, change enabling infrastructures such as dynamic capabilities, built-in flexibility, openness and a culture of learning.

Fig. 21 outlines that most existing change management frameworks fit into both paradigms but differ as for proportions (i.e. coordinates in fig. 21). Moreover, some proactive frameworks tell us primarily how to change (regardless of the content of the change process) whereas reactive frameworks have a content focus (i.e. the new concept) and consequently tell us primarily what has to be changed, with respect to both concept and context.

Transformation versus guided evolution

According to fig. 8, there are paradigms which differ in their intensity of intervention. Evolutionary transitions follow a non-intervention (i.e. non-management) paradigm. At the opposite end of the spectrum, the *transformation* paradigm implies a high intensity of intervention originally captured in the term "planned" change. A second management paradigm is hybrid (e.g. *guided or planned evolution*) and corresponds to the idea of *cultivating* change.

Rational design versus realistic comprehension

The sources of orientation for change management originate from two utterly different paradigms: One being the rational world of rules, norms, imperatives, and procedures that design change the way it ought to be (in order to obtain goals and meet requirements). The other being a comprehension of the ways (practices) change management is actually executed in reality. In other words, orientation comes either from a *"construction"* of a more or less ideal change management endeavor or from a *"reconstruction"* of typical change processes that have already taken place.

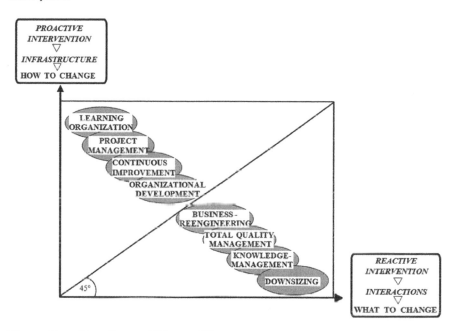

Figure 21:   Paradigms of Change Management

From the perspective of a BxB-approach the focus is on hybrid paradigms because there are a lot of pros for both the design and the comprehension paradigms. Choosing one of the two would mean not benefiting from the strengths of the other paradigm. In fact there are blending patterns: The logic of best practice learning for instance transforms reality into a rational norm.

3.3 Patterns of Change Management

3.3.1 Patterns of Implementation: Complexity Management

Due to its make-up, change management goes along with specific varieties of complexity that have to be handled (see fig. 3). On the one hand, the complexity of change processes is systematically underestimated. For instance, reducing change management complexity by exclusively relying on emergent self-optimising forces is dangerous. These forces may lead to path dependence, atavism and habits rather than change and innovation. Complexity management therefore has to focus on blending self-organization and management (see fig. 30). On the other hand, many companies are overwhelmed by the excessive complexity of radical transformation projects. These initiatives not only require the management of complex learning (see fig. 29) but in addition to this the management of *unlearning* (see fig. 22).

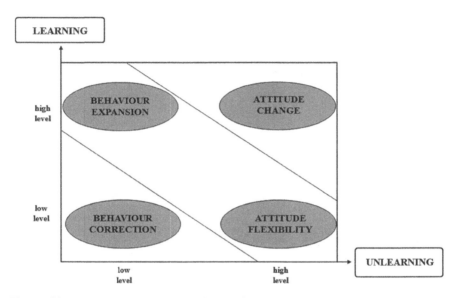

Figure 22:   Learning and Unlearning in Change Processes

Complexity and stress are caused particularly by the fact that in the transitional period, the processes of *building up a new order* are coupled with processes of *dismantling an old order*. If the hierarchy is dismantled as a coordination mechanism, then investment has to be made in alternative coordination mechanisms, such as teamwork, process coordination or internal markets. Deregulation– in the telecommunication sector via liberalization and de-monopolization – has to be accompanied by regulation (e.g. establishing supervisory authorities and formulating new ground rules for the competition). Due to this overlapping targets have to *unlearn*. When replacing hierarchical rules (between superiors and subordinates) with market rules (between internal customers and suppliers) the unlearning process is a hard struggle against the power of habit.

A reduction of complexity can be accomplished in two ways: if we want to do without learning processes, then only moderate changes, which minimize the delta between old and new, would be permissible. Take, for example, the moderate reduction of middle management. On the other hand, the unlearning effort could be minimized by preserving the existing regulations and adding new rules. These do not replace the status quo but complement it in terms of sedimented change. This principle of reducing complexity is also applied when an existing functional organization is overlain by product or process oriented committees. Since vested rights are taboo, resistance is avoided. It is likely that the existing order will die out to some extent during the course of time. Indeed, in many organizations, the hierarchically structured organization chart is only a facade. Decisions are taken in project teams and committees.

Against this background, the only appropriate *paradigm* for complexity management in change programs is not the *reduction of complexity* (e.g. eliminating dynamics by freezing specifications, following KISS-slogans), but the *optimizing of complexity* (e.g. optimized dynamics captured in the "edge of chaos"). Optimizing relies on principles of complexity fit (such as Ashby's law of requisite variety). Optimizing implies reducing as far as complexity in terms of an *unintended collateral* is concerned, e.g. inefficient conflicts in matrix structures or „throw it over the wall"-symptoms caused by overdosed specialization. So, migration management, conceived for the optimal transition from old IT-systems to new IT-systems, delivers valuable ideas for a complexity-conscious change management, also for non-IT change processes. The search for optimal complexity leads for example to approaches to combine top-down and bottom-up procedures (see fig. 25). Attempts to substitute the patchwork of separate change initiatives (cost reduction offensives, quality offensives, Program 2012, Program 2013 etc.) with a proactive long-term framework (e.g. learning organization) also arise from complexity optimization.

The paradigm of optimizing complexity is put into action by several *patterns of implementation*, e.g. step-by-step implementation and multi-track implementation.

Step-by-step-Implementation: The most prominent pattern of implementation is a generic two-step model containing a *pilot-* and a *roll-out* step (see fig. 23). The quantitative parameters to specify this simple pattern are a) relative size of pilot area (context coverage) and b) duration of the pilot step.

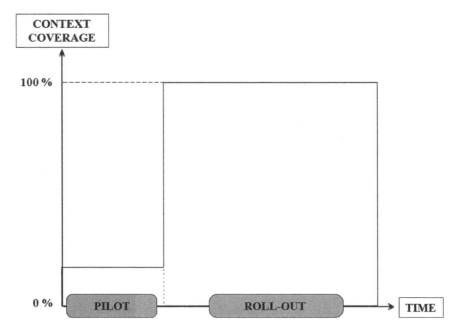

Figure 23:   Two-step Implementation Pattern

Figure 24 gives an illustration of the step-by-step implementation of an e-organization. It outlines the managed transition from a brick company to an integrated hybrid brick & click company.

Multi-track Implementation: Professional complexity management does not only stand for reducing complexity by incremental procedures. Sometimes optimal complexity management requires the exact opposite – an increase in complexity. This can be illustrated by multi-track patterns. With respect to the conflict between top-down procedures and bottom-up strategies, all attempts to reduce complexity lead to an either-or decision. However, change programs need *blended* "as-well-as" strategies. Only with the increase in complexity associated with these strategies, we can do justice to the learning requirements, the multitudes of impulses and so on. This can be demonstrated by the introduction of business process reengineering (see fig. 25 and chapter 7.3). The reengineering community often pleads for a rational *platform pattern*, whereby each successive step is placed upon the preceding platform. First, the basic principles and philosophy of process reengineering (internal customer-supplier relationship, holistic ways of thinking and handling, tear down walls between departments, disclosure of data, entrepreneurship in the organization etc.) have to be displayed. Then the organizational structures have to be adjusted from vertical functional responsibility to horizontal process responsibility (processes owners, case teams). Finally the techniques and tools of process modeling (such as Business Process Modeling Notation), customer surveys, process evaluation, process value analysis, process agreements and process costing are implemented.

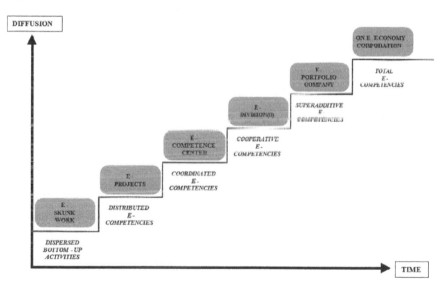

Figure 24:   Step-by-step Implementation of e-Business

The *mosaic pattern* is the exact reverse: first the techniques are trained and then the restructuring and philosophy of the supra-structure is tackled. A blended procedure uses the strengths of both of the single track strategies and at the same time avoids their weaknesses. This prevents the reengineering project from going on for centuries because we first have to wait for the cultural change before we can carry out the first process costing. This blended procedure also ensures that despite the detailed operative work, the point of the exercise is not lost.

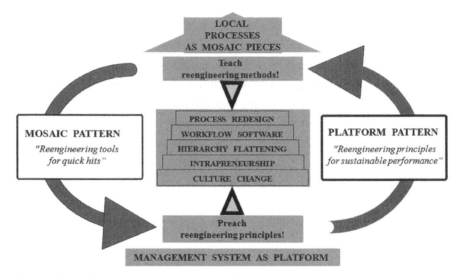

Figure 25:   Blended Implementation of Reengineering

3.3.2 Patterns of Implementation: Continuity

The diffusion paradigm claims a steady improvement of change management performance (see fig. 20). The relevant factors that determine performance and consequently serve as performance measure are *concept coverage* ("How many building blocks of the new concept have been successfully implemented?) and *context coverage* ("What percentage of target groups have committed themselves to the new concept?"). Change managers can follow three alternative patterns of implementation that differ with respect to the direction and continuity of obtaining coverage (see fig. 26).

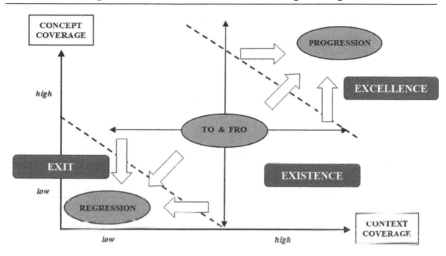

Figure 26:   Patterns of Implementation

The *progression* pattern relies on continuity, i.e. a steady approximation of an excellence level of performance. However, this pattern does not represent a realistic path-goal orientation. The inverse *regression* pattern may be quite realistic for mission impossible-projects and a source for learning from failure (e.g. bad practices). However it does not meet the requirements of a change management strategy. Nevertheless it is quite useful to understand the reasons for failure in terms of gaps in concept and/or context coverage that may eventually lead to the exit of a change project.

From a balanced resilience point of view, the unsteady *to and fro-pattern* appears most realistic. With respect to sourcing strategies this meandering is reflected in the insourcing-outsourcing-backsourcing-sequence. The gain ("plus") and loss ("minus") of building blocks as well as of targets reflects real life change management. Quite often, already implemented building blocks have to be modified or even abandoned in order to improve acceptance. Likewise certain modifications of concepts will most likely create some losers and thereby reduce context coverage. Fig. 27 illustrates the variety of "gains and losses" with respect to targets (context coverage) in terms of *migrations* between supporters, undecided, and opponents.

Recalling that the bottom-line of balanced resilience change manager is managing barriers, the roller coaster-pattern of performance (see fig. 20) should not enter the exit-zone (see fig. 26). In terms of context coverage, a minimum coverage serves as a barrier to failure: this critical mass of supporters of the new concept avoids change projects to be view as exotic niche initiatives or as a playground for revolutionists or idealists. As for dismantling success barriers, the required roll-out or context coverage may well rest below the 100% level: In order to overcome the barriers to success not all affected targets have to be won for the project. The missing rest of the targets will be captured e.g. by group pressure or by herding behavior.

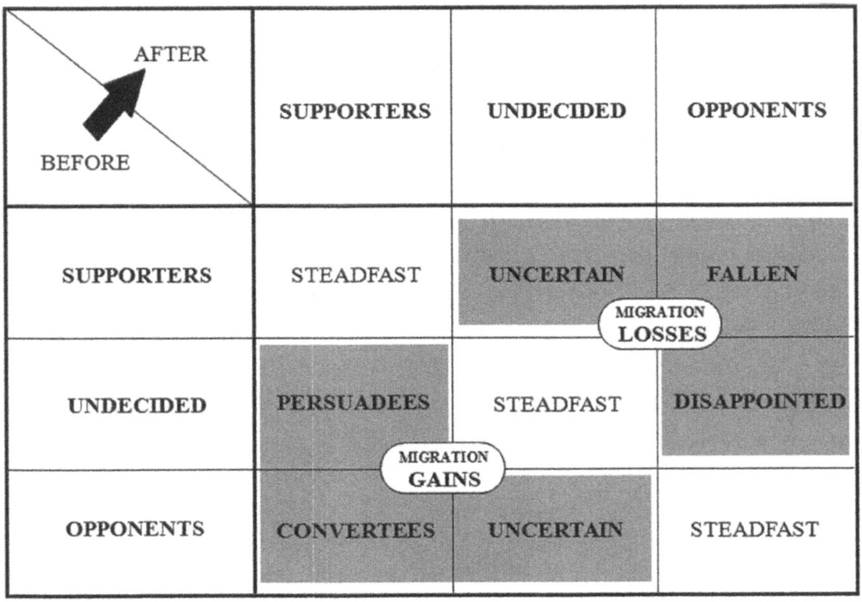

AFTER / BEFORE	SUPPORTERS	UNDECIDED	OPPONENTS
SUPPORTERS	STEADFAST	UNCERTAIN	FALLEN
UNDECIDED	PERSUADEES	STEADFAST	DISAPPOINTED
OPPONENTS	CONVERTEES	UNCERTAIN	STEADFAST

MIGRATION LOSSES

MIGRATION GAINS

Figure 27:   Migration amongst Target Groups

3.3.3 Patterns of Learning: Sources

Change requires ample learning. There is no one best way of learning but a scope of different learning patterns which change managers can utilize. One menu of learning patterns is built on the different *sources of learning*, answering the question: Where do the ideas for better ways of handling problems come from? Fig. 28 refers to four sources: learning by doing and by testing as well as learning within models and from models.

All learning systems use benchmarking to learn from successful models, i.e. from good or best practices. Furthermore, learning may take place in a simulated environment, sometimes supported by software („learning within a model"). Learning is also embedded in prototyping, where companies learn by testing and continuously improving earlier versions of a concept (product, process etc.). Last but not least, learning occurs on a trial and error basis in real time.

The four patterns differ with respect to the effectiveness and efficiency of learning processes. Learning by doing is rather costly but delivers solutions which are corroborated and customized to the learner's context. Contrary to that, best practice learning avoids costs on the one hand, since there is no need for costly trial and error-operations performed by the learner. On the other hand benchmarking causes a transfer problem because the practices should not just be copied but have to be customized to the specific learner context.

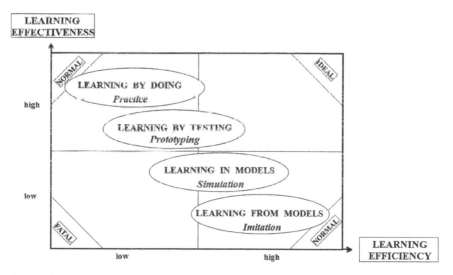

Figure 28:   Learning Patterns: Sources of Learning

A way of coping with the effectiveness-efficiency dilemma is *blended learning patterns*. So, learning in pilot areas combines learning by testing with learning from models: the (successful) pilot serves as a "home-made" role model for the rest of the company.

3.3.4 Patterns of Learning: Complexity

There are three levels of complex learning that change managers have to be proficient in: "single loop learning", "double loop learning" and "deutero learning" (see fig. 29). The respective complexity of these three patterns is determined by the scope and the content of learning.

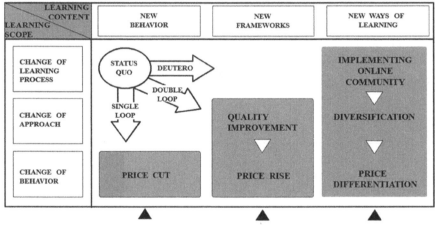

SHRINKING MARKET SHARES ARE COUNTERED BY. . .

Figure 29:   Learning Patterns: Complexity

Single loop learning: With "single loop learning" or "improvement learning" members of an organization try to identify and correct errors by changing their behavior. They learn new moves in a game that remains unchanged (e.g. price reduction within price competition). These processes do not affect existing rules, values, standards, norms, principles and routines. Fundamental cognitive changes necessary for innovation do not occur. Single loop learning occurs in continuous improvement processes and in a number of suggestion schemes. Very simple forms are reflected in learning curves.

Double loop learning: Double loop learning" or "renewal learning" involves fundamental changes in rules, norms, assumptions, routines or mental models (e.g. improving quality). Here, frameworks are changed: changes in the basic understanding of the business and values mean that traditional behavioral patterns are examined critically and - if necessary - adapted to the new view. This most likely provokes resistance from employees who want to hold on to old habits and are looking for continuity.

Deutero learning: This type of learning is also described as "learning to learn", i.e. acquiring new ways and methods of learning (e.g. implementing online communities). This enables the organization to improve its ability to learn. Online communities for instance enlarge the scope of sources for better strategies in comparison to traditional in-house sources considerably: the creativity of the "crowd", i.e. customers, suppliers, complementors, shareholders, or "anybody", can be exploited.

3.3.5 Patterns of participation

There is no one best way or pattern of leading change in people management. Instead, there are several patterns that differ with regard to the degree of participation of the change targets (see also fig. 12). There is some affinity to autocratic versus democratic leadership styles or governance structures (see fig. 30). In a way these patterns specify the hybrid paradigms of change management such as guided evolution.

The empowerment of targets increases from the left to the right in fig. 30. A high level of empowerment characterizes self-designed change where targets are empowered to design the new concept and are not just involved into workshops, Open Space events or blogs after the design job has been finished by others. In self-initiated change the targets trigger change activities after they have diagnosed the demand for change by themselves.

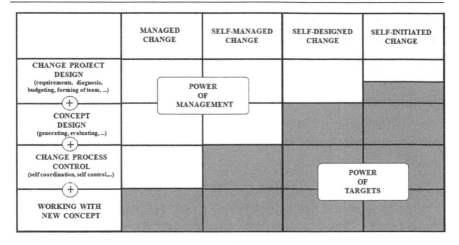

	MANAGED CHANGE	SELF-MANAGED CHANGE	SELF-DESIGNED CHANGE	SELF-INITIATED CHANGE
CHANGE PROJECT DESIGN (requirements, diagnosis, budgeting, forming of team, ...)				
(+)	POWER OF MANAGEMENT			
CONCEPT DESIGN (generating, evaluating, ...)				
(+)				
CHANGE PROCESS CONTROL (self coordination, self control,...)				
(+)			POWER OF TARGETS	
WORKING WITH NEW CONCEPT				

Figure 30:   Patterns of Participatory Change Management

Fig. 31 outlines a bidirectional and therefore more balanced pattern of participation.

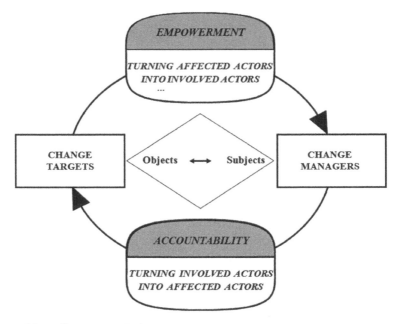

Figure 31:   Congruence Principle of Change Management

By this principle of congruence, the two-class system of change targets on the one hand, and change managers on the other hand, is more or less eliminated. Opportunities and risks are shared by both groups. Empowerment follows the credo of organizational development. The proportions between the „locomotives" and the „wagons" of the change are shifted in favor of the locomotives, which in turn increases the "promotion power" and vigor of the change program. Recently, the battle against the two-class system of players has yielded an inverse principle of participation, i.e. accountability: thereby the involved actors are turned into affected parties. This is achieved by integrating commitment to, and success of change programs in the change managers' MbO agreements. Together, the „congruence principle" of change management is fulfilled since rights and responsibilities in the change process are balanced.

3.3.6 Patterns of communication

The generic patterns of communication are also relevant to change management since communication serves as a critical determinant of change management performance (see chapter 5.6). On the one hand, configuration patterns such as 1:1 – communication (dyadic configuration) versus 1:n communication ("broadcasting", mass communication) have an impact both on effectiveness (customization of information contents) and efficiency (costs) of communication. On the other hand the communication channels turn out to be relevant: channel characteristics concern the direction of information flows (one-way or two-way communication) which impacts the credibility of content and senders. Moreover, channels determine the density and directness (immediate versus intermediated relationships) of communication: "chains", "wheels", "circles" and other centralized patterns enable fewer connections than decentralized networked patterns. Furthermore, communication media and infrastructures like face-to-face-communication versus telecommunication determine richness and reach of communication activities.

3.4 Parameters of Change Management

While patterns and - even more - paradigms are sparse, there is an abundance of parameters than can be utilized for change management purposes. They are located in the four *domains* of change management (see fig. 10 and chapter 4): The most common species of parameters are methods, techniques, and *tools*, e.g. workshops, surveys, kick-off meetings, blogs. In addition to this, *processes* serve as parameters, e.g. negotiating, communicating, solving conflicts or compensating losers of change. A third category of parameters is change management *skills* such as competence in project planning, empathy, trust building. Recently, levels of skills that differentiate between beginners and masters or experts have been defined, e.g. green, black and master black belts in quality management or D, C, B, and A-levels of project management skills ranging from Certified Project Management Associate (D) to Certified Projects Director (A). *Roles* complete the scope of essential parameters. Sponsors, experts, consultants, champions, Project Management Offices (PMO), third parties, or devil's advocates illustrate the broad spectrum of players needed for change projects.

Another taxonomy of parameters is based on the distinction between *soft factors* and *hard factors*. Visions for change initiatives (as part of reactive change management) as well as change cultures (as part of proactive change management) represent the most prominent soft ("cloudlike") parameters. In contrast milestone, resource planning, and organizational charts, stand for hard factors in change management.

Finally parameters are categorized according to their performance focus, i.e. either *effectiveness* or *efficiency*. So, on the one hand all devices that foster acceptance such as communication and motivation, yield effectiveness, although some of them in an inefficient, i.e. very costly and time consuming fashion. On the other hand, step-by-step processes, milestone planning, controlling of project costs and the like support cost and time efficient change projects but do not contribute to acceptance.

Within the 3P-framework, the choice of parameters must fit into the framing patterns as well as paradigms. Proactive change management utilizes parameters of "culture management" to establish a culture of readiness for change by applying manifestos, codes, and heroes which are not suitable for a reactive change management approach. Although both paradigms operate on guidelines, there are significant differences in timeframes to build up a) some generally accepted principles for handling all change processes at large as opposed to b) a slogan for a single change project.

4 Domains of Change Management

4.1 Scope of Domains

Paradigms, patterns, and parameters shape four different but interrelated domains of change management (see fig. 10 and fig. 32): Processes, tools, potential, and roles. Mapping the change management terrain according to these four domains follows a generic approach applied to all areas of management. Firstly, the four domains represent determinants of management performance: the design of procedures, the richness of toolboxes, the level of expertise and the existence of caretakers have an impact on success or failure of change initiatives. Secondly they represent views of modeling change management: the functional (process), personal (potential), instrumental (tool), and institutional (role) views. Within the process view for example, procedures are the foreground whereas the three remaining domains are (not entirely excluded, but) modeled less precisely as background. Processes and tools belong to the *task management* sphere of management whereas potential (a product of skill and will factors) and roles are part of *people management*.

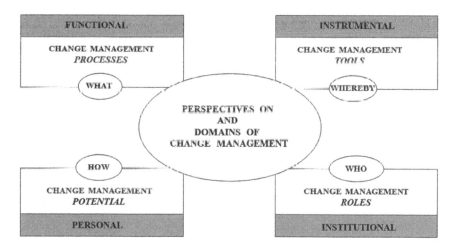

Figure 32:   Domains of Change Management

Consequently potential and roles together shape the domain of *change leadership*. As outlined in fig. 30, leadership is not identical with an autocratic or top-down way of managing change but also covers participation of targets. Whereas the term "change *managers*" denotes all players that impact change management in an authorized way, "change *leaders*" denominate the subset of managers who primarily deal with people such as members of a project team or targets. Leadership combines two notions of competence: *individual* competence (i.e. a potential in the heads and hearts of human beings) and *organizational* competence (a license to do something as part of a job or role description). Change agents fulfill management jobs by order of a principal, which characterizes for instance the relationship between steering committee and project managers. Unlike change agents who may exploit existing information asymmetries opportunistically, change *stewards* act (as "organizational citizens") for the sake of the greater good in terms of the performance of the change project.

Each domain contains the 3Ps as building blocks. Change leadership for instance is based on leadership paradigms (e.g. transformational or transactional leadership), patterns of participatory leadership (see fig. 30) as well as parameters, such as criteria and assessment centers for recruiting project managers. Likewise change processes may follow an internal marketing paradigm, an AIDA-pattern, and execute operations within the place, price, promotion, and product sectors of the marketing mix.

4.2 Processes

The *functional* approach focuses on optimized change processes, e.g. a better timing of pilot and roll-out phases and parallel instead of sequential communication with managers, employees, customers and other stakeholders affected by the change. In the (long) list of standard processes in change management, we find planning of activities, recruiting of multiplicators, diagnosing the need for change, dismantling barriers to success, milestone planning, preparing workshops, convincing targets, coaching, and many more. Obviously, the scope of change management processes incorporates *generic* management processes as well as *change specific* processes. Like management in general, change management relies on generic processes of problem solving or decision making. In contrast, implementation processes in terms of fitting a new concept into an existing context (see fig. 8) are change specific.

Process models are either embedded into the *rational design paradigm*, the *realistic comprehension paradigm*, or into a *hybrid paradigm* (see paragraph 3.2). Fig. 33 outlines three prevalent process models related to the three respective paradigms: the phase model of rational problem solving, the three stages of Darwinian evolution, and the (hybrid) three phase unfreeze-move-freeze model of attitude change. The latter model is not restricted to the unfreezing of personal attitudes, but can be applied to any attempt of destabilizing, including structures, relationships, beliefs, implicit theories, and business processes.

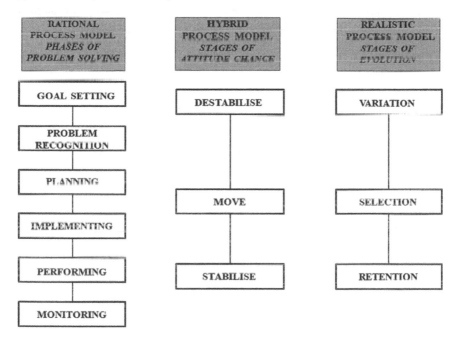

Figure 33:   Rational, Realistic and Hybrid Process Models

The respective process models can also be characterized by the typical environment for handling change: with the rational phase model this would be project management, with the hybrid model a social community (e.g. interactions on weblogs or forums) and with the evolutionary model certain intelligence activities such as benchmarking (to identify best practices), monitoring trends and mainstreams which also covers the identification of fads (finding out what the majority in the change community does) and "going with the flow".

Another hybrid blended model of change processes (on the company level) is *path breaking* or path creation in terms of a "planned path emergence". Fig. 34 outlines the generic four-stage pattern of path breaking, starting and ending with path dependence as a consequence of self-reinforcing processes, the economies of habitualisation (e.g. routine, efficiency, predictability) and bandwagon effects. The milestones of this pattern are a de-locking incident as well as a critical incident that eventually provokes a new lock-in. De-locking increases the scope of alternative options whereas selection processes have a reducing impact on diversity.

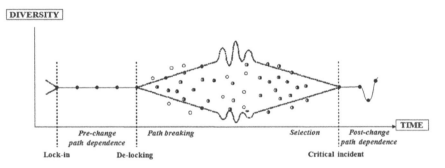

Figure 34:   Path Breaking as a Hybrid Process Model

When applying the path-breaking model to information processing strategies, information processing based on locally available soft- and hardware and cloud computing represent the pre-change and post-change paths respectively. De-locking is accomplished by DSL- and SOA-infrastructures, digital convergence, and good practices in IT-outsourcing with respect to cost savings. This triggers a variety of outsourcing-models, such as managed services with significantly different sizes of retained resources, private clouds, software-, network-, infrastructure-as-a- service models, etc. Spectacular failures of these hybrid approaches may represent a critical incident that creates a cloud computing mainstream.

The discrepancy between the rational and the realistic paradigms - and consequently process models - may be dramatic. Normally the mega difference is characterized by "unrealistic" procedures and "irrational" or "pathological" ways of handling change in reality. So, an irrational process may by the inverse of a rational procedure. In fact, real-world change processes sometimes follow a path-goal approach, i.e. the opposite of the rational goal-path approach. First, one decides to join a mainstream – for instance by introducing teamwork or shared services - and only afterwards, the specific advantages that teamwork brings are scrutinized.

Phase models are based on a thoroughly rational goal-path approach which relies on cybernetic thinking, primarily feedback and feed-forward loops as well as management cycles. It prescribes mandatory stages regardless of the specific contents of a project (see fig. 35).

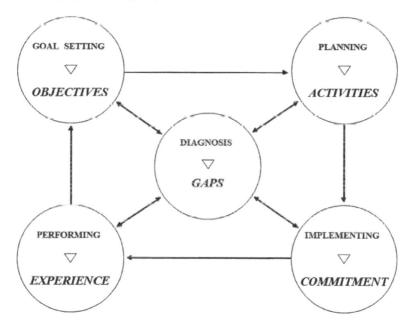

Figure 35:   Rational Phases of Change Management

In simplistic models, only diagnosis, design and implementation are differentiated. A more detailed structure differentiates the phases "setting goals" (vision), "recognizing problems", "planning activities" (concept), "implementing concepts", "performing activities", and "monitoring realization". Each phase provides *navigation data* such as goals, paths or gaps in terms of discrepancies between goals and anticipated or actual results. The power of orientation increases from goals to measures.

Within the reactive paradigm of change management, the core planning activity is *project planning*. Fig. 36 delivers a micro-view of project planning activities. Planning is either focused on the project *mission* or on the project *resources* (mainly human resources). So, cost planning deals with two complementary categories of project costs: Costs in terms of the monetary equivalent of resource consumption as well as cost in terms of (opportunity) costs (e.g. due to a contractual penalty) caused by an insufficient fulfillment of the project mission.

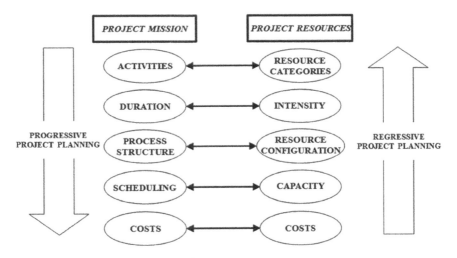

Figure 36:   Process Model of Project Planning

Besides project planning there are more change specific processes in the reactive change management paradigm: diagnostic processes of problem recognition and monitoring for instance deal with the identification of barriers to success (e.g. resistance, opponents) and barriers to failure (e.g. stamina, slack).

In addition to project planning, several *people management* activities are required to support the efforts for effective change management. To achieve a satisfying level of acceptance communication, training, motivating and organizing processes have to be conceived and executed. The specific dynamics of change performance (see fig. 20) require people management processes to cope with confusion (by coaching), diffusion (by internal marketing) and erosion (by supporting).

"People" in the reactive paradigm are change targets, e.g. employees and managers affected by a change project. "People" within the proactive paradigm stand for both managers and targets of change, in other words for all human resources involved. Hence generic *leadership functions* are also critical building blocks of change management processes (see fig. 37).

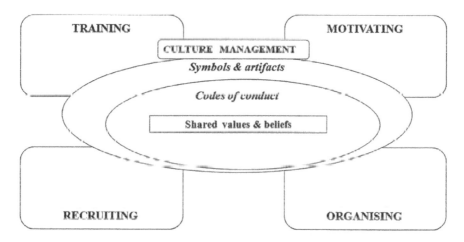

Figure 37:   People Management Processes

Recruiting in reactive change management refers to members of the project team. In proactive change management the recruiting of all employees is addressed: recruiting for change readiness is accomplished by selecting employees according to mobility, age, and learning capacity. According to aphorisms like "you can't teach an old dog new tricks", a juvenile manpower is more change-friendly than a graying workforce. *Motivating* in the reactive paradigm is often accomplished by compensating losers of change. In the proactive paradigm, motivation focuses growth, competence and affiliation needs. *Training* is focused on skills to cope with a specific concept in the reactive approach while focused on developing interpersonal skills and meta-competencies in the proactive paradigm. *Organizing* means either project organization or implementing flexible agile structures for organizational learning, e.g. flat hierarchies or communities of practice.

The proactive paradigm also covers processes of establishing a change friendly corporate culture. The management of culture differs from the four outlined people management functions because the ultimate object of culture, i.e. shared values and beliefs, can only be influenced indirectly via symbols, artifacts, and codes of conduct. The typical processes of culture management contain story-telling, working on the image of some "heroes of change", documenting and communicating on change-related values.

Another cluster of change management processes consists of *efficiency enhancing processes*. Controlling activities intend to cut change management costs and shorten project duration. This is accomplished via complexity management, e.g. step-by-step implementing which reduces error risks and thereby costs of change projects.

Despite the heterogeneous composition of the domain, all processes of change management have a common denominator: they create value by offering services (see also appendix A: Servitization). Recipients or "customers" of these services are stakeholders, principals, targets of change, and project managers. Unlike other value generating processes, service processes follow a specific logic: customers play a hybrid role. They are not only consumers of the services but also co-producers. These "pro-sumers" invest proprietary resources into the service delivery process, e.g. knowhow or budgets.

4.3 Leadership: Potential and Roles

Leaders or change are specified by their personal potential (skill and will) and their respective roles in the change process. Leaders are not exclusively positioned in top management (mostly characterized as "transformational leadership") but are distributed all over the company and sometimes even positioned outside the company. Although the need for leadership is not denied there is a lack of approaches to develop change leaders. This disregard can only be explained by the fact that change managers do not need to be supported: their skills and willingness to change are simply available without any special training or motivating activities. The idea that change leaders are "born" (and not trained) and that they are intrinsically "burning" for a change initiative (without being rewarded) turns out to be a myth that does not correspond to reality. In fact, leading change requires certain qualifications that not all leaders possess but which have to be acquired by specific measures. The first of these is being informed. Leaders, too, have to be aware of the contents, the reasons and the consequences of the impending changes. Furthermore, a not inconsiderable requirement of training has to be covered, especially in the new categories of change management, such as internal marketing, project management and controlling. This is the only way in which the required skills can be acquired. Motivation activities for change managers have to be worked upon intensively. The assumption that managers are "dying for" change initiatives despite the difficult times, massive barriers and frustrating experiences with implementation pitfalls proves to be too naïve. Adequate capacity planning has to ensure that change leaders have sufficient time to fulfill their roles in the change process despite the burdens of everyday business. This means that priorities have to be set for change projects and slack has to be ensured (e.g. promoter positions have to be shared). All companies are therefore well advised to invest a portion of their change budgets in „change management for change leaders".

The scope of roles change leaders have to play is multifaceted. They are needed as *promoters or facilitators of the change*. Two very different forms of support are expected of such „change agents". On the one hand, they are required as *visionaries, missionaries ("evangelists")* and *role models (" heroes")*. They have to convince the affected parties of the necessity of the change, develop guiding principles and actively set an example by visibly adopting new behavior. On the other hand, their methodological (search and replace) skills as *"craftsmen"* of the change are required. This includes for instance selecting suitable project team members and training schemes (for them), moderating in workshops, keeping people informed, planning project procedures, managing project costs, and marketing the change initiative, for example with road shows (presenting projects in subsidiaries and plants) or organizing idea competitions. Several surveys show that „visionaries" and

„craftsmen" have different attitudes to change initiatives: visionaries from top management are always more optimistic about the prospects of implementing changes than the craftsmen from middle management and staff departments.

The job description for change leaders outlined above raises the question whether the necessary skills are an automatic „joint product" of standard leadership qualifications or whether *additional qualifications* are required. There is every reason to assume that managers have to acquire various additional skills so that they are well prepared for their function in change projects: A good leader is not automatically good at managing change.

The broad functional scope of change leader roles automatically raises another question: How many persons are needed as leaders in change management? Interestingly, the views of the appropriate configuration of change leadership differ significantly, especially with respect to number and diversity of actors involved into change management. There are four levels of configuration complexity, ranging from simple to highly diversified configurations.

Champions of change: Here, change leadership is focused on one person ("Mister or Miss Change"). Some champions have turned into icons of the community of change managers (e.g. GE's Jack Welch).

Project team: Every member of a change project team is considered as a change leader, including experts and occasionally also external consultants. They are supposed to form a "strong guiding coalition". The leadership performance is usually measured by indicators of locomotion and cohesion.

Project supply chain: The extension of the configuration is mainly triggered by the triad model of promoters of change, i.e. *sponsors, champions*, and *experts*. Sometimes, sponsors are separated into a tandem configuration of initiating and sustaining sponsors. Only champions and some core experts are full time members of the project team. Sponsors are located outside of the project team in steering committees, some experts are involved into the change management process only part-time. This holds for staff and service departments (e.g. corporate development, strategic planning, human resources management, legal department). Some companies have set up internal consultancy networks or communities. *External consultants* play a critical role in the success of change management. They bring methodical routine into change management as well as authority based upon expertise. The entire configuration can be captured in a *supply chain* or *value chain* consisting of the project team, a downstream coordination super-structure and an upstream service-infrastructure (see fig. 38).

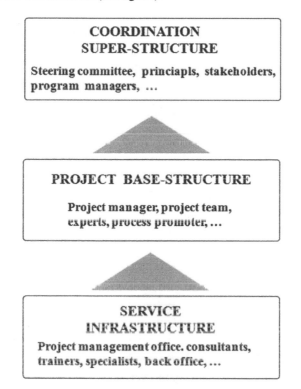

Figure 38:   Supply Chain of Change Leadership

Change Leadership Value Net: Unfortunately supply chain models are afflicted with a twofold deficit: First, they operate on *one-way* supply relationships between sponsors, champions, and experts. This contradicts the afore-mentioned logic of service processes where co-producers occupy two positions: a downstream position as customers (principals) and an upstream position as sponsors. Secondly, although they do cover vertical input-output relationships, they neglect horizontal relationships that are normally not based on transactions. Hence the influence of some actors outside the value chain is ignored. Change management is usually embedded in a multi-project management environment. Supply chain models do not take into account that some neighboring projects are complementary to a reference project while others are competing for budget, manpower, and attention of change targets. To overcome the two deficits a transition from a chain to a network approach is required. An appropriate network model is the *value net* model developed in strategic management. The adaption to change management yields a *change leadership value net*-model (see fig. 39).

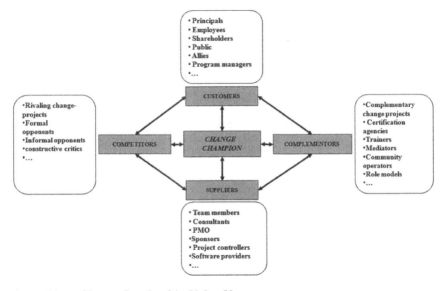

Figure 39:   Change Leadership Value Net

The change champion (project manager) serves as reference unit which is embedded into four network arenas. The two *vertical* arenas emulate the supply chain, however with fundamental modifications: on the one hand this concerns the hybrid role of top management as principals of change champions (customers) and as their sponsors (suppliers). On the other hand change targets are integrated into the customer arena: Change champions provide services for this target group in terms of supporting their efforts to cope with the change by communicating, motivating and training activities.

Project managers get support from two sources: the *suppliers* and the so called *complementors*. Complementors furnish complementary services to the customers. One cluster of complementors provides *infrastructures for interactions*, e.g. for collaboration, knowledge management, quality assurance, conflict management, or trust building. By definition, their services address several actors in the value net simultaneously. Another cluster consists of project managers of complementary change projects. Their service for the customers consists of their contribution to solutions, i.e. integrated configurations to meet customers' demands. Their service to the change champion is knowledge transfer which generates economies of scope, i.e. a reduction of overall costs of change management costs via good practice learning. Unlike the services from suppliers the majority of services from complementors are not systematically procured, let alone ordered by the project champions. Hence complementor relationships require sophisticated models of coordination beyond the familiar transactions along the supply chain.

Competitors are relevant for change leadership on the one hand, because they build up barriers to success for the reference change project. This is accomplished either in an official transparent way (e.g. by line managers, critics and devil's advocates) or in an informal clandestine fashion. Rivaling projects absorb both resources (from steering committees in multi-project management) and attention on the side of the change targets. However, on the other hand even competitors may support change projects. This paradoxical role is captured in the notion of the "good competitor". A TQM project and a knowledge management project may compete for budgets and attention but at the same time they cooperatively augment the sense of urgency for change.

In the balanced resilience framework, *barrier management* in terms of dismantling barriers and building up barriers to failure is a core job of change leaders. With respect to role assignment there are at least two options for allocating these jobs within the change leadership value net. The discovery of alternative assignment models is supported by analogies from team sports: In football there is a division of labor between a) defense and goal keepers who are in charge of building up barriers to failure ("risk managers") and b) forwards who are in charge of dismantling barriers to success ("opportunity managers"). In contrast, there is no organized separation between risk and opportunity focused players in basket ball, in other words: all members of the team act as risk as well as opportunity managers. When transferring these models into the change leadership value net, a division of risk and opportunity managers may be typical amongst complementors as well as suppliers (e.g. compliance officers and specialists for project risk management). In contrast, the remaining players in the value net, i.e. project base, super-structure, competitors and targets, are characterized by an entrepreneurial involvement into the change management process. Like all entrepreneurs, they simultaneously practice a balanced management change risks and change opportunities.

4.4 Tools

The tool approach represents the arena of change management with a maximum overlap of scientists' and practitioners' handling of change projects. The overall fund of tools is steadily growing. So are toolboxes in terms of actual configurations of tools for use in specific change projects. This augmentation is partly due to the activities of change consultancies, that develop and use tool innovations as a competitive strategy of differentiation (e.g. tool branding).

The tool domain is fundamentally shaped by antithetic *paradigms* of handling tool diversity: on the one hand, the *dogmatic* paradigm restricts tool application to a specific category of tools. A stringent preference for soft participatory tools for instance strictly prohibits the application of "manipulative" marketing tools. On the other hand *blended* approaches emphasize the advantages of mixing tools, in other words the advantages of diversity.

The prevalent *patterns* of tool development either follow the demand-pull approach (targets or sponsors determine tool utilization) or the supply-push approach (consultants determine tool utilization). All *push-approaches* imply the risk of generating "toys" (rather than tools) with questionable utility for users. In contrast, a *pull-pattern* assures implementation but restricts the creativity of the development process to very few sources. A *blended approach* advocates a hybrid pull-push pattern to exploit the strengths of the two models.

On the *parameter* level of the tool domain, the existing plethora of tools requires taxonomies to avoid complexity overkill that creates some "poverty due to abundance".

Furthermore, tools or media differ with respect to their *information technological ingredients*. Conventional tools rely on *non-digital,* paper and pencil devices as well as on non-virtual, face-to-face ways of interaction (see fig. 40). In contrast, *digital tools* exploit the power of software, hardware (e.g. devices for mobile telecommunication), and IT networks (e.g. Internet technologies). Software tools primarily support project management, presentations, and simulations. Some tools are provided via the Internet and cloud computing. For the time being, blended tools in terms of non digital-digital mixed tools represent (unlike blended *toolboxes*, see chapter 5) a niche in the spectrum of change management tools.

Figure 40:   Digital and Non-digital Tools for Change Management

Digital tools and especially Internet tools provide an electronic infrastructure that enables a twofold virtualisation of change processes, especially of communication, collaboration, and learning processes: *organizational virtuality* and *representation virtuality*. Fig. 41 illustrates the two categories of virtual environments from a learning perspective.

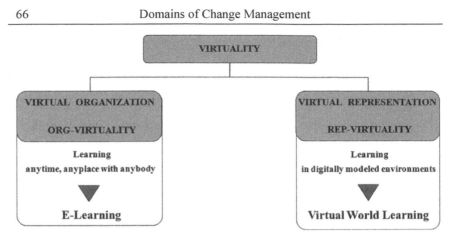

Figure 41:   Scope of Virtual Environments for Learning

Organizational virtuality dismantles temporal, spatial, and inter-organizational boundaries and enables communication and collaboration in an anytime-anyplace-anybody mode. So, a geographically dispersed (and mobile) manpower can be integrated into change management processes that bring together members from different enterprises in (more or less) open communities. This reduces travelling-, opportunity-, and transaction costs significantly. Moreover the effectiveness of some core change processes like learning processes is enhanced, since learning becomes more personalized. Notably web 2.0-tools such as weblogs, Wikis and social networks enable inter-organizational learning.

Representation virtuality utilizes high tech infrastructures. The elements of change processes, i.e. concepts (new products, buildings, etc.), contexts (competitors' products, natural environment, markets, etc.) as well as players are digitally represented in computer animations, simulations, morphing software, virtual reality or by avatars. Unlike mental models, dreams or fantasy of individuals, these tools create possible artificial worlds in a visual fashion thereby meeting the essence of change, i.e. visions of environments that do not - or at least not yet - exist in reality.

Different *clusters of change management tools* support the handling of two rather different objects: *Informational* tools help change leaders to source and process the information needed for solving change related problems. Relevant information for goal setting, diagnostic processes, planning and implementing cover three categories: models (e.g. reactance as an answer to regulation), methods (e.g. gap analysis), and data (e.g. frequencies of answers to questions in surveys). *Social* tools support the handling of interactions. The list of interactions encompasses teamwork, meetings, interviews, negotiations, workshops, event management (e.g. kick-offs, presentations), collaborative problem solving, and conflict management. Change specific tools for face-to-face team working are not restricted to small groups such as project teams or steering committees. There are also tools for handling certain interactions in large groups, e.g. Open Space (http://www.openspaceworld.org/) or World cafe'(www.theworldcafe.com/) for up to several hundreds of participants.

Chapter 5 delivers an in-depth analysis of toolboxes for implementation managers. The extended spectrum of demands on change programs calls for a wide range of change management instruments: These instruments are not restricted to the classic domains of human resources management and the project organization but also apply to other management sectors. These include various hard factors such as complexity management, marketing and controlling change.

5 Blended Toolboxes for Change Management

5.1 The Logic of Tool Blending

The BxB-approach to change management generates blended toolboxes. Whenever antithetic tools such as hard and soft tools are combined, blending yields hybrid toolboxes. There is evidence from recent surveys that blended change management is practiced via blended toolboxes. The majority of change managers advocate tool blending rather than substituting old by new tools. Only a minority concentrate on familiar face-to-face tools. Tool blending is predominantly guided by rational considerations, i.e. task features are more relevant than personal preferences (such as affinity to technology or tendencies towards familiar instruments) or experience.

The diversity of the blended components determines the hybridity of toolboxes: A combination of workshops, flyers, meetings and a letter from the CEO in the employees' magazine characterizes a *low* level of diversity (*homogeneous blending*) since all tools in the list rely on conventional communication via physical meetings or print media. The level of diversity *increases* when both face-to-face tools and digital media (e.g. e-mail, virtual communities and weblogs) are used. Diversity stems from the contrast between the blended tools (*heterogeneous blending)*, since electronic media, unlike face-to-face change management, go along with asynchronous communication and lack a face-to-face contact between the involved players.

Implementation tools provide an excellent illustration for blended toolboxes: Whereas proactive change management operates on *generic* management and leadership tools such as on-the-job learning, management of agile structures and recruiting contingent and flexible manpower, tools embedded into the reactive paradigm are *more change specific*. Within this paradigm *implementation* is focused on overcoming resistance to change, i.e. it deals with barriers to success rather than building up barriers to failure.

There are many arenas of tool blending in change management processes:

–   Change managers often utilize both the potential of *participative* Organizational Development (OD) tools and of "*manipulative*" marketing tools (e.g. "selling" change by means of awards, slogans, road shows, "deals", and advertising).

- Besides *soft* factors such as coaching, success stories, persuasion, role and theatre playing, *hard* factors like Balanced Scorecards or milestone planning are quite frequently applied within the same change project.

- *Top-down*-interventions (e.g. kick-offs, cascading information processes, corporate blogs) are combined with *bottom-up*-initiatives (e.g. suggestion schemes, continuous improvement process, communities, social software).

- Change management relies on physical *face-to-face* interactions as well as on *virtual* interactions via electronic media.

- Communication is based on unilateral *broadcasting* and on *interactive* environments such as team meetings, Open Space, workshops and video conferences.

- Acquisition of requisite skills is accomplished by *on the job-* and *off the job-* learning.

- Hybrid tools of *edutainment* and *infotainment* (e.g. Business TV, "gamification") help foster learning motivation.

Hence, most configurations of toolboxes imply numerous blending decisions. The *denotation* of blending emphasizes its hybrid make-up ("combining extremes") whereas the *connotation* of blending refers to the effectiveness of these mixes, captured in slogans like "best of both worlds-combinations". Blended models outside the management sphere such as blended materials (alloy), beverages or tobacco serve as good practices. Two arenas of tool blending are especially relevant:

Blended effectiveness-focused and efficiency-focused toolboxes: Bilateral face-to-face-talks (personalized 1:1 communication patterns) for instance are supposed to foster acceptance most effectively but cause considerable costs whereas e-mail communication (1:n-patterns) is very cost-efficient but not very effective. So the trade-off between effective and efficient change management may be handled by blending effective and efficient tools. One useful blended pattern is *mass customized communication* in change management: a combination of a standard content for all recipients (assuring efficiency) and an personalized content customized to different target groups (assuring effectiveness).

Blended digital and non digital toolboxes (see fig. 40): Blending creates a mix of real world activities and virtual world activities. For example, blending combines the *reach* of virtual communication and the *richness* of real world communication.

All species of tool blending cover three levels of blending (see fig. 10): On the *paradigm* level two principles of blending are applied: the *compound* paradigm operates on mixing complementary additive components in an "as-well-as"-fashion, primarily to reach excellence (best of both worlds): Only the mix of two (or more) tools warrants performance. This is for instance the logic of the (internal) marketing mix. In contrast, the *conjoint* paradigm combines alternative, .i.e. functionally redundant components in an "either-or"-fashion. In other words, each of the mixed tools is capable of solving the respective problem on its own. The blending does not yield excellence, but supports resilience in terms handling uncertainty, surprises, and turbulences by utilizing some slack in the blended toolbox. On the level of blending *patterns* there is a scope of several ways of mixing which are embedded either into the compound or the conjoint paradigm (see also fig. 44). A common conjoint pattern (frequently applied in blended learning) is sequential coupling: project work is often initialized by a face-to-face kick-off and continued in a virtual fashion supported by collaborative web tools and videoconferencing. On the *parameter* level the blending patterns are specified by fixing quantitative proportions, for instance the duration of face-to-face interactions in relation to virtual interactions.

Just like strategies, structures, systems or other building blocks of management, toolboxes are either a) the result of deliberate planning (engineered patterns of blending) or b) the result of unplanned activities (emergent patterns of blending) or possibly c) a (hybrid) combination of both, in the tradition of hybrid process models like guided evolution, logical incrementalism, organic rationality or organized anarchy. *Engineered* patterns of blending are created by a rational planning process. The objective of this process is achieving an optimal opportunities-risks ratio. *Emergent* patterns of blending are not determined by rational procedures. Like in all other fields of management, change managers are not necessarily guided by the rational evaluation of opportunities and risks. There are many other factors that influence blending activities. Some of them are apparently irrational from the standpoint of rational optimization. A prominent example is "change management follows fashion", with "hypes" (quite common in the lifecycle of electronic trends) representing an extreme species of fashion (e.g. incubators or "Apponomics"). However, go-with-the-flow behaviors in change management may have rational advantages for the situation of the individual change manager: for instance, mainstreams serve as an acceptable justification for individual decisions.

5.2 Evaluation of Tool Blending: Opportunities and Risks

Eclectic augmentation of toolboxes per se does not automatically mean enrichment, let alone a guaranty for enhanced performance. Neither is blending per se the reliable cure of weaknesses and drawbacks of some "second best" change management tools. A transfer of lessons learned from other blending arenas – both modern arenas such as blended learning, multimedia, multichannel distribution (brick & click- companies), or diversity management and traditional arenas like carrot & stick-leadership, dual leadership or interactions of intrinsic and extrinsic motivation – indicate that a "more means better" point of view is rather naïve. The message of these lessons is captured in a caveat: blending goes along with several risks of inefficiency or even ineffectiveness, e.g. over-load, lack of orientation, high costs and frictions.

To respond to the resulting ambivalent connotation of blending by a simple "blending: bane or boon-approach" turns out to be too superficial. Instead, the rational design of toolboxes should follow the principle of "no integration without evaluation". Evaluation delivers the orientation for interventions to strengthen the opportunities and to mitigate the risks related to tool blending. Fig. 42 illustrates a simplified evaluation of blending face-to-face and electronic tools in change management.

The evaluation model for blended toolboxes is hybrid the same way the objects of the evaluation are. The evaluation of the two tool clusters is focused on their respective *strengths* and *weaknesses*. From the perspective of the balanced resilience framework, opportunities (economies) are provided by the "productive tension" in a hybrid construction (area above the diagonal in fig. 42) whereas risks (diseconomies) come from "unproductive frictions" between the diverse components (area below the diagonal). In fig. 42, the evaluation is boiled down to just one typical strength and weakness of each cluster.

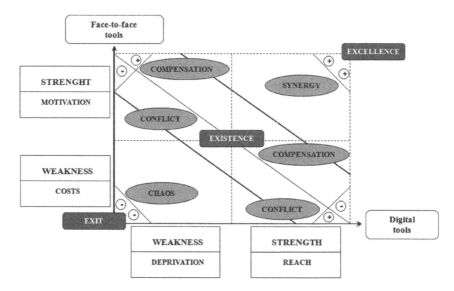

Figure 42:   Opportunities and Risks of Tool Blending

Face-to-face tools like group discussions or bilateral talks normally have a strong impact on motivation by offering the possibility to give immediate and personalized feedbacks and by satisfying social needs. These advantages, however, come along with high costs for travelling to physical meetings or seminars. Electronic tools like e-mail, intranet portals or social software typically have a high reach, since they are able to deliver information quickly and easily to all geographically dispersed employees, team members, or customers. However, this broadcasting bears the risk of social deprivation of the actors involved because emotional feedbacks in the change process are impaired. Thus, digital tools often leave social needs as well as security needs unsatisfied and fail in dealing with confusion, anxieties and other typical concomitants of change.

Tool blending enables excellent *synergetic learning* ("2+2=5") in terms of richness and reach of communication when communication via intranet and via workshops is combined. A *compensation* of weaknesses by strengths of the complementary tool is reached, when – for example - the time needed for seminars can be reduced by providing general basic information via electronic media prior to the face-to-face seminars. From a performance perspective, tool blending creates resilient learning systems.

One category of risk caused by blending is *conflict*: Providing redundant content by print and by digital media may provoke a conflict with project budget restrictions. Incompatibility may even cause *chaos*, for instance when contradictory contents are delivered via electronic media and physical meetings. This "mess" may be due to the fact that digital media are normally more up-to-date whereas print media (e.g. employee magazines) often distribute data that is obsolete, especially against the background of the typical turbulences in change processes.

Fig. 43 gives a more detailed evaluation of *augmented learning* where real world learning and virtual world learning are blended according to an augmented reality-pattern.

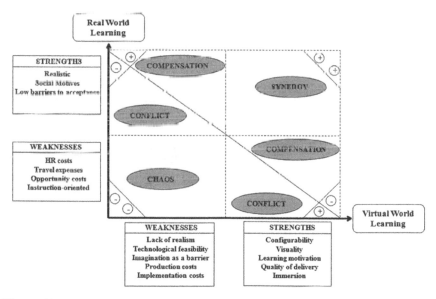

Figure 43:   Evaluation of Augmented Learning

Simulation tools, serious or educative games (mix of gaming and learning) and virtual reality (e.g. second life) as the major building blocks of virtual-world learning deliver a significantly better learning performance than no tech- or low tech-tools with respect to several determinants of learning performance. First, this holds for designability: virtual-world learning provides a better representation of possible, non-existing situations and more options for simulation than conventional tools like role playing or business theatre.

Moreover, the service level is higher since digital tools – unlike human trainers - are available in a reliable 24/7 mode and make quick responses whenever some requirements change. Furthermore, they foster learning motivation via immersion, the fun factor of gaming as well as edutainment.

5.3 Patterns of Tool Blending

Costs and benefits of tool blending depend on the way the respective tool components are coupled in order to create a high performing tool configuration. The manifold ways of coupling derive from a spectrum of archetypal patterns that determine the *architecture of a toolbox*. Fig. 44 outlines six blending patterns that are embedded in the compound and/ or conjoint paradigms of blending.

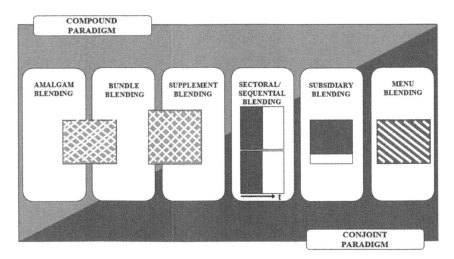

Figure 44:   Patterns of Tool Blending

Within *amalgam mixes* and *blended bundles* blending is performed in a "total" fashion yielding new genuinely hybrid tools that incorporate both genes of their parent tools: Project meetings are not either face-to-face or virtual, but semi-virtual (hybrid) with some team members participating physically, others virtually via videoconferencing (see fig. 41). Communication is neither purely top-down nor bottom-up, but takes place in an iterative down-up process. Whereas blending is mandatory in bundles, *supplement tool configurations* are based on optional blending: Whenever dialectical methods such as devil's advocates are applied the blending of thesis and antithesis (or first and second opinion) is supposed to yield a better synthesis.

In the case of *sectoral* and *sequential coupling*, change managers pick different tools out of a blended toolbox to apply them in distinct sectors or stages of the change project. By this strictly separated handling, tools can be adjusted to different segments of the context (e.g. different target groups like employees versus temporary manpower, top management versus lower management, silver workers versus digital natives), preferences of clients (reflecting their respective corporate culture) and modules of the change concept (e.g. redesigned business processes, organization charts, incentives systems, or company size). From a rational management point of view this corresponds to the idea of contingent management with respect to tool utilization. Likewise, face to face communication in the pilot phase can be combined with electronic communication in the roll out-phase which allows an adjustment to the respective sizes of the target groups. *Subsidiary blending* combines a default tool (standard) and a fallback tool (exception). For project leadership, self organization of the team is normally standard. Steering committees only interfere in a "management by exception mode", when the team fails in handling project problems. With team meetings, physical participation is the rule and virtual participation the exception in case travelling and opportunity costs prohibit physical participation. *Blended menus* offer at least two tools (e.g. e-mail or telephone, print media or electronic newsletters, physical workshops or virtual meetings on internet community platforms) as alternative options for ad hoc choices of tools. Providing menus is client-friendly but quite costly: Since tools are not pre-selected within a contingent change management approach, the whole range of diverse options has to be provided until change managers or clients make their choices.

Blending patterns are quantitatively specified on the *parameter* level. This is accomplished by fixing *proportions* of blending, i.e. the ratio of percentage of use of the tools in question. In sequential blending the duration of the episodes measures the intensity of tool application. 50:50-proportions stand for balanced blending (e.g. within bundles), while an 80:20-ratio indicates the dominance of one category (e.g. within subsidiary blending).

5.4 Implementation: Scope of Diagnostic and Intervention Tools

Implementation constitutes the craftsmanship sector of change management. The focal issues of implementation are not so much the visions of a change initiative, but the techniques, methods, and tools for its execution. All implementation efforts aim at aligning a new *concept* with an existing *context* (see fig. 45). The everyday business of implementers therefore consists of coordinating, harmonizing and fitting competitive strategies, e-business, business process responsibility, compliance programs, shared services, outsourcing, etc on the one hand, and existing structures, attitudes, career plans, claims to power, etc. on the other. What has to be controlled is the mutual process of alignment, in which both concept and context have to be modified: *accommodation* denotes the adjustment of the context to the new concept, *assimilation* the inverse adjustment of the new concept to the existing context. As a rule, implementation is effected through mutual adjustments of concept and context. These tasks are dealt with mainly in project teams, in bilateral negotiations with affected employees and – to a small extent – by deskwork.

Implementation activities apply to several sectors of the context simultaneously. *Technical* implementation makes sure that new software is compatible with the existing IT landscape. The object of *organizational* implementation is a fit, for example between the new principles of self-regulation and the existing principles of hierarchy-based management. Exactly which tools and measures should be used to achieve technical and organizational compatibility cannot be clarified in general terms. In contrast *people-focused* implementation always aims to achieve acceptance of the change through the affected targets by utilizing a *standard set* of implementation tools. Hence, universally valid statements about promoting acceptance can be made independently of specific concepts that are to be implemented. All *proactive* change management endeavors foster change readiness in the context and consequently reduce the delta between concept and context and hence the difficulty of implementation work.

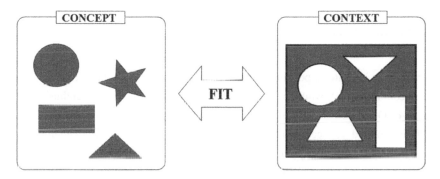

Figure 45:   Implementation as Aligning Concept and Context

Since ideas of concept and context are mostly represented by individual persons or groups of people, all implementation activities are also about handling conflicts. Here, instruments of conflict management are used. Sometimes, within the framework of one-sided *context adjustment* (accommodation) an enormous capacity for adjustment is expected of the affected workforce. The concept is not compromised, rather it is "pushed through". If this is successful, a manpower infrastructure for the new concept has been established which is conducive to implementation. *Concept adjustment* (assimilation) on the other hand involves more or less far-reaching modifications to the original concept. Negotiations are frequently the arenas at which an original concept is reworked and remodeled.

The successful organizing of this mutual adjustment process requires not only instruments to intervene in the concept and the context (*intervention tools*), but also *diagnostic tools*. Intervention tools which are supposed to make the affected managers, employees, but also customers, shareholders and suppliers, adapt their behavior to comply with the concept, represent the essence of implementation instruments. Four clusters of instruments that loosely correlate with four acceptance factors can be differentiated: *communication, training, motivation* and *organization tools* (see fig. 46).

Even the most perfect "know-how" to intervene cannot achieve the desired acceptance levels if it is applied at the wrong place. A „know-where"-support is therefore required to provide information about where exactly knowledge, capacity, skills, or willingness are available or are missing. Navigation assistance of this kind is provided by *diagnostic* tools. These intelligence activities include analyses of absenteeism statistics, employee talks and customer surveys.

Acceptance indicates a positive attitude to the change and is related in a way to the term commitment. It would be unrealistic to equate acceptance with enthusiasm (see fig. 14). On a realistic acceptance scale, forced cooperation and mere toleration are still interpreted as acceptance. Such levels of weak accordance signal however unstable attitudes. They can easily turn into evasive behavior, retreat, protests, strikes, boycotts and sabotages, as well as other manifestations of rejection (see fig. 27).

How can we find out whether the implementation activities have achieved acceptance? The question can be settled by bringing typical *acceptance indicators* into play. Behavior complying with the new order is a fairly good indication of acceptance. Think for example of the voluntary participation of employees in the activities of quality circles, communities of practice or of their investment in idea management-systems. By the same token, manifest refusal or retreat is a clear indication of non-acceptance. A controversial issue is the view that the number of employees who have taken part in introductory workshops (the so-called degree of pervasion) allows conclusions to be drawn about acceptance. In contrast, agreements, in which the affected managers and employees publicly demonstrate their backing for the reform by means of their signatures, can be seen as comparatively reliable indicators of acceptance. They represent not just non-binding lip service but rather formal agreements on targets; arrangements within the framework of promotional talks, contracts with unions, and employee surveys also provide indicators of acceptance.

Besides the acceptance indicators, *acceptance factors* are also of central importance to fostering acceptance: they determine the level of acceptance. At the same time they act as the starting points and target variables for specific change supporting activities. The section of a people management toolbox dedicated to influence attitudes and behaviors of people contains four core domains (see fig. 46). This classification is based upon the primary functionality of the tools, i.e. influencing the acceptance of change from employees, managers, customers, public and other groups affected by the transition. Within the balanced resilience framework, the four tool clusters serve as means to overcome the four categories of resistance to change, i.e. the four generic barriers of success of change management (see fig. 16).

To make people commit to new behavior and thereby accept or even embrace change both the ability for change (*skill factor*) and the willingness for change (*will factor*) must be taken care of. The tool domains of *information* and *instruction* complementarily determine the level of skill while *involvement* and *integration* determine the willingness of the change targets. Information and communication tools in change management are supposed to specify the content, the objectives, the consequences, and the progress of a change project.

Training is expected to develop the requisite personal competencies, and motivation tools to provide a commitment to the change project. Finally, organization tools such as participation and project organization integrate people actively into the change process by giving them roles which they are supposed to play, such as project managers, mediators, multiplicators, role models, or coaches. Acceptance is facilitated by getting the affected employees to know what the change is all about, know how to deal with it and also actually want it. It is also important to get as many affected employees as possible to adopt the new codes of behavior by having to take on certain roles in the transition process, e.g. as role models in prominent leadership positions.

The clustering of tools into communication, training, motivation and organization tools should not give the impression that individual tools can be exclusively assigned to a single acceptance factor. In actual fact, many measures are naturally multifunctional, i.e. they are attractive universal instruments. An employee survey can be used as a tool to gauge employee attitudes as well as a tool for communication between the affected parties and the involved parties. Workshops are distinguished by a special multiple functionality: they serve as information forums and as training events at the same time. Moreover, they are environments for participative organization and encourage motivation through transparency and involvement. Furthermore, wikis, and business or organizational theatre (see fig. 47) are versatile tools due to their capacity to inform, skill, motivate, and integrate simultaneously.

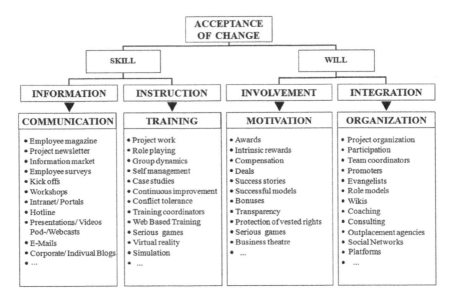

Figure 46:   Clusters of Intervention Tools

The four tool clusters in fig. 46 go along with two options of *tool blending*: In addition to *inter-cluster* blending of complementary tools, toolboxes are the result of *intra-cluster* blending, i.e. the configuration of functionally almost identical tools, such as workshops combined with bilateral talks and negotiations or print media combined with electronic media.

Communication, training, motivation and organization tools make up the *core tools* of implementation since their purpose is to foster acceptance within a given affected area. These core parameters are surrounded by *peripheral tools*. Some of them complement, others substitute the set of core tools:

Context and Concept Substitution: This involves dramatic interventions in which either the original concept or the affected context is more or less radically replaced (see fig. 48).

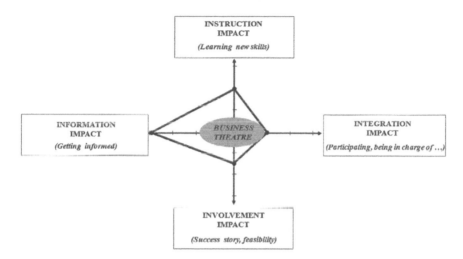

Figure 47:   Multi-Functionality of Implementation Tools: Business Theatre

On the one hand, ideas for change are withdrawn, offers of consultants disappear into drawers and drafts for agreements disappear from agendas.

On the other hand, managers and employees who do not want to lend their support to the change are decruited, e.g. via lay off. In less extreme cases, instead of introducing a concept in the headquarters as initially intended, the concept is implemented in a less difficult overseas branch. All these last-resort eliminations of reform programs and opponents are an expression of resignation. If a person responsible for the implementation has to put the brakes on in this way, then he is proving his own shortcomings. He is fails in turning bureaucrats into managers or managers into intrapreneurs.

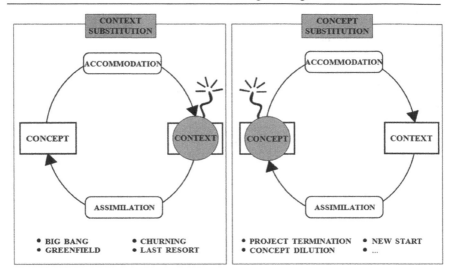

Figure 48:   Radical Fitting Activities

Creating Flexibility in Context and Concept: The exact opposite of such radical, zero-base interventions is constituted by the measures which on the one hand sensitize the affected workforce to changes in their environment, the necessity for change, to training requirements etc, and which on the other hand, "prepare" a given concept for the expected resistance from the affected workforce. Built-in flexibility serves as a powerful tool in both cases. As for the potential for adjustment in the context, the proactive paradigm of change management provides the required readiness for change by building-up dynamic capabilities (see fig. 19).

The scope of implementation tools also comprises complementary people management activities (see fig. 37) and tools since implementation tools require human resources. Hence, tools (e.g. assessment centers) for recruiting experts, trainers, moderators and external consultants are also part of the implementation toolbox. For professional recruiting a market survey of the scope of external consulting, training and outplacement services as well as HR-skills in manpower redeployment and, if need be, replacement of opponents are required. Moreover, on completion of change programs, full-time project employees have to be re-integrated into the line.

5.5 Diagnostic Tools

"Is a change project needed at all?"; "What sort of resistance has to be expected?"; "To what extent has the desired acceptance been achieved?", "Are there enough promoters of change available?" These and similar questions can be answered by means of diagnostic tools. For diagnostic purposes, employee, customer and expert surveys, trend extrapolations, variance analyses, correlation analyses, and standard weak-point analyses are carried out or applied. The use of standard tools improves assessments merely based on gut feeling. Nonetheless, the available diagnostic instruments have not been tried and tested to such an extent, that intuitive guesses are no longer relevant.

Diagnoses serve to detect the need for action. If flyers, workshops, Intranet pages and training programs are used without a prior check of the necessity for such action, the risk of overdosing interventions is high. This results in blind "actionism" and wastefulness through wrongly focused interventions. On the other hand, an insufficient investment in intelligence, analyses and diagnoses can also lead to insufficient intervention. Then no signals, which might point to a need for training or to an information deficit, are registered at all. Change managers would miss opportunities for change, e.g. a change in top management or the adoption of best practices. Concrete implementation requirements (i.e. information, training, motivation, and organization requirements) can only be determined by more or less systematic diagnostic activities. Among these requirements, the determination of training needs within the framework of personnel development is the most developed and firmly established. Different diagnostic tools are needed to fulfill the four basic functionalities of a diagnostic system (see fig. 49).

Prospective diagnosis takes place before implementation tools (see fig. 46) are employed. With regard to risks they serve as early warning systems. The diagnosis shows *strong* (i.e. clear and validated) signals of risks and opportunities ("gaps"), in some circumstances also *weak* (i.e. vague and conjectural) signals for possible deteriorations in the industrial climate, changes in trade union strategies etc. As a preparatory activity) it supports the proactive optimization of an implementation project.

FUNCTIONALITY	PROCESSES & TOOLS
FIND	Discover signals *Scanning, simulation, what-if-reasoning, ...*
FILTER	Elimate unlikely and irrelevant signals *Validating, screening, evaluating, ranking, ...*
FORMAT	Compose or decompose signals *Cluster & discriminant analysis, partitioning, ...*
FOCUS	Identify typical and eteological signals *Cause-effect analysis, pattern recognition, ...*

Figure 49:   Functionalities of Diagnostic Tools

Retrospective diagnosis is the evaluation after communication, training, motivation and organizational measures have been taken. However, it does not only serve as a performance control and post-assessment tool. At the same time, it also indirectly helps to identify the errors and disruptions that have to be dealt with "in the next round" of the change management cycle.

Finding and Filtering

To identify existing action needs, tools are needed that will scan all the sectors from which signals for a necessity for change and for change processes can come. These tools are construed as "radars". Two types of radars are needed for change management:

A *change radar* records information that signals the necessity for a change program. Such change impulses come from in-house sectors as well as from the environment (see fig. 2). An *implementation radar* ascertains all indications of existing implementation requirements. It is only employed after a change concept has been formulated and facilitates a "feasibility study". A scan covers three diagnostic areas: the concept to be implemented, the affected context and the available implementation competence. The appraisal of the implementation requirements to be dealt with is effected in several steps.

First, an analysis of the *concept* to be implemented provides first-hand knowledge of its feasibility according to scope, compatibility and familiarity. An investigation of the *context* based on this analysis then provides information about the situation of the affected workforce, the inherent inertia within the system and the learning capacity in the context. A *competence* analysis provides details as to which qualitative and quantitative capacities are available for the implementation project. This competence scan covers for example the availability of sponsors, the range of services offered by external consultants, and the possibilities of outsourcing training programs. Clues to the competence and availability of promoters can be obtained via questionnaires which include for example the following items: "Is the sponsor aware of how many people and /or teams will be affected by the change?" and "Is the sponsor giving the project his constant support?" Concept-context discrepancies tell us about the gross demand for implementation activities. An estimation of the net demand can be obtained by subtracting the available implementation competencies from this gross demand.

Diagnostic analyses provide data with very different diagnostic content. On the one hand we get ambiguous data from HR information systems, and customer and employee surveys which in this raw form, do not allow conclusions to be drawn about specific implementation requirements. On the other hand, we get specific information about the reasons for resistance and can then initiate specific interventions based on this information.

Surveys and forecasts can only provide data about existing facts or future states that may be relevant to the implementation job. This data is the result of employee and customer surveys, employee talks, market surveys, and trend and scenario analyses. Participation in suggestions system provides appropriate indicators for the willingness to learn; modest degrees of job satisfaction – surveyed by job satisfaction questionnaires – can be taken as an indicator of a willingness to change. Absenteeism statistics and the frequency of complaints also transmit ambiguous signals that first have to be analyzed. If we want to identify the group of affected employees in this way, then we will encounter dangerous errors of judgment. More meaningful information can be obtained from standardized questionnaires that provide data about resistance. Questions could be along the lines of "Was the change clearly explained?", "Do you think that this change is really necessary?" and "Does the change threaten your personal interests in any way?" Informal "opinion leaders" (or "outsiders") can be identified with the aid of socio-metrical methods or by screening friends and buddies lists in social networks.

Employee surveys play a central role because not only do they provide surface data ("find"-functionality, see fig. 49) but they also help to identify reasons, opinions, subjective views and future developments ("focus"-functionality). This explains the frequency with which employee surveys are currently carried out in participative change programs. It is not uncommon that in very traditional companies, the first employee surveys were only carried out 100 years after their foundation. In contrast to some customer surveys, employee surveys provide a representative set of opinions, because here a response rate of well over 50% can be expected. Moreover, employee surveys are multifunctional tools. Besides being diagnostic tools, they are also suitable as evaluation tools to monitor success, and as tools for sourcing ideas and encourage motivation. Sometimes, in the form of a referendum, they can legitimize certain management decisions in the face of workers' representatives or shareholders.

Deviation data can be obtained by comparing established facts with specific standards. Any downward deviation signifies a risk, an upward deviation means that the criterion has been more than met and therefore signifies an opportunity. Significantly different benchmarks serve as standards. Objectives (e.g. performance measures in the form of spans of control or service levels) are used in controlling the change process. They are applied in retrospective target-performance comparisons as well as in prospective comparisons between target and forecasted performance (gap analysis). Comparisons among two target performances examine the compatibility amongst several performance measures, such as budgeted working hours lost through absenteeism on the one hand, and machine availability on the other. Moreover, in an inter-company comparison, the frequency of complaints is compared with the industry average or with best practices, in an inter-temporal comparison with the figures of previous projects. In many sectors (e.g. idea management system) institutions exist which have specialized in surveying such standards.

More information can be obtained from deviation data if it is evaluated according to the *degree of deviation*, for instance less intense or highly intense conflicts or by the help of so called traffic light systems. Alert stages, which trigger various intervention measures, can be defined in this way: high conflict intensity in negotiations necessitates the inclusion of a mediator, whereas lower conflict potentials can be settled bilaterally.

Important diagnostic information can also be obtained from a comparison between promotional forces (change enablers) and oppositional forces (change disablers). The delta between the promotional potential and the oppositional potential tells us about the feasibility of a change project. An appropriate tool is force field analysis. Here the promotional forces (e.g. dissatisfaction with the status quo, a crisis) and the inhibiting forces (e.g. fears, lethargy) are measured on a three-tiered scale (weak, average, strong) and then the aggregated forces are balanced (see fig. 15).

Formatting and Focusing

The collected diagnostic data can be dealt with more easily if the whole host of signals is clustered ("format"-functionality). Clustering results in a taxonomy of several types of resistance (e.g. will barriers and skill barriers) as well as categories of complaints (delays, unfriendliness, incomplete deliveries, errors etc). Moreover, syndromes of combined risks that appear simultaneously can be discovered more easily (pattern recognition tools). A frequent syndrome is the coupling of employee dissatisfaction and customer dissatisfaction.

The distinction between causes and symptoms is particularly useful ("focus"-functionality). A diagnosed "internal emigration" can only be treated if fears or burn-out - and not a strong orientation towards leisure - have been identified as the cause. Some tools which support the focus functionality are digital tools dealing with digitals signals, e.g. data or text mining and heat maps. Intervention plans should therefore always focus specifically on the suspected causes of resistance. Failure due to curing symptoms can only be avoided in this way.

5.6 Communication Tools

Communication has a critical impact on the performance of change initiatives. The design and selection of communication tools (see fig. 46) is embedded in different communication patterns (see paragraph 3.3). To encourage participation and motivation and to enhance the credibility of communication, management is advised to set up opportunities for *two-way communication* and not restrict itself to one-sided promotional campaigns. The more developed the communication culture, the better information activities can be carried out via existing formal and informal communication infrastructures (portals, Intranet, employee magazine, regular formal meetings, talks, informal meetings etc). Consequently, investment into communication infrastructures is an integral part of *proactive* change management. In addition, *change-specific* information tools such as workshops, hotlines and consultations are used.

Pragmatic considerations favor an aggressively open information policy and prohibit a policy of news embargos and camouflage tactics: as a rule, every affected person has access to *several* information channels. Thus, there is the risk that employees will learn of an imminent change from unofficial sources (Internet, newspapers, colleagues, union representatives, etc). This leads to authorized information sources losing credibility and to a practically uncontrollable grapevine.

Besides tools to provide information about the affected employees, tools to inform the affected workforce about the change are the focal point of communication. Informational offensives are aimed at several target groups including managers, shareholders, the public, suppliers and customers. The entire spectrum of communication tools is illustrated by examples in fig. 50.

The two dimensions in fig. 50 represent two dimensions of communication performance. The *horizontal* dimension stands for the effectiveness of communication which increases from the left to the right whereas the *vertical* dimension stands for efficiency increasing from the bottom to the top.

The top left quadrant contains the "cheap" instruments of communication since change managers rely on existing information channels in which data are transmitted in one direction (e.g. top down) only. Moreover, to pass on information to senior staff according to the cascade principle, standard vertical channels are used as channels of change communication. In contrast, the bottom right quadrant contains the "expensive" instruments of communication. On the one hand, they represent dedicated tools activities that have been developed specifically for the change project. Moreover, they have been designed to facilitate two-way communication. Change communication must cover four compulsory components of communication (see fig. 51).

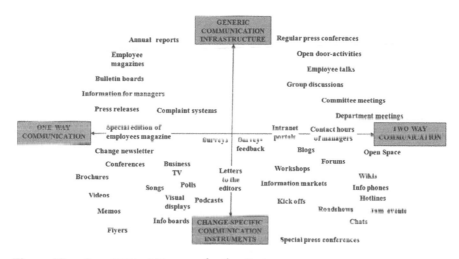

Figure 50:   Spectrum of Communication Instruments

The affected workforce should always be informed about the *reasons* for the change, the concrete *contents* of the change project, all relevant *effects and consequences*, and by feedback procedures about the *performance*, i.e. successes and if need be, about the failures of the implementation activities. Projects to dismantle corporate hierarchy for instance therefore have to deal with hierarchy levels as cost drivers ("hierarchy levels for which the customer is reluctant to pay"), the desired extension of the span of control (from an average three to eight direct subordinate employees), positive consequences (shorter chains of communication) as well as negative consequences (fewer promotion prospects), and finally with successes (successful transfer of "bosses" onto the professional career path) or failures (overtaxed superiors).

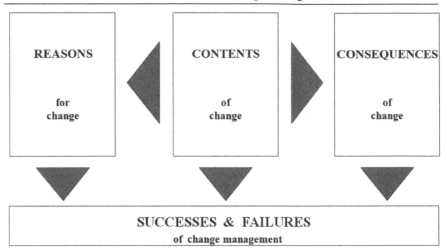

Figure 51:   Mandatory Contents of Communication in Change Management

The utilization of communication tools is embedded in the existing corporate infrastructures for communication. They are composed of hard factors (*technological infrastructures*) and soft factors (*cultural infrastructure*). To increase both reach and efficiency, *technological* communication infrastructures are needed that enable virtual communication. So, a diversified infrastructure facilitates communication by offering options for selecting or blending communication tools with respect to the positioning of senders and receivers in space and in time (see fig. 52).

The *corporate communication culture* has a huge impact on all aspects of the information policy in the change process: the more developed the communication culture, the more information activities that can be carried out via existing formal and informal infrastructures (e.g. regular meetings, management by walking around). The important factors in the choice of media is the technical infrastructure (web 2.0, Intranet, available kiosk systems on which videos can be operated via touch-screens, business TV) as well as the stage of development of the visualization culture, e.g. the familiarity of the lower level employees with various presentation media.

DISTANCE	SAME TIME	TEMPORAL	DIFFERENT TIME
SAME PLACE	o FACE TO FACE - COMMUNICATION o FLIP CHARTS / WHITE BOARDS o GRAPHIC DISPLAYS o DEMONSTRATION SYSTEMS o VOTING - SYSTEMS o MEETING SUPPORT - SYSTEMS o ...		o ASYNCHRONOUS COMMUNICATION o KIOSK SYSTEMS o DOCUMENTATION MANAGEMENT- SYSTEMS o BULLETIN BOARD - SYSTEMS o INFORMATION MARKETS o ...
SPATIAL			
DIFFERENT PLACE	o SYNCHRONOUS TELECOMMUNICATION o TELEPHONE / TELECONFERENCING o VIDEOCONFERENCING o VIRTUAL MEETINGS o CHATS o REMOTE SCREEN SHARING o ...		o ASYNCHRONOUS TELECOMMUNICATION o FAX o E – MAIL/ VOICE-MAIL o GROUPWARE o INTRANET/ PORTALS o SOCIAL SOFTWARE o FORUMS o BLOGS/ WIKIS o ...

Figure 52:   Communication Infrastructures

Closely connected to communication culture are "disclosure versus secrecy"-issues as well as "defensive versus offensive information policy"-issues. Think of open communication as the expression of a culture of trust, and of the immediate provision of information, which goes beyond legal disclosure requirements. Yet, there are also pragmatic reasons that favor an aggressively open information policy instead of a policy of secrecy (see fig. 53).

It is becoming increasingly difficult to prevent information from leaking out of the specific channels for which it is intended. On the one hand, this increases the risk that "classified" information is diffused via unofficial channels, e.g. via social networks or whistle-blowers. Authorized information sources can do very little about the associated rumor mill, not even by denying reports. On the other hand, it is becoming increasingly difficult to disconnect different official information channels from each other: the workforce for instance can often access information intended for the supervisory board. The appropriate means of protection against these risks is an *offensive, open information policy*.

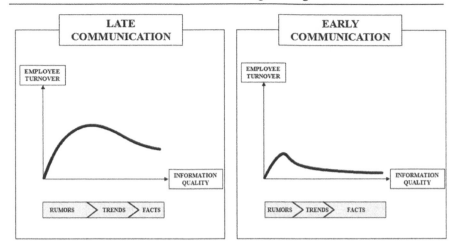

Figure 53:   Consequences of Late and Early Timing of Communication

When blending communication tools – according to compound or conjoint principles - the effectiveness and the efficiency of the various instruments have to be taken into account. Using standard tools from the existing communication infrastructure (e.g. employee magazines) proves to be cost efficient but only manages to attract modest attention. In practice, one compromise solution is to produce a "special edition" of the periodically appearing employee magazine. Efforts at tailor-made information policies for the affected individuals also quickly come up against cost restrictions. Individual talks or "fireside chats" in small groups can usually only be justified if the involved parties sacrifice some "after-work" hours, which keeps opportunity costs low. Some information systems (e.g. portals, Intranets, information markets, information-on-demand systems) are a cost-efficient means by which employees can retrieve information to cover their individual needs. In addition, digital media are more time-efficient, i.e. up-to-date, than print media. It has to be ensured however, that the information can actually be retrieved. Another challenge for information policies is that the credibility of the information is an indispensable prerequisite for the acceptance of the basic message. This is put at risk if the information is exaggerated or depicted in gross "black and white" terms. Testimonials in the employee newsletter should therefore include not only success stories but also reports about the difficulties encountered in implementation.

Again, the blending of digital and non-digital tools turns out to be powerful device for obtaining both effectiveness and efficiency of change communication. Beyond these efficiency and effectiveness considerations, the morphology of communication itself advocates the blending of hybrid media. Besides the content aspect there is always a relationship aspect (meta-communication). This morphology of communication drives media mixes, since not all tools cover both functions of communication. To foster a relationship between sender and receiver, face-to-face communication is usually more appropriate while content can be delivered more efficiently via electronic communication media. Thus, covering all communication purposes and simultaneously paying attention to the performance requirements (effectiveness and efficiency) can best be accomplished by blending several media.

5.7 Training Tools

Training activities are supposed to develop the skills necessary for dealing with a new IT system, a new structure, a new competitive strategy or other new concepts. Training covers all areas of skills, since acceptance requires training in methodological skills (e.g. presentation techniques, mind mapping, web competence) and interpersonal skills (e.g. ability to cooperate, empathy, trust building, customer relationships) together with professional skills. Training in general is subjected to a paradigm shift *"from teaching to learning"*. Consequently training patterns shift from interaction-based training (e.g. teacher-student-interactions in seminars and oral exams) to infrastructure-based learning (e g student-controlled learning and monitoring of learning performance supported by infrastructures). Finally this shift impacts the relevance of interaction-supporting tools (e.g. beamers, flip charts, classrooms) compared to infrastructural tools that enable learning processes (e.g. portals, learning management systems).

The training toolboxes have been considerably *enriched* by digital learning tools ("new media", see fig. 40) which are *computer*-based (e.g. CBT, CD/DVD), *web 1.0*-based (e.g. WBT, Computer Supported Cooperative Work-groupware, chats, forums, virtual classrooms) or *web 2.0*-based (wikis, podcasts, social networks, micro-blogging, etc.).

Simultaneous requirements for both effectiveness and efficiency are the drivers for the use of hybrid learning concepts combining onsite learning and e-learning. The demand for efficiency results from the specific organizational conditions for training in change projects: a comparatively *large number* of learners have to be trained within a *short time-span* that is *synchronized* with the milestones of the respective project. Contrary to standard training for HR-development, there is very little space for individualized timing of training activities and at the same time a high pressure to avoid opportunity costs caused by the absence of numerous employees from their workplaces. This determines the configuration of blended training toolboxes. *Blended learning* is basically used to gain benefits in terms of efficiency as well as of effectiveness (see fig. 54).

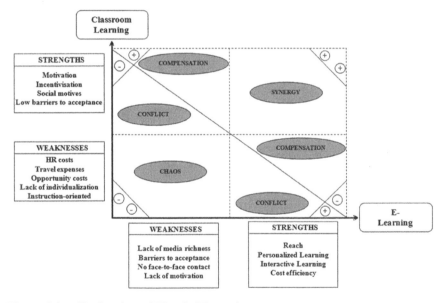

Figure 54:   Evaluation of Blended Learning

E-learning increases training *efficiency* by cost savings which, in turn, build upon their virtualization potential. E-learning can lead to an organizational virtualization of teaching and learning by overcoming temporal and spatial boundaries. This enables an anyplace-anywhere-working mode in a project management-environment. Thus, travel costs, facility costs, and payments for trainers can be reduced significantly. The increase in learning *effectiveness* is mainly based on the deployment of a diversified mix of methods and media. Thereby, didactical concepts can be improved by using the adequate mixes with respect to different learning contents and different groups of learners. This approach eventually leads to a higher degree of personalization of learning processes. The advantages of blended learning can be accomplished by the mutual compensation of weaknesses of extremely diverse learning forms and by bundling their strengths to generate synergy.

Skilling programs are also based on blending *off-the-job*, *near-the-job* and *on-the-job training* (see fig. 55), a taxonomy that refers to the intersection of work processes and learning processes.

On-the-Job-Training	Near-the-Job-Training	Off-the-Job-Training
• JOB INSTRUCTION TRAINING • JOB ROTATION • INTERNSHIPS • ASSISTANTSHIPS • SPECIAL MISSIONS • MENTORING • MULTIPLE MANAGEMENT • ...	• PROJECT WORK • COMMITTEE WORK • QUALITY CIRCLES • COMMUNITIES OF PRACTICE • ...	• WEB / COMPUTER-BASED TRAINING • PROGRAMMED INSTRUCTION • DISTANCE LEARNING • READING • LECTURES / SEMINARS • CLASSROOM COURSES • OUTWARD BOUND PROGRAMS • OFFSITE WORKSHOPS • CASE STUDIES • MANAGEMENT GAMES • ROLE PLAYING • SENSITIVITY TRAINING • ...

Figure 55:   Scope of Training Tools

Companies with a highly developed secondary organization and a team-based primary organization focus training processes which take place on-the-job or at least, near-the-job. This means that to a greater extent, *superiors* and, in part also *colleagues* have to act as trainers. Moreover, skilling requirements also apply to the leaders responsible for implementing change. This is mainly accomplished by training moderators and project managers.

5.8 Motivation Tools

The use of *incentives* to obtain acceptance of the change is central to all motivation activities (see fig. 46). In contrast to toolboxes for communication, training, participation and collaboration in projects, only few motivational tools can be imported from existing tool pools for "business as usual". Incentives and other motivation tools can be *intrinsic* advantages in the respective change itself, e.g. job enrichment via empowerment, or in change-related communication and training. Intrinsic incentives are a very good way of motivating the „winners" of a change program. New working-time models will be approved if they allow employees more personal control over working hours. *Extrinsic* incentives such as financial or symbolic awards (in imitation of the Oscars in quality management) stimulate and gratify exceptional performances of subsidiaries, teams, managers and other players in the implementation process. The amount of the bonus offered by implementation awards plays a minor role however. These awards honor record achievements of quality teams, departments or plants that have successfully come to grips with the change. The awards are often tied up with competitions. These competitive events additionally stimulate the "Olympic" ambitions of the participants. The costs of designing and carrying out such competitions (caused by jury, experts, communications etc) have to be taken into account though. Moreover, loss compensation payments are made for material disadvantages associated with a change. These are supposed to encourage „toleration" of the change by *losers* of the transition. With *counter business and trade-offs* (e.g. within the framework of agreements safeguarding a plant or other locations), a return (e.g. job security) is offered for a certain period as compensation for a stipulated change in behavior (e.g. increase of working hours).

Sufficient transparency of the change processes must also be ensured: Motivation is not only dependent upon tools in terms of incentives but also upon the likelihood and the attainability of these advantages. Appropriate tools to create transparency are clear rules about reward allocation, e.g. for improvement suggestions, for awards or for (loss) compensation for losers of the change. Agreements on targets are a tested means of creating transparency and one that is increasingly being applied in change processes (see also fig. 31).

Motivation activities to encourage acceptance of a change pursue two goals (see fig. 56). Certainly, *accordance* to the change has to be promoted on the one hand. This can be done by using best practices in change management that should be emulated, through motivating success stories or quick hits (successful pilot areas), as well as active involvement (participation) in the change process, the intrinsic rewards potential of the change, and the prospect of „awards" for excellent commitment to the implementation. On the other hand, *rejection* of the change by „losers" has to be inhibited. Top management has to issue appeals and threats, willful destruction of established systems has to be prevented, trade-offs have to be negotiated and loss compensations paid.

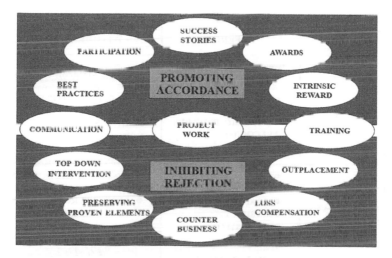

Figure 56:   Scope of Motivation Tools

With *counter business* a return is offered as compensation for necessary changes in behavior or for a sacrifice. Superiors for instance will experience the adverse effects of empowerment projects when their control is reduced. As compensation, superiors are offered jobs as senior consultants and mentors, along the lines of "less boss and more expert". The idea behind these *deals* is to prevent the affected leaders from obstructing initiatives to dismantle the hierarchical structure. Whenever change implies job cuts, outplacement services (including transfer companies) serve as a critical tool for inhibiting resistance by losers of the cost cutting or outsourcing project.

Motivation turns out to be the sector of the change management toolbox where *blending* is most common. This signals that there is no superior tool of motivating, although "money matters" and similar slogans claim that they exist. Besides the blending of intrinsic and extrinsic rewards, the numerous blending operations concern combining "carrots" (pleasant stimuli) and "sticks" (unpleasant stimuli) to foster acceptance. The patterns of blending positive and negative motivational tools must take account of the fact that the two clusters of motivating stimuli can be either offered or withdrawn (see fig. 57).

HANDLING CONNOTATION	OFFERING	WITHDRAWING
PLEASANT STIMULI	**POSITIVE REINFORCEMENT** ● LOSS COMPENSATION ● BONUSES ● INTRINSIC REWARDS ● RECOGNITION ● AWARDS ●...	**PUNISHMENT** ● REDUCED BONUSES ● ISOLATION ● LESS SALARY ● LESS STATUS ●...
UNPLEASANT STIMULI	● STRESS ● MORE WORKLOAD ● MORE WORKING TIME ● LIABILITY ● STIGMATIZING ●... **PUNISHMENT**	● LESS COST ALLOCATION ● LESS STRESS ● LESS SUPERVISION ● LESS JOB RISKS ●... **NEGATIVE REINFORCEMENT**

Figure 57:   Blending of "Carrot"- and "Stick"- Tools of Motivation

Whereas *offering* incentives as well as unpleasant stimuli covers standard positive reinforcement and punishment practices, the *withdrawal* of rewards and threats represents a more subtle, but sometimes more relevant method of motivating new behaviors. So, implementing intrapraneurship in companies goes along with diminishing supervision from superiors. In addition to these intrinsic motivators, change management also exploits the potential of eliminating extrinsic threats such as loss of income or jobs. Both globalization and several production technologies represent de-motivating job killers, unless their threat is reduced or even eliminated by job security agreements.

5.9 Organizational Tools

5.9.1 Extended Change Leadership Value Net

Organizational change has to be organized. The aim is to actively integrate as many of the affected people as possible: The goal of the project is more easily reached when the "project train" has as many active "locomotives", not as many „wagons" ("fans") as possible. The more locomotives, the more risk sharing can be practiced which supports the resilience of a change initiative. The list of organizational tools (see fig. 46) contains project organization, consultants, participatory arrangements (see fig. 30), role models, evangelists, and coaches. The scope of relevant players is captured in the Change Leadership Value Net-Model (see fig. 39).

To spot all relevant roles serving as "tools" (caretakers) in the organizational toolbox, an extension of the CLVN is needed, particularly with respect to the vertical dimension of the change management service production, both downstream and upstream the value chain (see fig. 58).

A downstream extension in the Extended Change Leadership Value Net (ECLVN) substantiates the position of different customers, primarily different stakeholders of change. Whereas the steering committee represents the immediate customer of change champions, the committee (or company top management) has external "tier two" customers, shareholders, and the public who expect a service related to the change project from them. Representatives of town or county councils for instance will expect a minimum raise of regional unemployment rates caused by plans to close down plants. The upstream extension differentiates between different tiers of service supply. So, external providers (e.g. consultants, outplacement companies, cloud services-providers) support internal tier one providers of services for the project manager. Upstream allies as members of vertical business networks may provide financial support (solidarity) for a challenged supplier partner company or offer employment options for laid-off employees. On the level of collective labor relations (unions/ employers), public agencies such as law makers, employment agencies, public funds, (insurance communities), etc. are expected to contribute to mitigating the hardships that come along with downsizing and other cost cutting change initiatives. Otherwise, benefits of change with be "privatized" (by companies) and costs ("losses") will be allocated to society (i.e. tax payers).

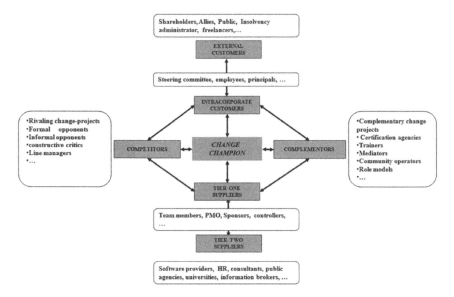

Figure 58:   Extended Change Leadership Value Net

In a global economy, in addition to local or regional agencies also national and supranational agencies are relevant sources for change management services, such as regulatory frameworks (for unemployment insurance, "flexicurity", social criteria for redundancy, etc.). From a balanced resilience point of view, the service job of public agencies is not restricted to risk management, i.e. builder of failure barriers. They also have to play their role as facilitators of change, both as the legislative body (deregulation, protection against (wrongful) dismissal, institutions to settle differences of interest, antitrust law, intergeneration agreements etc) and as sponsor of change friendly cultural activities (e.g. culture of experimentation and non-conformity, culture of entrepreneurship, anti red tape reforms). These services create opportunities for change by dismantling barriers to success. All things considered, the Extended Change Leadership Value Net signals that part of the change management workload is shifted to the society level (see fig. 1).

As a matter of fact some infrastructure services for change management are not provided by suppliers, but by *complementors*. This holds especially for mediators, arbiters, and courts of justice: Due to the considerable potential for conflict in change programs, their services are frequently needed. The "relationship services" of these complementors address several players along the supply chain simultaneously. To entail these services, an XXL-extension of the CLVN is required that covers both the vertical and the horizontal enlargement. The *horizontal* extension of the CLVN towards competitors signals, that change management is not just the art of integrating promoters and the affected workforce into a program. At the same time, it is the art of being able to exclude certain opponents and to protect the project from the influence of these opponents. To this aim, various organizational measures are taken in practice. The spectrum ranges from diverting the information stream ("bypassing") right through to curtailing powers, transferral to unattractive positions, and the withdrawal of status symbols.

5.9.2 Holistic Project Organization

Surveys clearly show that dedicated structures - mostly in the form of *project organization* - shape the core of the change leadership network. The tools, methods and procedures of a transition or interim organization of this kind are adopted with considerable investment in the group-dynamic processes of forming (coming together), storming (establishing roles), and norming (establishing rules of the game). Only then the performing processes can be started (see fig. 104). With respect to roles, power promoters (sponsors from top management), professional promoters (e.g. legal, strategy, IT, and tax experts), and a process promoter as the coordinator in the project organization have to be integrated. A „project core" or "project base" is set up for the project (see fig. 38). All other involved parties remain in their line functions and ensure that the link between project and line is operational.

Several *"archetypes"* of project organizations exist. In the line-integrated-type of project organization and the line-staff organization, the project has few dedicated resources and a very modest amount of autonomy. The great majority of project workers retain their line functions and collaborate in projects alongside their dominant line activities. In contrast, the "pure-type" project organization has a high level of autonomy and self-sufficiency. Matrix-type project organizations make up the fourth archetype and represent a spectrum of very different forms of power distribution amongst project managers and line managers.

Line-integrated-type and pure-type project organizations are not suited for change initiatives: the former doesn't have enough clout; the latter does not provide enough scope for participation on the part of the affected workforce. A blending of these two archetypes is therefore called for: the hard core of the project team is made available for the project as in the model of the pure-type project organization. All other involved parties retain their line functions and ensure smooth operations and transfer of new concepts between project and line. In a way, they represent the virtual manpower for the project.

The project leader (as "Mister Reengineering" or "Miss Outsourcing" for example) and the project team represent the focus of the implementation process so often that they are mistakenly seen as embodying the project organization as a whole. In actual fact, the project organization is made up of three levels (see fig. 38). The core team of the project acts as the *project base* and is responsible for implementing the change program. In restructuring projects, leadership is often assumed by the HR department and the corporate development department. The core team is backed up by numerous process owners, experts, multipliers, moderators, trainers, external consultants and neutral research institutions, all of which are involved in the project work on a temporary basis. All of these constitute the *project infrastructure* level, i.e. the "infrastructure of services" for change projects. The range of functions found in the third level, the *super-structure*, includes the initialization or stopping of change projects, selection of project leaders, provision of the necessary project resources and budgets, and the coordination of different projects. At the center of this coordinative superstructure is the steering committee composed of customers (e.g. users), employee representatives, representatives of senior staff and possibly other project stakeholders.

Triad of promoters of change: A project organization should, first and foremost, provide the required power to a change project. This is essential in order for the project to be carried through in the face of daily operating business, line management and opponents. This promotional power is provided by three types of promoters (see fig. 59).

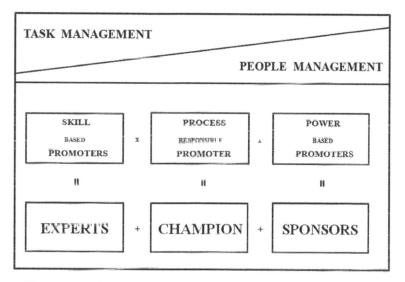

Figure 59:   Triad of Promoters in Change Management

Power promoters (e.g. representatives of top management) support the change through the power of their positions. They act as sponsors or mentors of the change program. *Professional promoters* bring in their expertise (e.g. in labor law or IT) and process promoters - project champions - bring in their skills as coordinators within the project, project leaders, moderators and as process owners. The project organization always complies with the formula "two engines, one transmission", with *process promoters* have the role of a coordinating transmission. As a rule, there are several experts and sponsors: The CEO for instance who, as the "advocate of the change" kindles enthusiasm for the change in the first place (initiating sponsor), often transfers the role of sponsor to a colleague (sustaining sponsor). In spite of this tandem change management is not a matter of "leading in pairs", but in triads.

5.10 Planning and Controlling Tools

5.10.1 Arenas of Implementation Planning

The link between planning and change formed the beginnings of change management in terms of "planned organizational change". However, the planning tool sector of the change management toolbox is not a relapse into the mechanistic steering approach (see fig. 33). Planning in change management – like planning in general – is primarily the answer to two challenges: On the one hand, *flexibility* requirements resulting from existing (endogenous and exogenous) uncertainties. On the other hand, there are specific *integration* requirements due to ubiquitous conflicts as well as to interdependencies between several change projects in a multi-project management approach.

In all implementation projects, managers are also called upon to be project planners and controllers (see fig. 38). With complex integral concepts, in particular, sound *scheduling* is needed for the stepwise introduction of „Reengineering, ERP-software, Shared Services, Green, Virtual & Co". First, one needs to find out with the participation of local managers, which areas of the organization are suitable as „construction sites" or "learning fields" for the implementation. In addition, the optimal sequence in which to introduce the respective modules of the concept has to be established. Procedural planning is not a matter of an exact scheduling supported by sophisticated planning techniques, but rather the handling of complex interdependencies between teamwork, business processes, visions, remuneration systems, cultures, and other elements of concept and context in order to obtain acceptance.

Controlling is seen as an integral information and controlling instrument. More and more areas of an organization have been incorporated into the „controlling terrain". These do not only include „hard" and operational areas, but also „soft" and strategic areas such as HR controlling, R&D controlling, and project controlling. Against this background, it seems less and less plausible that change management be excluded from the realm of controlling. This means that the fuzziness and incalculability of change processes has to be taken into consideration when selecting suitable controlling tools. The enlightened practitioner knows that any form of trust in numbers is misplaced when investing in change programs. Particularly in change management, performance measures represent *estimated values* only. Nevertheless, controlling is invaluable when handling hidden but relevant costs. Such iceberg-shaped compositions of costs are typical for the costs of the project organization (see fig. 66).

On the one hand, there are several generic issues that concern all activities of implementation planning and controlling such as tools for resource planning, change performance metrics, and cost management. On the other hand, some tools only cover certain areas of the implementation process: The traditional core of the toolbox for planning implementation consists of tools for project planning, but only covers the intra-project arena of implementation planning. More tools are needed for planning the extra-project and the inter-project arenas.

5.10.2 Resource planning

This planning activity is dedicated to the provision of human resources for the entire extended change leadership value net, i.e. also to the provision of external consultants and trainers. Within the organization, capacity planning has to distinguish between project participants in the base of the change project, in the super-structure and those in the infra-structure of the change project. The required promotion capacity consisting of top management sponsors, multiplicators and moderators is often underrated because of the lack of tool application. To ensure continuous availability in human resources, also slack capacities have to be planned. For instance, substitutes for assigned promoters have to be appointed (see fig. 19).

Guaranteeing the *availability of promoters* is a particular challenge. With all part-time involved people, availability is always threatened by obligations in day-to-day business or in other projects. This is true for all project members in the super-structure and infra-structure of a project, who are not exclusively assigned to a particular project. Special problems are encountered when trying to secure the availability of power promoters who always operate in an area of tension between strategic importance and operational urgency. To make sure that the capacity of power promoters is not consumed by day-to-day business, clear *priorities* have to be set in favor of the change activities, daily business has to be delegated, several mentors have to be recruited and the entire implementation workload has to be suitably partitioned into work „packages".

A particular availability risk arises in turnaround, downsizing and hierarchy-flattening projects. These frequently result in the *early* dismantlement of middle management. It gives rise to capacity bottlenecks in project management. In principle, middle management has a "transmission function" for impulses which go from the top down or from the bottom up. In hierarchical, cumbersome organizational structures, considerable transmission capacity is necessary to disseminate the ideas of the „chiefs" amongst the „Injuns". Significantly less transmission capacity is required in a lean powerful organization because there, the „companies within the companies" are primarily self-regulating and only have to be tuned to certain synergies by coordinators. Whenever middle management is „thinned out" in anticipation of the rules in a lean organization, there is a lack of transmission power in the transitional period, i.e. a lack of change agents who convey the ideas of the new order from the „still-chiefs" to the „still-Injuns".

Just like in very many other sectors of management, *outsourcing* is an essential option for resource planning. Outsourcing is not only triggered by efficiency requirements (e.g. costs) but also by effectiveness criteria (e.g. expertise). Fig. 60 illustrates the scope of external or "managed" services for change management.

The interaction of internal and external promoters goes beyond the scope of classic *make-or-buy* reasoning. Rather, it is about *blending* intra-corporate and extra-corporate resources in optimal *make-and-buy* solutions for providing the necessary promotion power. The interaction of external consultants and internal promoters often has the character of a symbiotic relationship. Internal promoters appoint external consultants as impartial outsiders. Sometimes the external consultants have to take on the role of an unassailable authority; sometimes they also have to be the scapegoats for failures or unpopular measures. On the other hand, external consultants need the insiders as sources of information and liaison devices for their inquiries.

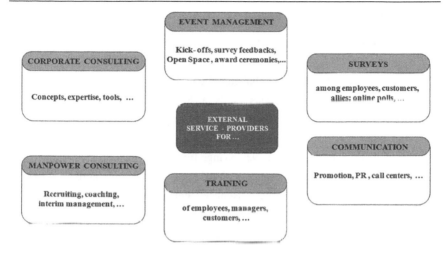

Figure 60:   Outsourcing of Change Management Services

Fig. 61 illustrates both the respective strengths ("I") and weaknesses ("-") of internal and external promoters and proportions of blending the two sources of promotion power as well as their typical outputs.

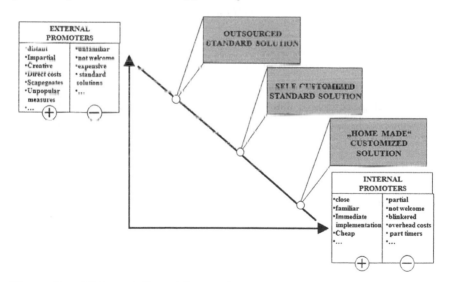

Figure 61:   Make-and-Buy of Change Promoters

5.10.3 Change Performance Metrics

Besides controlling project costs, change agents also have to know how to use „soft" performance measures. Finding appropriate *indicators* to evaluate improvement and learning processes illustrates the challenge behind "soft performance metrics": the „number of submitted suggestions" tells a lot about the involvement of the employees, but little about the quality of the improvement process. The implementation quota primarily indicates the upward acceptance of new ideas developed at the grass roots level. Net savings figures provide information about the productiveness of the suggestions from the business perspective and are a suitable indicator of the quality of the ideas. Bonuses and employee shares (redistribution quota) are of interest from the motivation point of view. Some companies however reject these savings-based bonuses for suggestions as „bribes". Instead, they only employ symbolic rewards and consequently do not work with this performance measure.

The common denominator of all performance measurement systems for change management is complexity in terms of multi-indicator systems and multi-rating systems (see fig. 65). There is no way of reducing complexity to one super-KPI. Multi-rating is a lever for *balanced performance measurement*. Fig. 62 outlines the metrics of implementation performance by a simple tool (kiviat diagram) that balances on the one hand indicators of *effectiveness* (acceptance) and *efficiency* (costs and speed of different implementation processes) and on the other hand the *concept focus* (left section) versus *context focus* (right section) of these indicators. A particular challenge arises when trying to answer the question „How can the effectiveness of change programs be measured?". Performance can be measured at two points: First, the extent to which the planned concept (teamwork, flattened hierarchy etc.) has actually been put into effect can be deduced from the proportion of implemented components (concept coverage: total/ major/ partial) and the customization of the concept (perfect/ approximate/ modified/ reduced). Secondly, the extent to which the affected context has been won over the change can be determined by the degrees of diffusion (context coverage) and accommodation of the concept.

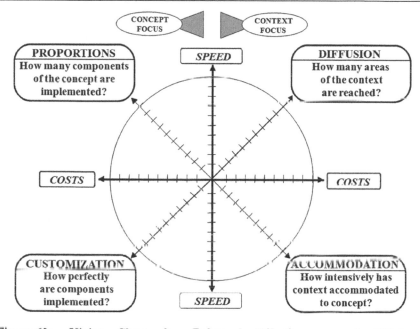

Figure 62:   **Kiviat   Chart   for   Balanced   Effectiveness   and   Efficiency   Measurement**

The degree of *accommodation* indicates the extent to which the change has been accepted by the individual employees, managers, suppliers or customers. The degree of acceptance depends upon four factors: the more the affected individuals are *acquainted with* the change, are *able to* handle the change on the basis of appropriate skills, *want* the change and *have to* actively participate in the change process, the more positive the attitude towards the change will be. To ensure the effectiveness and efficiency of change processes, change managers have to know how to use a fund of „soft" and „hard" tools.

Performance indicators constitute valuable orientation data for controlling and assessing behavior without restricting the behavioral scope too much. Performance measures are not only the subject of top down demands but also of agreements. The *commitment to targets*-model, which derives from management by objectives, can also be applied to change processes. This is true for all levels of the organization.

Agreements on targets constitute an integral component of promotion talks with leaders as well as of continuous improvement processes both on the group level and on the individual level. Level-specific performance measures have to be applied so that all persons affected can comprehend the essence of this form of controlling. Furthermore, working with performance measures facilitates comparability. However, this comparability is only possible to a certain degree whenever organizational units (e.g. teams) are empowered to select the performance indicators by which they want to be measured, i.e. are not subjected to a system of standard performance indicators.

The idea of a balanced performance measurement is essential to a standard tool, the so called balanced scorecard (BSC). It balances four perspectives of performance and offers performance measures for each perspective (see fig. 63).

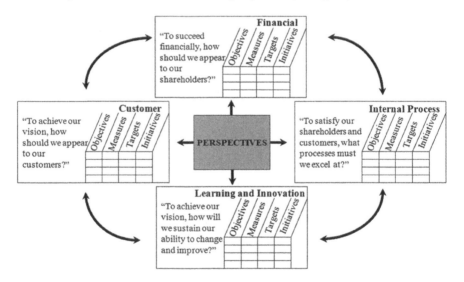

Figure 63:   Change Implementation Balanced Scorecard

The learning and innovation perspective explicitly refers to change management, not only within the reactive but also within the proactive paradigm. When applied to project or implementation management, "process" refers to project processes and "customers" to both internal and external customers (see fig. 58). However, with the

ECLVN as a benchmark, (even) the four perspectives of the BSC do not sufficiently cover all relevant stakeholder perspectives of change management performance.

Since implementation is project focused, also tools for evaluating project performance are relevant. One of these (rare) measurement tools, the *project excellence-model* (IPMA) is adopted from business excellence modelling (see fig. 64). It balances *performance criteria* and *competence criteria*. Competencies correspond to performance determinants from the simple "success factor type". In other words, the handling of barriers (see fig. 18) is neglected in this model.

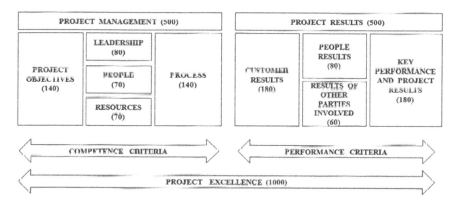

Figure 64:   Tool for Measuring Project Excellence

Finally, some performance measurement tools support the *appraisal of actors* in change project management, such as the project manager. The balanced versions of these tools are usually based on a „360-degree assessment": they not only cover multiple perspectives (such as "customer results" or "people results" which are also implemented in existing multi-rating systems, see fig. 63 and 64) but moreover involve multiple *raters* that assess performance according to the specific value generated by the project, e.g. assessed by customer satisfaction feedbacks, evaluation by principals or upward evaluation of a project leader by members of the project team. This balanced multi-rating can be easily integrated into the CLVN which also represents a 360 degree-approach (see fig. 65). *Competitors* from other projects assess not only expertise but also the utility of the project for their purposes.

So do *complementors* by assessing positive spill-overs ("cross utility effects") or externalities for their activities.

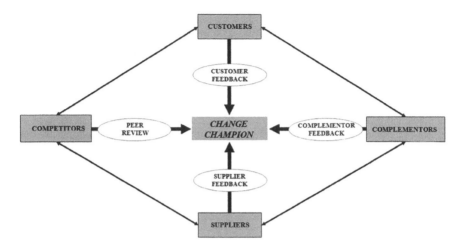

**Figure 65:   Balanced   360-Degree   Rating   Tool   for   Project   Managers'
Performance**

5.10.4 Cost Management

The huge budget volumes for restructuring programs point to a need for the management of the *costs of implementation projects*. Cost awareness in this field must not however lead to a preference for low budget projects which may just survive, but yield hardly any results (see fig. 13). At the same time, cost management must get rid of naive fallacies: the frequently applied rule that a consultant may only cost as much as he saves in personnel costs, is an inappropriate basis for controlling change project costs.

Cost transparency is an indispensable prerequisite for all types of cost management. This requirement applies specifically to the costs of the project organization (see fig. 66). Although the costs of external consultants can be determined by their invoices, and the costs of in-house project members of a core project team determined by transfer prices (hourly or daily rates), project management causes a lot more cost categories than these two. Fluctuation costs in the switch between line work and project work would remain unaccounted for (see fig. 36). Furthermore, it is extremely costly to try to establish the exact costs of the super-structure of a project (costs of the steering committee and the involvement of top management in kick-off events, road shows, meetings, workshops, blogs etc.) and the infrastructure of a project organization (e.g. temporarily involved experts, moderators, trainers and others of the kind). Above all *coordination* or transaction *costs*, i.e. costs of a relationship lifecycle-management of all relationships between the actors involved in the change leadership value net, defy exact calculation.

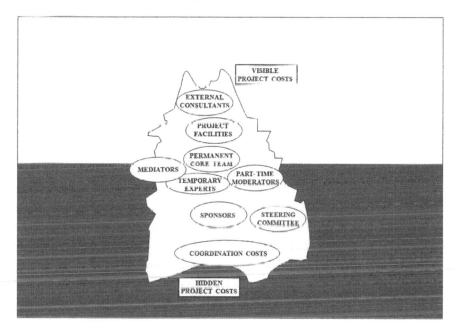

Figure 66:   Iceberg of Project Costs

Managing implementation costs is not a matter of comparing costs of several consultancy offers or the cost impacts of make-or-buy decisions for training activities. Here we are actually dealing with *make-and-buy* decisions. For each problem, the optimal *mix* of outsourcing and in-sourcing has to be determined (see also fig. 61). The *multiplicator principle* constitutes a frequently practiced example of such a make-and-buy blend: in order to cover an existing need to train the workforce, only a small percentage of employees are trained externally. Participants in these outsourced seminars and workshops then themselves function as the trainers and moderators within the company. Cost savings can only be achieved if the costs for internal multiplicators include lower transaction costs than transaction costs caused by relying on external manpower. Moreover, travel costs can be reduced by holding in-house events. This last advantage becomes irrelevant if external trainers also offer in-house seminars or if training is based on e-learning. When comparing the hourly rates of external full-time moderators and internal part-time moderators, the opportunity costs caused by the internal multiplicators also have to be included in the calculations.

All things considered, tools for managing implementation costs should not primarily focus on the cost *level* because these amounts can only be vaguely estimated (see fig. 61). Cost accounting for cost *structures* turns out to be more meaningful. Cost structures determine the composition of overall costs with respect to a) fixed and variable costs, b) direct and overhead costs or c) production and transaction costs. With communication tools for example, an investment in communication infrastructures (e.g. Intranet, employee talks, employee newsletters) primarily causes a higher percentage of fixed costs. In contrast, team meetings or bilateral talks are characterized by high variable, yet low fixed costs. Sourcing decisions in change management (see fig. 60) mainly determine shares of high variable costs and fixed costs: outsourcing increases the percentage of variable costs. As fig. 67 suggests, the management of cost *structures* serves as heuristics for the traditional management of cost *levels*: the higher the percentage of variable costs, the better the cost reactivity and eventually the better the chances to decrease costs.

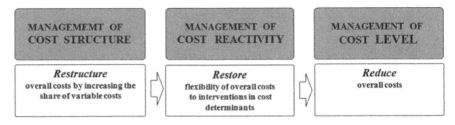

Figure 67:   Heuristics for Project Cost Planning

5.10.5 Tools for the Intra-project Arena

A look at the "interiors" of project planning reveals that (apart from cost planning, see paragraph 5.10.4) the core planning activities are *process* planning and *resource* planning (see fig. 36). The respective tools primarily support the change champion (project manager).

Process planning determines the sequence of implementation activities. Executing steps in the wrong sequence can bring about massive cost increases and time delays. A manufacturing company implemented manufacturing cells in the following sequence: a) reconstructing the manufacturing facility (,,concrete phase"), b) investing in machining centers ("steel phase"), c) setting up a production control centre ("software/hardware phase") and d) introducing the new work organization ("org phase"). The "org phase" was started too late however, because the building-up of soft factors (new work organization) takes longer than building-up hard factors. Thus, the whole project was delayed by more than a year. Delays of this kind can be reduced by running parallel operations. However, the parallel execution of different activities is associated with two preconditions: sub-projects have to be decoupled, and sufficient manpower has to be available (see time efficient upheaval projects in fig. 13).

The multiple uncertainties in the change process can only be countered by flexible planning. Some of the *flexibility requirements* that have to be dealt with stem from the context of change programs. This holds for economic changes that can occur during the course of the project. A recession encourages change because a sense of urgency is created which might lead to a destabilizing of existing structures and attitudes. On the other hand, a recession also inhibits change. Projects fizzle out because project resources are "axed". Ongoing projects might be delayed because of the reduced availability of employees yet to be trained or the dismissal of project employees.

When planning *project team resources*, the nominal and the factual availability of project members must be differentiated. Project employees are not actually available according to their nominal project assignments (e.g. four days a week). The factually available capacity is significantly smaller as the result of a (repeated) switch between project work and line work (plus absenteeism). The switching pattern triggers considerable re-orientation processes for the respective employees. Likewise, teams do not immediately work efficiently the moment they are installed. Before teams reach the actual performing phase in the team life cycle, they have to go through the forming (orientation), storming (finding roles) and norming (establishing norms) phases in which they operate with a significantly limited efficiency.

5.10.6 Tools for the Extra-project Arena

These planning tools support the super-structure of the change project management with respect to decisions that deal elements of the surrounding extra-project arena, mainly assigning manpower from line jobs to projects, stating project missions derived from competitive strategies, stopping projects and the like.

Timing of implementation projects: With technical changes in IT or construction projects, there are standard rules for the optimal timing of implementation activities: Here, (extended) weekends and holidays are used for implementation activities that are normally accompanied by power cuts as well as server downtime. Deciding upon the best timing for *organizational* change projects is by far more difficult. The relevant criteria for a decision lead to contradictory recommendations: With respect to the availability of promoters and to the readiness for change, a start in a *downturn* period appears to be optimal. The situation most likely creates a sense of urgency and leaders might be less absorbed in daily business. However, if we want to keep the designing scope as open as possible then we should start the project as early as possible, i.e. not wait for times characterized by symptoms of crisis. In no way does it appear opportune to introduce a change program in a crisis.

There is also no consensus whether a short (and intensive) project is preferable to a drawn-out project. At least there are rules of thumb for establishing project milestones: there should not be more than half a year between two milestones. This is the only way to guarantee a timely feedback both for project planning and for learning processes of individual employees and project teams.

Planning horizon of change projects: Is implementation planning over as soon as the fixed final date of the change project has been reached or is implementation an open-end job? In the latter case, the rules of project planning would not cover the entire implementation process (see fig. 68). Considering the phenomenon of *erosion* (see fig. 20), change management does indeed take on the character of an on-going activity. *Fluctuations* in the workforce also require that new employees have to be briefed, trained and motivated according to the implemented concept in a permanent fashion. Also changes in the concept due to higher expectation and levels of aspiration (*expansion*) and *innovation* (alternative new concepts or new fads), make implementing a "permanent" job. Expansion is typical for change management integrated into quality improvement: they oftentimes are triggered by ISO certification necessities. However, top management frequently augments the purpose from mere compliance to quality standards to enhancing quality performance in order to generate customer satisfaction. Apparently, this expansion exemplifies a balanced resilience approach that does not only build up barriers to failure (i.e. non compliance) but also dismantles barriers to success in terms of opportunities to improve quality competitiveness.

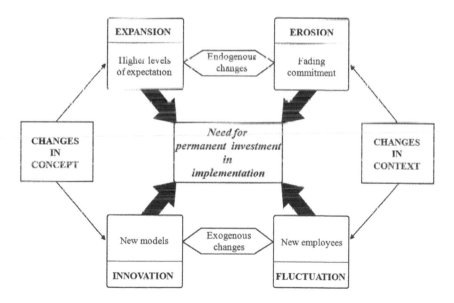

Figure 68:   Drivers of Implementation

5.10.7 Tools for the Inter-project Arena

These planning tools support multi-project management or project portfolio-management which is a job of the super-structure of change project management. This arena takes account of the fact that at the same time several change projects are on their way. As a rule, none of the respective change projects is an island since there are numerous connections between them. First and foremost, tools are needed to discover the four categories of *interdependencies* between projects (see fig. 69).

	COMPLEMENTARY INTERDEPENDENCE	COMPETITIVE INTERDEPENDENCE
OUTPUT CONNECTION	SYNERGY	CANNIBALISM
INPUT CONNECTION	ECONOMIES OF SCOPE	RIVALRY

Figure 69:   Interdependencies between Change Projects

Resource *rivalry* concerning project manpower represents the focus of traditional interdependency analysis. This problem is aggravated by informal poaching of excellent project manpower. Moreover, if several projects are started at the same time – e.g. customer relationship projects and outsourcing projects – this can lead to the *cannibalization* of attention between projects, with respect to attention from both steering committee and targets. On the other hand, *economies of scope* reduce overall project costs because of a transfer of methodological and specific knowledge between projects as well as a sharing of a common knowledge infrastructure (data base, toolbox, procedural models, project software, best practices, etc.) that is build up once and utilized many times. *Synergies* are typical of complementary projects whenever a configuration of two or more projects triggers more commitment than an isolated single project. Sometimes, synergies even originate from competitive relationships between projects (e.g. lean management and agility projects) provided the respective cluster of projects detracts attention (and budget) from other project clusters (i.e. CSR-projects). The discovery of interdependencies is supported by "soft" tools such as mind mapping or by "hard" tools like cross impact analysis.

Once the interdependencies have been clarified, an infrastructure for an integrated multi-project planning can be installed. Organizational infrastructures focus on program managers, coordination councils or linking pins, i.e. people participating in two or more change projects which facilitates the transfer of implicit knowledge between the two projects. A challenge to multi-project planning are the significant differences in the duration of interdependent change projects, such as a short-term IT-device substitution project (from single purpose to multiple purpose devices), a mid-term cloud outsourcing project and a long-term project for cultural change (e.g. open Innovation). Even with sequential planning and parallelization, these time span differences are difficult to harmonize. Premium integration tools for multi-project change management come from change project *portfolio management*. For example, these tools support the cross-subsidizing between projects which yields economies of scope.

Maturity level	Description
OPTIMISED	There are fully defined project, program and project portfolio standards, structures and processes in place which are fully applied throughout the organization, which the management actively controls and continuously improves.
MANAGED	There are fully defined project, program and project portfolio standards, structures and processes in place which are fully applied throughout the organization, which the management actively controls.
STANDARDISED	There are fully defined project, program and project portfolio standards, structures and processes in place which are mostly applied throughout the organization.
DEFINED	There are partially defined project, program and project portfolio standards, structures and processes in place which are partially applied in the organization.
INITIALISED	The achievements of project management are at a personal level. There are individuals who perform well, but project, programme and project portfolio performance is coincidental. The organization has no formal project, program and project portfolio standards, structures and processes in place.

Figure 70:   Project Management Capability Maturity Model Integration

The inter-project arena also has an *inter-temporal* facet concerning the development of change management competence over several consecutive change projects. Tools like the Capability Maturity Model Integration (CMMI) applied to project management (see fig. 70) help measure the progress in project management competence. The key indicators of project competence originate from the sectors of a project management infrastructure, i.e. standards, structures and processes.

5.11 Marketing Tools

5.11.1 Marketing Change: Paradigm, Patterns, and Parameters

Every change manager has something to sell: the appropriate managerial style in change management is rather „selling" than "telling". To master this difficult task, several skills in so called *internal marketing* (as opposed to product marketing) are required. This includes directing implementation activities towards the various target groups ("customer segments", see fig. 71) such as different categories of managers, winners or losers, affected persons inside or outside the company. The target group determines which tools from the marketing mix are used: even with the *branding* of the change project, attention should be paid to finding a concise motto, catchy messages, and to packaging suited to the concept (e.g. abandoning hierarchical wording and charts). The penetration of marketing thought into change management is manifested superficially in the growing dissemination of marketing terms in the vocabulary of change managers. Even in change management, the talk is increasingly about "promotion", "kick-off events", "road shows" etc. The convergence of marketing and change management can be explained by the remarkable expansion of generic marketing: marketing not only addresses external markets but all sectors *inside* an organization by a so-called internal marketing strategy. "Professional marketing" has yet another facet: some companies have decided to market their in-house developed and tested change concepts to external customers. For external marketing of this kind, service catalogues have been conceived and trademarks occasionally protect relevant products. However, the marketing paradigm is only legitimate in a change management framework, if there is no interference with the existing tools in the implementation management toolbox.

Change programs are not helped by operating with false labeling, deceptive packaging and other "manipulative" marketing tricks.

What can change managers learn from marketing? In order to master the difficult task of selling change, existing approaches can be enriched by the marketing *paradigm* and by marketing *patterns*. So, change managers benefit from moulding the change implementation process into a buying process. Buying behavior models such as the *AIDA pattern* (Attention, Interest, Desire, Action) emphasize that acceptance (Desire, Action) can only come about if, beforehand, we have gained sufficient attention from the persons affected. This becomes all the more difficult the more the affected persons are inundated by messages on change subjects and consequently switch off. In view of the numerous fads in current management thought, this reaction is most likely. All attempts at achieving acceptance therefore have to be expanded by information-disseminating activities to gain attention. The post-decision phase (i.e. the processes after the buying procedure) is of equal importance to implementation. In the post-decision phase, so-called *cognitive dissonance* emerges (see also fig. 84). Supporters of the new concept begin to question their „purchasing decision". It might have been better to stick with the old conditions or a less radical change might have been more suitable. Such mental tensions are reduced by mechanisms which are supposed to align the factual decision and the assessment. Attempts at ridding themselves of the burdening dissonance frequently lead to gross and dangerous distortions of reality in the form of condemnations or glorifications as well as overly simplistic black-and-white modeling.

Marketing change is about finding the optimal mixture of generic messages on the one hand and target group-specific messages on the other. The latter are articulated in the language of the respective target groups (managers, customers etc). The generic messages have to use pithy marketing language and work with catchy slogans and images in order to reach all targets affected by the change. Opinion leaders play also an important role in the „*distribution*" of innovations. They have to be identified and won over as „marketing agents". Without the professional use of promotional media (portals, videos, brochures, screen savers, etc.), insufficient attention will be drawn to the initiative and thus implementation of the change will not be successful.

5.11.2 Focusing on Target Groups

A fundamental lesson learned from marketing reads: before running advertisements, sales promotions and marketing operations, the market has to be segmented so that the different target groups can be identified. If only the overall market is addressed, the success of the marketing activities is at risk because one is focusing on the phantom of the "average customer". Analogously in change management, change managers must be aware of the fact that the circle of persons affected is composed of very different groups each of which needs to be treated differently (see fig. 71).

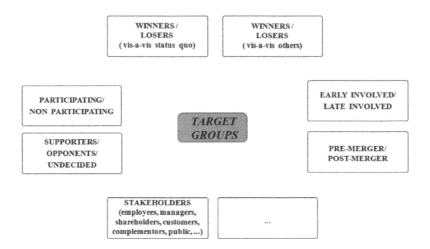

Figure 71:   Target Groups for Implementation Management

To roughly estimate the challenge of an implementation project, the targets should be divided into three groups: the *supporters*, the *opponents* and the *undecided* („ditherers"). A high percentage of opponents for any kind of change signals a general reluctance to change. With cost cutting programs – which are naturally characterized by a high percentage of opponents – it is chiefly a matter of finding out the percentage of true supporters. With concepts of restructuring towards customer orientation and towards a cultural change, one should start with realistic proportions. Experience clearly shows that ditherers constitute about 50%.

Another change specific taxonomy of target groups differentiates between *winners* and *losers*, either based on a comparison with the status quo or on other groups as benchmarks. These two groups have to be handled with significantly different instruments (see fig. 72). Whereas winners are trained intensively, motivated by intrinsic advantages of the change, and actively involved in the project organization as moderators, success stories and role models, the attitude towards losers is more one of leaving them in the dark, radically re-training them, where necessary indemnifying them, and within the scope of the project organization, bypassing them. Despite the plausibility of the winner-loser differentiation, there can be great disparity between the *objective* and the *subjective* classifications.

☞ LOSERS	☞ WINNERS
weaken resistance by...	strengthen enthusiasm by...
o keeping things secret	o keeping people informed
o retraining	o training
o compensating loss	o motivating intrinsically
o bypassing	o utilizing

Figure 72:   Dealing with Winners and Losers of Change

It is possible that in an empowerment project objectively, the proportion of losers (e.g. managers of corporate service centers, first-liners) is very low. On the subjective level however, 100% of the persons affected might feel like losers because they have to change their conduct and cut out habits of which they have grown fond. Furthermore, the *selectivity* of this clustering must not be overestimated: in projects to promote entrepreneurship in the organization, future intrapreneurs will feel like both losers and winners of the restructuring, depending on the economic situation of their businesses in question.

The identification of winners and losers requires a sophisticated definition of target groups according to the degree to which they are affected (e.g. in an M&A-project

pre-merger employees versus post-merger employees), the timing of their involvement into the project (early/ late) and to the way in which they are affected (positively/ negatively). Moreover, generic definitions of target groups are also relevant for change marketing: the target groups correspond to the *stakeholders* of a change project that are located in the ECLVN (see fig. 58).

5.11.3 8P-Toolbox of Marketing Tools

The target group definition determines which tools from the marketing mix are used. Since change management is about marketing a *service* and not a "product", the traditional 4 P-toolbox has to be a) enlarged to an 8 P-toolbox (see fig. 73) and b) the "Ps" have to be customized to change specifics. The four extra "Ps" are characterized as follows: the *participating customer* denotes the customer (see fig. 58) as a co-producer of change services such as training. *Process* means the interaction between a service provider (e.g. change champion) and the various

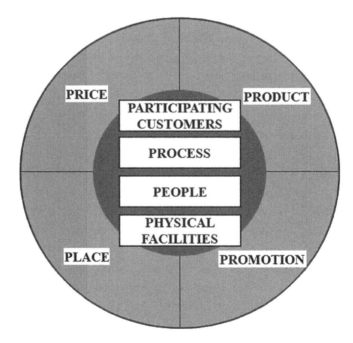

Figure 73:   8P-Toolbox of Change Management

Customers - as opposed to some self-servicing of the customers within a "change warehouse". *People* refers to (interpersonal) skills of service providers. *Physical facilities* cover all infrastructures that enable face-to-face or virtual interactions (e.g. locations for kick-off events, portals, Internet communities) as well as hardware devices that support the customer in dealing with the change project, e.g. computers, mobile devices and networks for Web Based Training.

There are certain correlations between the soft implementation tools (see fig. 46) and the *core 4P-marketing mix tools* (see fig. 74).

Figure 74:   4P-Marketing Tools in Change Management

In the case of communication policies ("promotion") we even have a 1:1-correspondence. Furthermore, there is a fairly close relationship between motivation and terms policies ("price"), between organization and diffusion policies ("place"), and between product policies ("product") and concept design.

Communication tools: The essence of promotion via communication is an optimized media mix. Again, the area of conflict between the effectiveness and the efficiency of the various tools should be taken into account. Separating or combining information activities for different target groups has a major impact on both effectiveness and efficiency of communication: Should different or identical messages and media be used to communicate with shareholders, customers, suppliers, managers, employees and the public?

The question can be answered by a rule of thumb: the same information-release date and the same basic message, but differing degrees of detail and forms of presenting the information, as well as differing information channels. A more or less synchronized timing for information activities for different target groups is advisable if the various target groups have access to several channels. This applies to employee representatives or employees as shareholders of the company, all of who have access to shareholders' newsletters. In general, decoupling internal communications from external communications is hardly feasible. This would provoke the risk that employees find out about restructuring programs in their own company from the news papers or from their union representatives before they do so from their superiors. The basic message should be the same for all target groups. This includes the components of the vision and mission of the change programs, symbols and symbolic figures on screensavers or posters. The design of the texts should make sure that they can be understood by the larger part of the affected employees. In addition, differentiated communication via investors' newsletters, annual reports, customer journals, supplier days, press releases etc. is called for.

Information which is presented by a short list of catchy slogans is easier to accept and implement than complicated, academic and far too sweeping statements. This marketing principle is contravened if one operates with a catalogue of more than five fundamental messages, principles, etc. We should keep in mind that many people find it difficult to remember all of the Ten Commandments, for example. Furthermore, communication policies should not constitute one-way communication. This is clearly shown in external marketing by customer surveys (analogous to an employee survey) and the great importance of feedback via customer complaints management (i.e. call centers and hotlines) or open idea management systems.

Concept Design Tools: Designing customer-oriented change begins with branding and wording. We are looking for an attractive motto with high valence and potency.

Furthermore, it is of great importance that the change program is specific to the organization and not a consequence of a bandwagon effect or some me-too approach. Now and again, change programs have to be focused just so they can stand out from previous projects: so, risks of confusing reengineering projects and initiatives of overhead cost management should be avoided. In principle, however, a broad interpretation of a change program should be given priority over narrow specification (focusing quality, costs, etc. only). "Cultural change" or "new models" are particularly suited as an umbrella for diverse subjects. New challenges do not force the program to be altered but rather, they force the otherwise unaltered program to take up these new trends. Even refreshment programs can be brought under the original umbrella.

The overall change project has to leave sufficient scope for adaptation and customization to the specific contexts in the different areas of an organization. For instance, variable tariff agreements are suited to this. Adaptation to local conditions can be achieved partly as a service offered by internal consulting, and partly by the respective areas customizing the basic concept themselves.

Packaging also plays an important role in marketing change. Projects to flatten hierarchies for example cover more than just the elimination of some hierarchical levels (see fig. 75). The organization chart should also be changed from a hierarchical pyramid form to a non-hierarchical form with the aid of concentric circles. Located at the centre of this chart and not at the top of a pyramid is a corporate center with its coordination and shared service functions. Assembled on the periphery and therefore directly at the interface with the customers, are the business centers. An even more radical visual packaging is accomplished by inverted charts: these depict the so called right-side-up organization with sales representative at the top and CEOs at the bottom of the hierarchy. Just like the graphic packaging, the verbal packaging is also very important: in non-hierarchical structures, rank-based job descriptions (e.g. head of department) are replaced by function-based descriptions (e.g. coordinator, senior consultant), management teams or "circles" of managers and intra-company markets replace hierarchical relationships between superiors and subordinates.

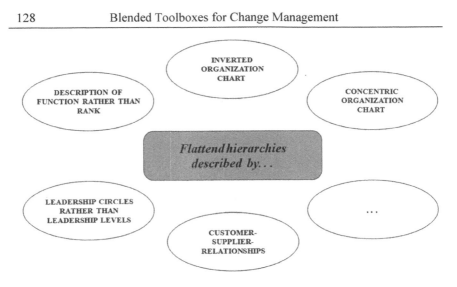

Figure 75:   Optimal "Packaging" of Hierarchy-Flattening Programs

Diffusion tools: Diffusion is about the "distribution" of change management services by "interpolating" intermediaries in between the players in the ECLVN (see fig. 58). Just like distribution channels, diffusion channels or paths describe the spread of acceptance for changes within the organization. Contrary to classic marketing, the direction of the diffusion of a change is not clearly defined. Besides top-down diffusion also bottom-up diffusion is relevant. In corporations which grow via acquisitions, diffusion can take place horizontally on the level of existing and acquired business units or go from the new subsidiary via headquarters to the other subsidiaries. Diffusion is based on mechanisms of imitation (bandwagon effects, learning from successful models), sometimes also of "viral marketing". On the organizational level, marketing agents or intermediaries are called in. Some of them are already installed in the organization (superiors, staff, committees) or they have to be established specifically for the project. Mentors are suitable for this purpose. Informal opinion leaders are predestined for this function, as are groups such as communities of practice (thematic groups) or workshops. In accordance with customer-oriented marketing, the customer has to be „picked up" on the spot. This purpose is served by decentralized informational, presentation and training events, e.g. road shows.

Terms Design Tools: They concern the "terms of business", which are agreed upon with the various target groups. From winners, one demands a reciprocal service, be it active participation in change processes, increased commitment (agreements on targets) or compromises in other areas of conflict. The undecided may be reached via Oscars to be won by pioneers who are particularly committed to the change program. The losers are offered loss compensation. The tool of *counter business*, i.e. balanced combinations of stipulated contributions and conceded rewards are illustrated in fig. 76. Fears of (possibly self inflicted) job loss (via improvement suggestions) can be reduced by job guarantees. To compensate the cuts in

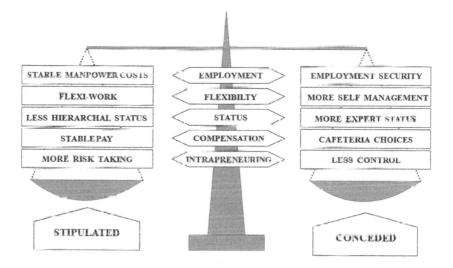

Figure 76:   Counter-business in the Implementation Process

remuneration (along with cost cutting projects), so called cafeteria models are designed. They offer a greater choice for the individual who is configuring his total compensation by combining salary, deferred compensation and fringe benefits. Counter businesses in working hours frequently allow for higher flexibility on the part of the employer (e.g. agreement on total annual working hours) in return for increased flexibility on the part of the employee (e.g. flexitime models).

Terms policies cover not only contribution and rewards, but also the *time factor* of the settled agreements. The *contract periods* of collective wage contracts and contracts on the company level play an important role for determining costs and benefits with respect to changing business cycles. The option to postpone drastic measures (e.g. outsourcing, job-cuts) is often also important. Such a delay allows the affected employees to better prepare for serious changes in their employment situation.

5.12 Tools for Managing Complexity of Change

Tools for handling change complexity are embedded in paradigms (e.g. reduction or optimization of complexity) and patterns (e.g. step-by-step implementation, migration) of complexity management (see fig. 23 and 24). They intersect both with tools for planning for *flexibility* such as milestone plans, slack resources, redundancy, scenario technique, and contingency planning (considering changes in mission and resources like requirements, human resource fluctuation, etc.) and for *integration* (agreements instead of command-and-control tools): by definition (see fig. 3), complexity in terms of ambiguity is the intersection of risk and complexity management and complexity in terms of variety the intersection with integration planning.

Complexity management must not be equated with "simple" complexity reduction. Rather, it requires the competent handling of complexity, which covers the competence areas of modularization, focusing, approximation, and the professional use of provisional arrangements and versions.

Modularization in terms of breaking down the whole change program into small building blocks is the key to step-by-step patterns of implementation. Modularization is applied to the *concept* as well as to the *context* of a change project (see fig. 77). The concept is decomposed into *components* (e.g. career concepts, teamwork, centre models, ERP modules, etc.), the context is decomposed into *sections* (e.g. departments, business units, plants, subsidiaries, etc.). Whenever both ways of modularization are applied simultaneously, implementation will take incremental steps, the contrast to the non-modularized procedure normally characterized as the "big bang"-pattern.

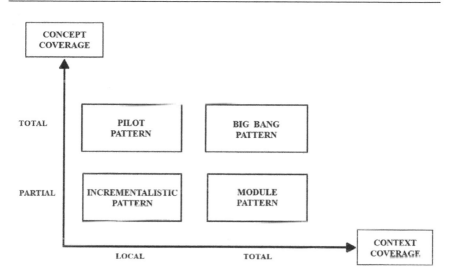

Figure 77:   Modularization for Step-by-Step Implementation

The art of modularization consists of minimizing the links between components as well as between sections. Otherwise modularization would cause a boomerang effect in terms of a high complexity caused by laborious activities to integrate the building blocks. An interface analysis can be made by using the so called influence matrix as a tool. The matrix includes the intensity of influence between several modules (intensity levels: weak, medium, strong), and differentiates between active exertion of influence and the passive state of being influenced.

Compromise solutions reduce the time needed to reach an agreement. However, with some pragmatic compromises the overall duration of change programs may also be paradoxically extended: they are very „vague" and consequently require considerable investment in interpretation and conflict resolution in the (likely) event of controversial interpretations.

Focusing change activities on the essential elements, i.e. components of the concept and sections of the context, also has the effect of reducing complexity. The remaining modules will most likely adjust themselves to the prior installed modules. The influence matrix support the identification these so called "active" modules.

Approximations: Step-by-step procedures sometimes yield approximate solutions which do not lead to the complete implementation of the original concept. Within the scope of intrapreneuring projects for example, the implementation of reward systems has to be accomplished. A thoroughbred entrepreneur is – just like the head of a medium-sized enterprise – paid directly by the customers; his remuneration is highly dependent on market performance. A good approximation is constituted by reward systems which are based on the performance of cost, revenue, profit and investment centers. The degree of approximation increases from cost to investment centers. A rougher approximation of a reward system based on center performance is a bonus system. Bonuses are calculated upon corporate performance (as opposed to center performance). Performance based remuneration systems based on the appraisals of employees by superiors – and not by the (simulated) market – contain only trace elements of entrepreneurship which makes them a poor approximation of an entrepreneurial reward system.

The million-dollar question with all complexity-reducing approximation strategies is: Which *level of approximation* must be reached in order to obtain the desired performance improvements? The assumption that implementation performance increases steadily with the degree of approximation is rather unrealistic. Sometimes, the required performance is only achieved when the level of approximation is high, in other words, only after the optimal solution is implemented.

Provisional Arrangements and Versions: Provisional or interim arrangements are temporary concepts which are quick and cheap to install and give the change program its first, performance relevant impetus. Later, these „crutches" are no longer needed. This holds for instance for interim managers or transfer companies which take over valuable functions in the process of downsizing and yet are not needed any more thereafter. Examination of the life cycle costs of the entire project reveals that the dissolution of provisional arrangements often gives rise to considerable follow-up costs. The inherent momentum of such objects means they become established and resist voluntary self-dissolution.

Step-by-step implementation is completed much more elegantly with the aid of the *versioning* concept. As with successive versions of software products, the maturity of the concept increases successively as a result of improvement processes. Such sophistication takes place for example in the transition from part-time to full-time responsibility for business processes in reengineering.

Portfolio-Management: Portfolios are embedded into the paradigm of complexity optimization: This tool is most recommendable for selecting pilot areas (see fig. 23).

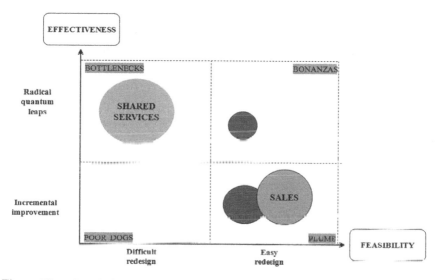

Figure 78:   Portfolio of Pilot Areas

These are sectors of an organization that can serve as nuclei or models in the diffusion of changes throughout the organization. Despite the catchiness of the basic idea of pilot procedures, the selection of a concrete pilot area can be a headache since there are two most plausible, but contradictory recommendations: In view of a quick and uncomplicated implementation, one pleads for *plum areas*, which promise quick hits – because they have already achieved the status of a benchmark and/or no or only negligible resistance has to be overcome. Some greenfield sites represent such plum areas. Despite of the pros, some cons are against picking plums: they have only modest improvement potential und moreover they are not accepted as representative models by the rest of the organization. On the other hand, good reasons for the selection of „big nuts" or *bottleneck areas* can be produced. They are convincing because of the high gains in productivity, namely a high change volume (e.g. the attainable increase in customer value) and the sustainable model function. Nonetheless, considerable resistance has to be overcome, which may lead to a prolonged pilot phase. In view of these bright and dark sides of both procedures, it is advisable not to consider them as alternatives but to blend them in such a way that pilot areas are selected from both categories respectively. The blending of these antithetic types of pilot areas can be accomplished by a portfolio (see fig. 78). Indeed, the quick successes in the plum areas "subsidize" the tough reform projects in the bottleneck areas, at any rate motivationally and sometimes, also financially via the attained cost savings.

6 Management of Opportunities and Risks

6.1 Taxonomy of Opportunities and Risks

The essence of the balanced resilience framework is the *combination of risk and opportunity management*. According to the 3E-performance model, the impact of opportunities is reflected in the opportunity impact zone whereas the impact of risks is captured in the risk impact zone (see fig. 15). From a change management point of view the specific categories of risks and opportunities have to be identified. The awareness of these determinants enables balanced resilience change managers to both build-up barriers to failure via handling risk factors and to dismantle barriers to success by exploiting opportunity factors.

OPPORTUNITIES	RISKS
SENSE OF URGENCY	*FOCUS ON SURVIVAL*
DARWINISTIC SELECTION	*LACK OF MONEY*
SOLIDARITY	*HECTIC RUSH*
LEGITIMATION FOR UNPOPULAR MEASURES	*PSEUDO ACEPTANCE*
ATMOSPHERE OF DEPARTURE	

Figure 79:   Crisis: Opportunity and Risk Facets

Risk and opportunity intelligence, i.e. the identification of the determinants of failure or success of change management, is complicated by two challenges. Both are related to complexity in terms of ambiguity (see fig. 3):

Fuzziness: There are several determinants that cannot unambiguously be identified as either risk or opportunity factors. This lack of differentiation is familiar from many other management areas: so, all investments have both an opportunity and a risk aspect. Since there is no way to tell whether the risk facets or the opportunity facets prevail, an unambiguous either-or-classification is not feasible.

A notorious example for an ambiguous element in change management is *"crisis"*. Fig.74 lists typical facets of crisis related risks and opportunities.

Another change-specific example for the hybrid character of change-related issues is greenfields (see fig. 80).

OPPORTUNITIES	RISKS
MINIMUM RESISTANCE	*TEETHING PROBLEMS*
NO NEED TO UNLEARN	*CONSTRUCTION SITE STRESS FACTORS*
PIONIEERING SPIRIT	*MAJOR INVESTMENT*
HIGH POTENTIALS	*TWO SEPARATED WORLDS*
ROLE: NUCLUES OF CHANGE	*IMAGE: EXOTIC EXCEPTION*

Figure 80:   Greenfields: Opportunity and Risk Facets

Transparency: Very many factors, that actually impact change management performance are difficult to identify at all, regardless of their positive or negative impact. This intelligence deficit is caused by the highly conjectural character of the relationship between causes and effects which reflects the maturity level of the change management body of knowledge (CMBOK). Consequently, they represent "untransparent", "hidden" or "obscure" - as opposed to evident or transparent - opportunities or risks.

Whenever change managers do something evidently highly risky, in other words: something that most likely provokes the failure of the change project, they are bound to commit an error. The categorization as an *error* or a "sin" is justified if the cause-effect-connection in question is transparent, i.e. it has become part of the CMBOK. So, neglecting communication, denying participation of change targets, forgetting to provide top management support or to compensate the loss of losers (and other "commandments" of change management) is like committing a sin because – according to the existent CMBOK - targets will most certainly not support or even sabotage the change.

In contrast, there are "inevitable errors" that change managers cannot be blamed for. The list of these errors contains the following challenges: a) dilemmas, b) paradoxes, c) pathologies and d) "white spots" or "gaps" in the CMBOK.

Dilemmas in Change Management: Inevitable errors go along with *dilemmas* which - by definition – are handled by activities that are "wrong" in at least one respect. This risk is illustrated in fig. 81 by the example of the dilemma of trust in change management.

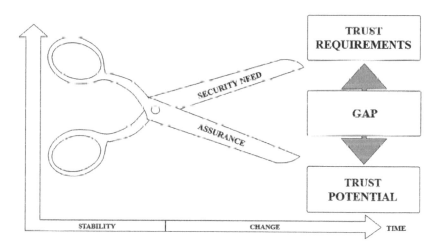

Figure 81:   Dilemma of Trust in Change Management

Change processes are characterized by an exceptionally high need for trust. This results from the need for security on the part of the targets, e.g. the affected employees. The more drastic the change however, the less one is able to reassure the affected employees. This results inevitably in a confidence gap. How can change managers help to build up trust so that the de-motivating effects of a confidence gap can be avoided? One standard activity of trust building is providing transparency. This requires however that the change managers themselves know exactly how the change project will proceed and what the results of this process will be. Unfortunately, this prerequisite cannot be met in many change projects. A merger project for instance is designed in a nontransparent fashion, e.g. in order to avoid insider trading and related adverse effects on the stock market. At the beginning of post-integration management, it is normally unclear how many employees and which employees are affected by the merger. Often, it is only with considerable delay that the principles of manpower cuts ("fifty-fifty" amongst the merging companies, transfer companies, redundancy payments, etc.) can be disclosed.

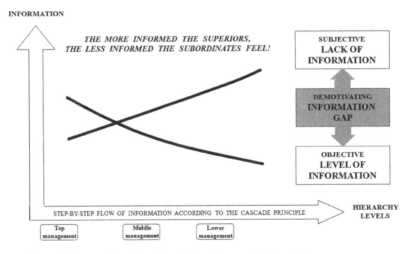

Figure 82:   Information Gap due to the Cascade Principle

Developing trust is perforce at a low level: transparency is often reduced to the announcement of the *dates* on which management will inform the affected employees about the content and scale of headcount adaption. Another standard measure of building up trust is to cushion the severity of the change. This can be done for example by employment assurance contracts. These normally create security for (only) one to three years. Apparently there are narrow limits to building up trust in the change process. It is evident that dilemmas are one category of challenges in change management for which there is frequently no satisfactory solution.

Paradoxes: The top-down cascade model of communication, as depicted in fig. 82, is supposed to improve the knowledge of targets about the change. However this common pattern of information flow paradoxically causes a de-motivating information gap: Subordinates systematically feel more badly informed about important changes (decentralization, mergers, personnel cutbacks, etc.) than their superiors. One way to remedy this is to simultaneously provide all the affected parties with a rough idea of the key data of the change. The details can then be provided later, following the cascade principle.

In addition to these change specific paradoxes change management has to tackle some generic paradoxes of management. Most relevant for change management is the so called vicious *circle of bureaucracy* or *bureaupathic behavior*. Fig. 83 outlines that (change) managers respond to chaos by regimentation (guidelines, handbooks, codes of conduct, performance indicators, etc.) that is intended to establish order. Regulation triggers reactance in terms of finding loopholes, bypassing rules, creating a shadow economy, etc. which altogether generate chaos. So paradoxically regulation creates chaos.

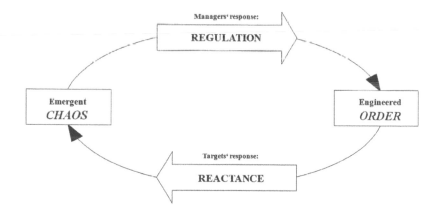

Figure 83:   Change Management Paradoxes: Bureaupathic Behavior

Pathologies: Of equal importance are (pathological) patterns such as "paralysis by analysis" or patterns of eliminating so called *cognitive dissonance* (see fig. 84): Targets that made up their minds to oppose change have to deal with a dissonance between their decision and the expectations of change managers. This dissonant perception (of a dissonant reality) is sensed as unpleasant. Mechanisms of eliminating the mental dissonance are triggered in order to get rid of this unpleasant constellation. These mental mechanisms are irrationally assimilating (the perception of) reality to the desire for consonance: this is for instance accomplished by downgrading the advantages of change and upgrading the advantages of the status quo, e.g. by a nostalgic approach. The process increases resistance to change and the likelihood of failure of the change project.

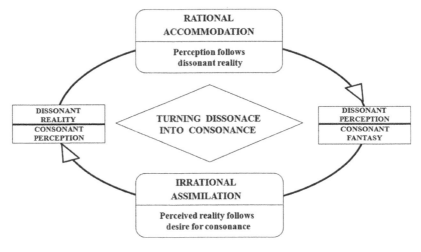

Figure 84:   Change   Management   Pathologies: Eliminating   Cognitive Dissonance

Pitfalls: Unlike "errors" that are triggered by deficits such as a) lack of activity (e.g. shirking, lethargy) or b) lack of managerial preparation of activities, pitfalls represent risks only to dedicated, sometimes overly active change managers. Activism makes these managers enter terrain covered by numerous hidden pitfalls, occasionally also deliberately set traps. Change managers do not comprehend that they provoke failure by their activity and dedication. Instead they are rather proud of their commitment and consequently extremely frustrated by their failure.

The demarcation between "errors" and "pitfalls" is not categorical but depends on the maturity level of the CMBOK. The NIMBY phenomenon (acronym for: *N*ot *I*n *M*y *B*ackyard) serves as an ostensive illustration. NIMBY describes a survey-related risk of asking unspecific questions which result in misleading answers: Targets may agree when asked questions like "Do you think things have to be changed?" but actually disagree as soon as change requires sacrifices on their part. So cost cutting may be accepted but cost cutting in the immediate organizational unit ("backyard") is rejected. As soon as the knowledge about pitfalls is incorporated into the CMBOK, pitfalls turn into errors, i.e. risks change managers are held accountable for. Consequently, attribution of failure to "Murphy's Law" or "black holes" is no longer justified. In other words, as soon as an awareness for pitfalls is created, the intelligent handling of these pitfalls becomes a touchstone of competence in change management. It is becoming more difficult for change managers to exculpate themselves through ignorance.

6.2 Change Opportunities: Scope and Management

The intelligence of change opportunities is effectively supported by listing *standard opportunities* for change management (see fig. 85). The listed events represent a favorable ambiance and an appropriate starting points for change initiatives since resistance is low, pressure high, resources available, and change readiness assured.

More favorable occasions for change initiatives are changes in the environment that compel companies to change (e.g. introduction of the Euro or compliance regulations) provided these necessities are considered as opportunities for performance enhancing projects. Likewise the implementation of ERP-software or e-business represents an opportunity to examine business processes. Linking optional "performance projects" to mandatory "compliance projects" appears particularly opportune with SOX compliance projects, IFRS projects and ISO certification projects.

Figure 85:   Selected Opportunities for Change Management

Management of opportunities should not be restricted to some *reactive* discovery or predicting of opportunities. In others word, professional opportunity management is not just a job for hunters and gatherers or prospectors (see fig. 86).

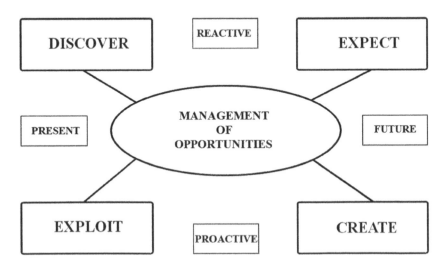

Figure 86:   Proactive and Reactive Opportunity Management

In addition, management must focus interventions to *exploit* or *create* opportunities, such as exploiting the opportunities of a crisis (see fig. 74) or creating opportunities by timing product launches according to internal needs for change or by terminating contracts with top managers that are change reluctant.

Whenever change management on the company level is embedded in a generic trend or fashion, there are primarily two options for strategic opportunity management (see fig. 87).

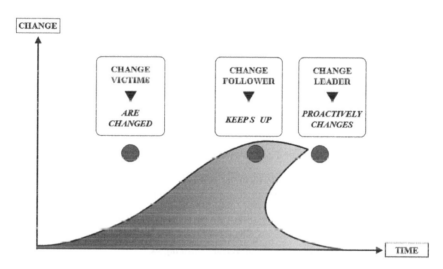

Figure 87:   Strategic Management of Change Opportunities

These two options are adopted from innovation strategies and competitive strategies: On the one hand, the position of the change leader (first mover), which IBM for example assumed in business process management in the 1980s. On the other hand, the early change follower who keeps up-to-date with changes. In contrast, those who restrict themselves to operative opportunity management (motto: „me too") can easily maneuver themselves into the role of change victims who can only reactively adjust.

6.3 Change Risks: Scope and Management

6.3.1 Errors

First, investment in intelligence activities to identify the typical errors is required (see also appendix E). From a risk management point of view, change managers can decide upon the wrong *therapy* on the one hand, and make incorrect *diagnoses* on the other. As a rule, diagnostic errors trigger intervention errors. The risk of incorrect intervention (e.g. choosing chapter 7 instead of chapter 11 in bankruptcy cases, sunk cost fallacy) was discovered earlier than the risk of an incorrect intelligence. In cases of wrong therapy decisions, *type I- and type II-errors* are differentiated, corresponding to alpha and beta errors in statistics. Very frequently, in the area of conflict between a *revolutionary* intervention or an *evolutionary* intervention for example, the wrong decision is made. The rejected option would have led to success while the selected option (most likely) leads to failure.

Two (more) archetypal errors are associated with wrong diagnoses. *Type III-error* denotes the risk that the wrong problem is tackled. When outlining a change project, it is possible that top management concentrates on the (objectively) wrong stakeholder front: shareholder-value disciples for example localize the bottleneck for long-term corporate development principally in the capital market. At the same time, however, the customer market or the labor market for IT specialists in numerous industries are also characterized by massive bottlenecks.

Type IV-error describes the risk of misjudging the context in which the new concept has to be implemented. This form of diagnostic error results from incorrect answers to the key question: „Who is affected by restructuring, to what extent and in what way?". When making an outsourcing decision for example, management focuses on suppliers and sales partners that have to be prepared for close collaboration. Often they overlook the fact that their own procurement department is developing huge resistance to the new outsourcing rules. Another variety of type IV-error arises when the winner or loser status of the affected employees is not diagnosed thoroughly (see fig. 88).

Of the current employees, an array of sacrifices is required by a change project. The spectrum ranges from sacrificing leisure time to the notorious sacrifice of „making oneself superfluous". Because of the delayed effect, many pioneers of change in the workforce will not fully profit from the change measures which they actively helped to draw up. In this respect, they represent the *sacrificial* generation. The circumstances of future employees are frequently the exact reverse. They can reap the fruits of the investment of their predecessors. In view of this inter-generative distribution of benefits and sacrifices, there are considerable difficulties in motivating the current workforce for the change project. At best, this can only succeed if the good and the bad years are more or less even in the passage of time.

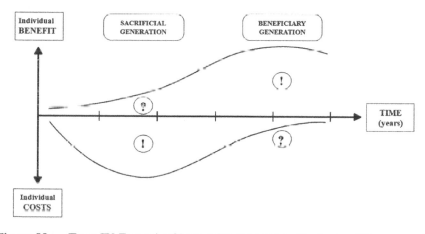

Figure 88:   Type IV-Error in Change Management: Confusing Winners and Losers

It is not enough however to just identify archetypal errors. The ethics of professional change managers demand a clarification of responsibility: To what extent can change managers be held responsible for the typical errors in change projects? There are two answers to this question: Change managers *must* assume responsibility if the errors have arisen because they do not rely on the CMBOK. Even if the corroborated knowledge in change management is fairly modest, there exists a catalogue of „professional malpractices", „sins", „infringements" or at the very least „negligence". This concerns violations against the universally known rules of good implementation activities, such as one-sided concentration on hard factors or soft factors respectively, on one-sided top-down or bottom-up implementation, disregard for typical resistance or barriers, or the lack of involvement of power promoters from top management. On the other hand, change managers are *not* responsible if the errors have arisen for reasons unknown, due to insurmountable resistance or barriers, or due to unforeseeable changes in the underlying situation.

6.3.2 Pitfalls

In addition to errors, risk management has to deal with less discernible dangers in terms of pitfalls. It is the brand of change agents, who totally identify themselves with their roles and thus put their heart into it, who especially have to contend with these pitfalls. It is not a lack of commitment, but overzealousness that is the most frequent reason for running into typical pitfalls of change projects. The following catalogue of generic pitfalls is supposed to contribute to the create awareness for these subtle risks of change projects. The pitfalls in this catalogue are clustered into *dosage, orientation and timing pitfalls*. Awareness is supposed to safeguard against those risks that are particularly frustrating because the affected change managers are not aware of having done something wrong.

Dosage Pitfalls

The *actionism pitfall* arises from an overdose of change offensives. Behind every action is activity and thus the basically welcome attitude of managers to actively see to changes. Overdosing occurs when several managers start their own initiatives but not in coordination with each other. One negative consequence of actionism is cost- and time-inefficiency of change processes. Moreover, acceptance of changes is not encouraged but inhibited. Instead of an intensified shake-up, targets cut themselves off from the „flood" of uncoordinated change initiatives. The affected employees become immune to changes, i.e. are less open or receptive to various communications of change. The image of promoters and consultants can also suffer under actionism. This is especially true when hyperactivity is not seen as commitment but as helplessness.

Doping pitfalls arise when - from the very outset - change managers take advantage of extensive top management support to push through a project in order to achieve broad acceptance as quickly as possible. This acceptance however is like the effect of performance enhancing drugs in sports: it is artificial. It quickly diminishes when the drugs are discontinued. From time to time, such a setback can be detected shortly after kick-off when the initiating sponsor becomes less visible.

Likewise, the well-known and undoubtedly very useful placebo effect can lead to a *placebo pitfall* (see fig. 89). Typical placebos in change management are the use of myths, gurus and renowned consultants, as well as going along with a management-hype. These do indeed create a high degree of confidence in the short term: for instance: „If everyone is into knowledge management, then we are on the right track". However, this placebo effect is normally short-lived. In the long-term, disillusionment and a drastic drop in the acceptance curve have to be reckoned with. This is particularly abrupt when a management fashion clearly finds itself in a downward trend or a role model (e.g. Japan) that one has copied later turns out to be a flop.

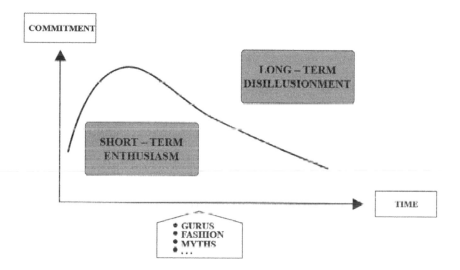

Figure 89:   Placebo Pitfall

Incorrect dosage also underlies the *pitfall of success*. Fig. 90 shows that past successes of an organization play an ambivalent role in its willingness to change and - closely coupled with this – in the future prospects for success. „Small" successes have a positive effect and do not diminish the readiness to further improve. This category includes, for example, success stories from the organization's pilot areas which can be used to encourage support for the roll out. In contrast, „huge", e.g. long lasting successes turn out to be very dangerous. They result in a state of being spoilt by success and complacency. With respect to companies this is also known as the Icarus *paradox*. Managers, who are evaluated in terms of success, find it difficult to understand that there can be an overdose of success. The only escape from the pitfall of success is finding an „optimal" level of success.

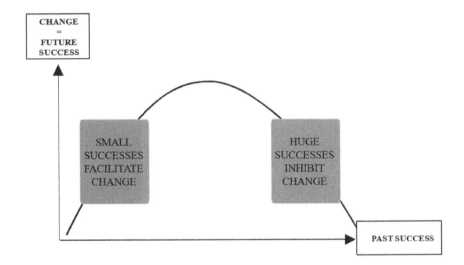

Figure 90:   Pitfall of Succes in Change Management

Orientation Pitfalls

Some pitfalls provoke a *lack of orientation* or misdirection. Anyone who is caught in this category of pitfalls is operating with inadequate navigation data.

The *breakdown pitfall* leads primarily to a lack of bearings. This risk arises a) when one tries to break down decrepit structures and b) in the struggle against the lethargy of organizations spoilt by success. What turns out to be particularly dangerous is the – intuitively plausible – view that a high degree of unrest and insecurity is sufficient for the still intact self-managing employees to set the organization on a new course towards its target. As we know from the unfreeze-move-freeze paradigm in organizational development (see fig. 33), a new departure requires not only a breakdown (unfreeze) but also additional intervention to set the course (move). This especially includes investment in a vision pointing the way.

Improvisation in terms of using provisional solutions is generally regarded as the epitome pragmatic management. Many change managers are not aware however, that provisional arrangements have several unpleasant drawbacks. They are therefore taken by surprise by the *pitfall of provisional arrangements* (see fig. 91).

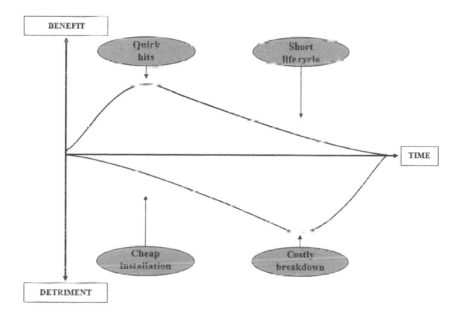

Figure 91:   Provisional Arrangements Pitfall

If, for example, in New Public Management, centralized controllership is first installed in an authority, but is meant to be replaced later by decentralized controllership and self-controlling, this usually results in high costs when it comes to dissolving this provisional arrangement at a later stage. Experience shows that provisional arrangements vigorously defy dissolution.

Provisional arrangements have a more negative effect when the „patient", who is only supposed to use these „crutches" as walking aids as a temporary measure, gets to like them in the long run and consequently can no longer live without them. In these all but seldom cases, the pitfall of provisional arrangement manifests itself in paradoxical circumstances, as shown in fig. 92. Organizations whose idea management is based on idea-reward schemes but who want to shift to the Continuous Improvement Process paradigm, also aim at reducing the costs of idea management: employees are supposed to provide the organization with ideas free of charge and be happy with immaterial recognition. Many organizations offer (modest) financial rewards as a temporary initial aid for the new suggestion scheme. Experience has shown that without incentives of this kind, there will be insufficient motivation for any form of change. Unfortunately, the principle of the protection of vested rights sees to it that these temporary additional bonuses cannot be completely eliminated at a later stage. Paradoxically, the result is *not the intended reduction but an increase* in the costs of idea management.

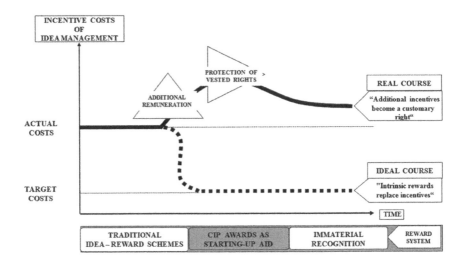

Figure 92:   Pitfall of Provisional Arrangements within Changing Idea Management

One specific *cost cutting pitfall* has to be dealt with when attempting to increase shareholder value (see fig. 93). This pitfall does not lead to a lack of orientation but to *misdirection*. In shareholder value management, the desired improvement in the return of investment as an output-input relation can be achieved by a) cutting costs ("denominator-focused management") and by b) developing competency ("numerator-focused management"). Change managers who consider these two options as equivalent, ignore the existing *asymmetry* and will become rather frustrated. Whereas the measures for competency development (e.g. knowledge management, learning culture, benchmarking, training) also support the cost cutting efforts (use of experience curve effects, minimizing stocks, reducing overhead costs, etc.), all downsizing measures serve primarily to confuse and discourage. The result is that they inhibit efforts to promote innovation, i.e. offensives for new products, procedures and markets. It is questionable therefore whether a sustainable increase in the shareholder value can be attained by these cost cutting measures.

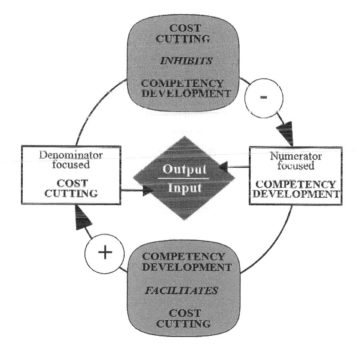

Figure 93:   Cost Cutting Pitfall

The *panic pitfall* arises from plausible yet damaging reactions to the typical deterioration of performance measures in the early phase of an implementation process marked by confusion (see fig. 20). If, in this phase, managers really are confronted with deterioration rather than the expected improvement, they will likely panic. They increase pressure and intensify controls. We know from research in bureaucracy that this reaction, which is completely "normal" for business as usual, often gives rise to a real deterioration (see fig. 83). The confusion risks are also intensified when, in the face of failure reports in the initial implementation phase, some promoters abandon ship in a panic so as not to "go under with the project". By doing this however, they withdraw the support which is critical for the success of the project.

The *nostalgic pitfall* has similar effects. When faced with teething troubles of the change project, change promoters cultivate a – thoroughly justifiable – longing for the "good old days". When these promoters distance themselves mentally or publicly from the project, the project's chances of succeeding will decrease tremendously.

Anyone, who concentrates only on quantitative performance measures (e.g. number of submitted suggestions, number of workshop participants) - in accordance with the plausible maxim "No management without measurement" - will easily fall prey to the *Gresham pitfall*. The soft, but acceptance-relevant performance measures of the change are neglected, e.g. results of employee surveys or improvements of climate. In many cases, this leads to misdirection in the conduct of the promoters.

Timing Pitfalls

The risk of a *postponement pitfall* arises if a change project that goes along with unpopular measures (e.g. downsizing, cost cutting, off-shoring) is implemented as late as possible so as to increase the pressure to accept the change and thereby reduce costs of mobilizing (see fig. 94). This is justified by the fact that without pressure nothing happens. What is overlooked however is that in trying to reduce resistance, the change costs that have to be dealt with increase: instead of few employees a major part of the entire manpower has to be laid off. The frequent result is an explosion in the project costs.

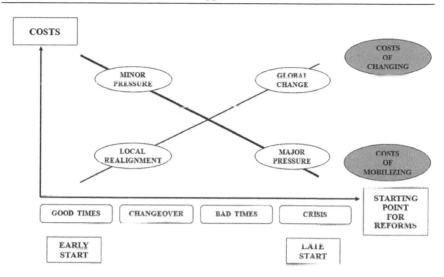

Figure 94:   Postponement Pitfall

A change leader will maneuver himself into a *last resort pitfall* if he keeps putting off unpopular measures such as cutting jobs because he sees them as the last resort. Such conduct rates as „realistic" or even, on a superficial level, as „social". However, this delay usually brings about a simultaneous increase in the change requisites that have to be dealt with. If the economic situation of the organization worsens, then even more jobs have to be shed. A dangerous gap opens up between the essential change requisites and the actual adjustments.

An *early start pitfall* exists when, for example, a change project (i.e. empowerment) is introduced in a very *hierarchical* organization via a *non-hierarchical* structure installed in the *transition phase*. This happens for example by introducing a dual career path with a non-hierarchical project organization, whenever this type of structure is unknown to the company. By this, change promoters hope to conduct a (salutary) "shock therapy". Inevitably, the anticipation of non-hierarchical working modes causes considerable turbulence (confusion). This possibly jeopardizes the success of the project.

Often, the momentum of a change program is overestimated and the "life expectancy" of old ground rules underestimated. Change managers then fall into an *inertia trap*. Here too, change measures are fundamentally rational but their timing completely inappropriate. The restructuring from a monolithic corporation into a decentralized management holding model is usually implemented by a project organization established in headquarters. The standard catalogue of such restructuring projects normally includes several centrally-designed concepts for the formation of profit centers, flexible working hours, concentrating on core competencies via outsourcing and partnership programs with suppliers. Immediately after the installation of these profit centers, the newly appointed center managers make it clear – in complete accordance with the assumed responsibility and self-controlling rights –, that they do not feel bound by the headquarters' concepts of outsourcing, working hours etc, but want to take direct control of developing tailor-made models for their centers themselves. Obviously, when planning the new corporate structure, it was incorrectly assumed that development would be sluggish thereby ensuring that some old rules would still apply in the new structures. This is inconsistent however with the considerable momentum of such „revolutionary" approaches of decentralization.

Evidence from product development has made us more aware of the *time pitfall*. Similar risks also arise with organizational innovations, as illustrated in fig. 95. The average life span of many change concepts becomes shorter. At the same time, the average time to implement a change tends to get longer.

The short life span of change concepts can be put down to very diverse reasons. Some of these reasons are exogenous in nature and are associated with the fashionable character of many change concepts, e.g. Shareholder Value Management or outsourcing. Sometimes however, the reasons for short life cycles are of one's own making. Take for example the cannibalization of several programs: a merger often results in TQM or IT projects being aborted or fizzling out. It is the „innovative" and restless change managers in particular who maneuver their organizations into an *„acceleration pitfall"*: the life span of an organizational change is systematically shortened by a constant series of new change projects. This "creative destruction" reduces the desired chances of acceptance on the affected employees.

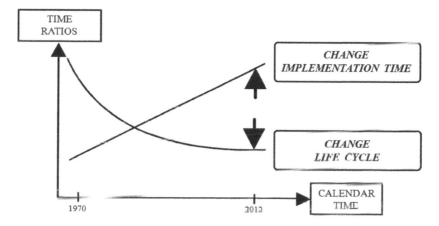

Figure 95:   Time Pitfall in Change Management

6.3.3 Misconduct

A third category of risks derives from specific *willful* behaviors of the actors involved in the Change Leadership Value Net that impair change management performance due to *impairing* relationships to other actors. For instance, change champions or service providers practice misconduct that is beneficial to their personal interests but detrimental to the interests of sponsors, other service providers or others. They do not behave as *stewards* of the change project but as opportunistic *agents* who want to profit from the information asymmetry that accompanies their relationship to principals. Stewards try to create an atmosphere of trust by stabling a maximum of transparency and fairness. Fig. 96 outlines typical categories of misconduct in partnerships. The information asymmetry that is opportunistically exploited by one partner is either a) *emergent* or b) *deliberately provoked* by activities of hiding, camouflage, or deceptive signaling. "Hiding" creates nontransparency and impedes partners' intelligence activities. Provoking information asymmetry (e.g. via hiding agendas) constitutes one category of misconduct that enables follow-up opportunities for more opportunistic (mis-) conduct (e.g. moral hazard).

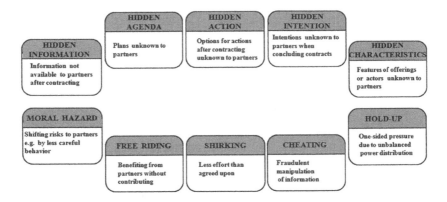

Figure 96:   Misconduct-Induced Risks to Relationships in the CMVN

Free riding in complementor relationships (see fig. 39 and 58) takes place when complementors (e.g. trainers) do not compensate their partners (e.g. project managers) for the costs of acquiring customers or project budgets, i.e. costs remain exclusively allocated to the project managers. *Hold-up* situations are quite often the result of tailoring services to the needs of either principals or complementors. This yields unbalanced power distributions since the providers of customized change management services will not be able to sell these services to other clients.

Whenever relationships in the CMVN are contract-based, misconduct impedes the fulfillment of contracts. Fig. 97 provides an overview of typical contracts concluded to control the business relationships along the project supply chain.

Also non-contractual complementor relationships in the CMVN bear risks, some of them due to information asymmetry amongst change champions and complementors or amongst several complementors. Project complementors quite often have hidden agendas or execute hidden actions that concern their business relationships to other "third" parties (e.g. in multi-principal constellations). Moreover, trainers or community operators may know more about the requirements of sponsors or the needs of targets than project champions do. This asymmetry may induce shirking or cheating.

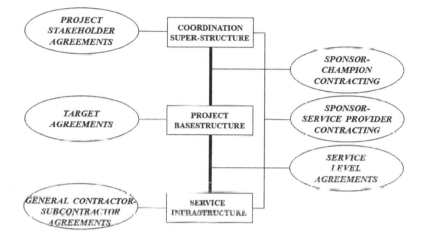

Figure 97:   Contract-based Relationships in the CMVN

Already by definition, competitors' behaviors are a source of risks for the success of the reference change project. Consequently, "misconduct of competitors" only denotes the violation of rules for fairness of competition, e.g. poaching of project manpower. In general, relationship risks in this arena of the CMVN are caused by a transition from *good*, i.e. rule abiding to *bad* competitors who keep violating rules.

7 Change Management Frameworks

7.1 Virtual Organizations and Organizational Networks

7.1.1 Virtual Organization: From Enterprise to Interprise

Researchers from MIT have outlined two scenarios of 21st century organization: one they called „virtual countries", the other „small companies, large networks". The first scenario has to do with global companies, for which the local-global distinction is somewhat obsolete. A new species of global companies are dotcoms. These operate Internet-based beyond political or geographical frontiers. The second scenario deals with the borderless company. These companies are network-shaped. Networking goes beyond the traditional boundaries of a firm. Networks are the core of various management concepts, such as „extended enterprise", „open industry", „(extended) supply chain management", "eco-system", "clusters", "business web", or „virtual company". The major drivers of complexity in virtualization are fuzziness and volatility.

The concepts of „virtualization", „virtualness" or „organizational virtuality" (see also fig. 41) must first be refined since the notion of a *virtual company* is ambiguous (see fig. 98). On a micro-organizational level this also holds for the concept of a *virtual team* (project team), a *virtual department* (e.g. R&D, HR) or a virtual event (e.g. conference, meeting), on a macro-organizational level for a *virtual market*. On the one hand, virtualization refers to the *electronic infrastructure* of the company, creating „electronic companies", "digital companies", "Internet companies" or „E-companies". Virtual is not necessarily digital, but also comprises non-digital infrastructures for telecommunication like teleconferences. On the other hand, virtualization reflects the *network shape* of a boundaryless organization. The end customer is increasingly aware of the fact that there is not one producer but a value network of several enterprises behind many products (e.g. personal computers, cars or mountain bikes), numerous services (e.g. health services, business travels or a package holiday) and solutions (e.g. logistics, telecommunication, energy supply). This is sometimes made transparent by ingredients marketing (e.g. "Intel inside", "Goretex inside", "sent from BlackBerry"). The term "network" has been adopted for such cross-company cooperation among several, legally independent enterprises.

Sometimes, they are also referred to as "quasi companies", "open" or "disaggregated" value-adding systems. Organizational networks are not about conventional companies or familiar bilateral forms of cooperation (e.g. joint ventures), but about the combination of a larger number of legally independent partners. The number of interfaces increases hand in hand with the increase in partners and thus the complexity of the entity.

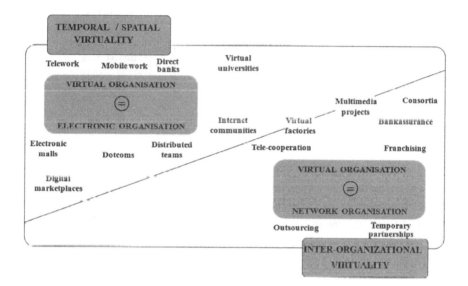

Figure 98:   Concepts of Virtual Company

The two concepts of virtual company have „flexible and agile organization" as a common denominator, as shown in fig. 99. Spatial and temporal virtualization are both Internet-enabled. Spatial virtuality provides flexi-space, i.e. the capability of doing work *anywhere*. Temporal virtuality stands for flexi-time, which is reflected in the philosophy of *anytime*. In addition, temporal virtuality enables business „round the clock" in a „company that never sleeps". Inter-organizational virtuality means *flexi-contracts*, i.e. primarily loose contractual relationships across company borders with varying partners (with „anybody"). The fluid character of virtual organizations gives rise to a number of difficulties in clarifying what is „internal" or „external", or which actors are „insiders" and which are „outsiders".

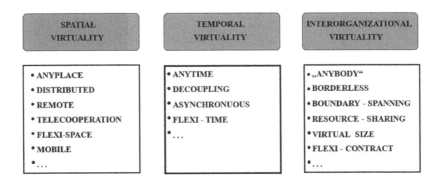

SPATIAL VIRTUALITY	TEMPORAL VIRTUALITY	INTERORGANIZATIONAL VIRTUALITY
• ANYPLACE • DISTRIBUTED • REMOTE • TELECOOPERATION • FLEXI-SPACE • MOBILE • ...	• ANYTIME • DECOUPLING • ASYNCHRONUOUS • FLEXI - TIME • ...	• „ANYBODY" • BORDERLESS • BOUNDARY - SPANNING • RESOURCE - SHARING • VIRTUAL SIZE • FLEXI - CONTRACT • ...

Figure 99:   Three Dimensions of Organizational Virtualization

We will concentrate on the *inter-organizational, institutional* or contractual *virtuality* of virtual companies. In this aspect, some, but not all virtual companies define themselves by the electronic infrastructure of their business. We refer to the extended (network) enterprise as an „*interprise*". Fig. 100 is a synopsis of current trends all of which result in interprises.

Quite a number of well-known companies as well as a plethora of (as yet) no-name micro companies have adopted the term „virtual". For example, big businesses such as Dell, Nike, Benetton, Airbus, some of the global auditing companies, and firms in the media industry (i.e. news agencies, movie studios, multimedia companies) all use the label „virtual". An additional growing number of internet communities (Social networks such as Facebook or open source Communities such as Linux, Mozilla, etc.) complete the list of virtual organizations.

All virtual companies, in the *broader* sense, lack certain characteristics of conventional companies, e.g. extensive vertical integration (which has been replaced by outsourcing to suppliers, value added resellers or other business partners) and the mono-centric concentration of power at group headquarters. In the *narrow* sense, virtual organizations are regarded as particularly flexible forms of IT-enabled

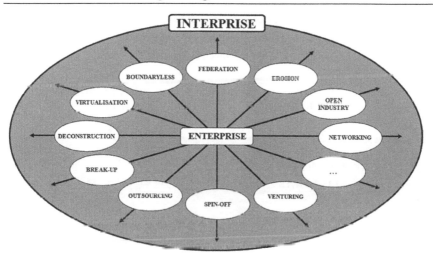

Figure 100:   Trends towards the Interprise

cooperation of limited duration among several legally independent companies and persons with the mission of fulfilling customer orders. It is true that Internet-enabled "non-permanent organizations" of this type are found mainly in the innovative high-tech and service industries (e.g. in the media sector). Yet there is every reason to believe that this specific organizational form can also gain ground in large areas of traditional industries, namely in all primarily informational development activities that occur there (e.g. worldwide at Ford and AT&T) and in service processes Virtual organizational forms in the narrow sense manage without the physical and legal features of a traditional organization: they are not physically concentrated in specific buildings and offices, they do not have comprehensive organizational manuals, they have no legal form connected with ample overhead (but only streamlined coordinative positions that function as brokers) and the like. "*Virtual size*" in terms of all available network assets (manpower, facilities, know-how, customer data, etc.) replaces conventional criteria of size, such as the number of employees and total assets (see fig. 101).

Thus, virtual network structures also lack a number of features and mechanisms that conventionally define the corporate identity of an enterprise, such as a proprietary legal entity, physical locations, dedicated resources and a specific corporate culture. In other words, the identity of virtual networks is primarily defined by their mission, i.e. by the products developed or by the services provided.

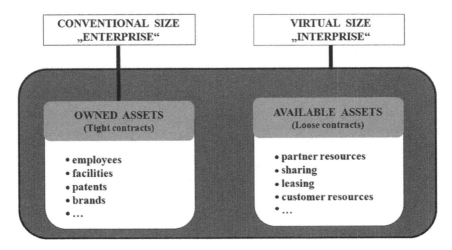

Figure 101:   Virtual versus Conventional Size

7.1.2 Scope of Network Organizations

Intra-company and inter-company networks: Distinctions are made between national and international, intra-industry and inter-industry as well as between intra-company and inter-company networks according to partners' origins. Intra-company networks take into account that within the company itself, the rules for collaboration among the partners also shift towards a "federation of divisions and departments". The significance of intra-company networks is underlined by the revaluation of informal, self-regulating networks. Intra-company network structures are the result of various forms of change:

Segmentation: Cell division into "plants within the plant" or into an "atomized", "molecular" or profit center organization constitutes an indispensable requirement for the emergence of networks in general. These business units have to be empowered at the organizational level (more autonomy) as well as at the resources level (more autarky).

Internal markets: Coordination among „entrepreneurs within the company" or „intra-corporate entrepreneurs" is based on market interaction patterns between internal customers and suppliers rather than hierarchical supra- and subordination: Horizontal service level agreements between market partners replaces hierarchy. However, internal markets are not based on exactly the same coordination principles as external markets. The coordination principles for the latter are based more on economic textbook markets. Special terms that may deviate from typical terms in real markets often exist between internal customers and suppliers, e.g. a "last call" or a purchase commitment. In view of the close link between spin-off and affiliation processes, the distinction between in-house and cross-company networks is increasingly fuzzy and thus less relevant.

Long-term and project-based networks: Long-term networks not only comprise long- term basic agreements (e.g. with suppliers and customers or in franchising systems), joint ventures, financial or management holdings but also associations (e.g. industrial and professional associations) and personal networks. Apart from long-term networks, there are networks of limited duration that are tied up with fixed-term projects. Sometimes, they are called "dynamic networks" as opposed to "stable networks". One variety of this type of "fluid network" that has already been dealt with is the virtual company. Consortia (e.g. in the banking or construction sector) have been in existence for a long time.

At the intra-company level, temporary networks are commonly found in community and project structures. They represent a "tent organization", i.e. project teams, working groups, crisis management tasks forces, communities of practice (thematic groups) and the like. A tent organization is strikingly different from the „palace organization", which is built to last and leans towards bureaucracy. If business operations in general are project-based ("management by projects", "projectification", also see appendix B) – like in management consultancy or in the movie industry – then the result is an ad hoc network organization.

Important transitional patterns between the two network variants exist in the dynamic development of network structures. "Long-term networks" often function as pools, from which short term network partners are recruited for a specific project.

Conversely, temporary forms of collaboration are often prototypes for long-term network organizations.

Traditional and modern networks: The emergence of network organizations undoubtedly represents a radical change. From the organizational viewpoint however, these loose and complex forms of association are not *innovations* in the narrow sense. Rather, they are the renaissance of an organizational principle that was prevalent in the pre-industrial era (see fig. 102).

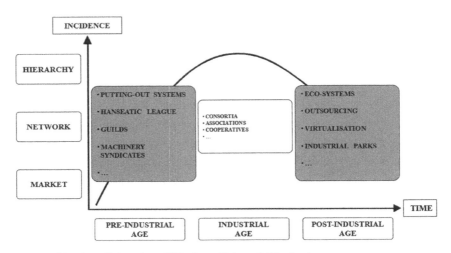

Figure 102:   Traditional and Modern Network Variants

The majority of "historical" network forms emerge on the resources front. It is typical for the putting-out system construction, for example, that the resources (buildings, machines, know-how etc.) required for a project or a business transaction are not brought in by a single dominant unit and thus by a single entrepreneur (as in the industrial manufacturing system), but by a multitude of entrepreneurs. A fundamental difference between traditional and modern network forms is the relevance of IT support. This is impressively illustrated by virtual "digital" organizations in the narrow sense.

7.1.3 People Management in Virtual Companies

People management covers all activities of „handling" people i.e. recruiting and "decruiting", skilling and development (training), motivating and organizing (see fig. 37). People management represents a combination of so-called *interactive* leadership (face-to-face feedback and rewarding, selecting, criticizing, assigning, etc.) and *infra-structural* leadership (culture management, managing labor relations, building trust, implementing pay systems, conceiving grievance procedures, etc.).

Along with the differences between traditional enterprises and virtual interprises, people management in virtual companies is also supposed to be different. The „*distance*" between leaders and subordinates in all virtual organizations is a major cause of differences, as well as of stress, insecurity, resistance, etc. According to the three facets of virtualization (see fig. 99), there are three types of distance that enforce new leadership patterns: *spatial* distance (working remotely, „e-lancing", mobile work), *temporal* distance (working asynchronously) and *Inter-organizational* distance (e.g. soft contracts, constraints to governance). Some experts consider the differences to be moderate. Others consider them to be quite fundamental. Consequently, either *modifications* or *substitutes* of traditional leadership can be differentiated in accordance with the required extent of change.

Modifications: Leadership problems in virtual organizations can be dealt with sufficiently by making incremental alterations to traditional leadership patterns. Project management techniques, for example, are also valid in a virtual environment, provided they are adapted to the fact that team members are from several independent companies, and that steering committees represent all stakeholders of the project in question. Another typical modification refers to „new" labor relations: this describes the shift from collective bargaining towards more individual relationship management as a concomitant of the diminishing power of unions in the new economy.

Substitutes: These are needed if people management in virtual companies is considered to be totally different from familiar patterns. Applying traditional patterns would not only be inappropriate, but detrimental and dangerous. In practice, a very broad range of substitutes is applied in interprises. First, there is a trend to replace *interactive* leadership (face-to-face communication) with *infrastructural* leadership (culture, organigrams, reward systems, etc.). Then there is the substitution of *hierarchical* structures with *heterarchical* structures. Skills in interprises are not primarily provided by training (like in traditional companies), but by recruiting already available skills, since there is no room („slack") for extensive training in lean and only temporarily configured project networks. Last but not least, the *„interpreneur (interprise-entrepreneur)"* replaces the „employee" - the target of leadership activities in traditional companies.

Some moderate versions of substitutes are „surrogates". Surrogates are similar in design to standard leadership patterns, but adjusted to the virtual environment. For example, we are familiar with *intra*preneurship, which serves as a surrogate for (genuine) entrepreneurship (see also paragraph 7.2). *Inter*preneurs represent entrepreneurs who are involved in varying ad hoc projects and not in a long-term exclusive relationship with the same company (as is the case with intrapreneurs). Analogously, expert *power* is often a surrogate for formal power. *Careers* in virtual organizations do not exist in terms of a management or professional career ladder. Still, we do find opportunities for personal growth, in terms of a sequence of participation in different virtual companies over time. Promotion can be measured by the (increasing) size, budget or reputation of the respective assignments. These indicators of promotion and personal growth serve as surrogates for traditional careers. The pattern resembles career paths in project management established by a number of (innovative) enterprises.

Hybrid leadership patterns: The two types of change (modifications and substitutes) outlined above are not, however, mutually exclusive options. As a rule, leaders in interprises have to practice both traditional and virtual leadership, i.e. work with modifications and substitutes more or less simultaneously. The idea of a blended hybrid design also holds for the entire company: interprises very often operate as so-called *brick-and-click hybrids*. *Split location work* (home office and company office) illustrates the hybrid character of virtual companies on the work level of individuals.

The hybrid leadership approach is enforced by a typical *splitting of human resources* into two clusters. Modifications of traditional leadership patterns are applied to one cluster comprising *core personnel*. The second cluster of independent *partners* is handled predominantly with substitutes (see also fig. 105). As a consequence, a *two-class system* among the involved manpower emerges in many virtual companies. One class enjoys more job security, but less independence. The other class pays the price of less security for more independence.

7.1.4 Recruiting for Virtual Companies

Recruiting (as well as decruiting) activities aim at sourcing the manpower required for a virtual company. As in traditional companies, recruitment is primarily performed by search, selection and placement, such as implacement, new placement, replacement or outplacement. Flexible recruiting in traditional companies is based on a hire & fire policy „around" employment contracts. In virtual companies flexibility of recruiting is achieved by *configuration* and *reconfiguration*. Targets of configuration activities are teams, networks, pools, companies, or communities (e.g. online-communities). Configuring manpower sometimes means *modifying* employment contracts, e.g. from full-time to part-time or long-term to short-term.

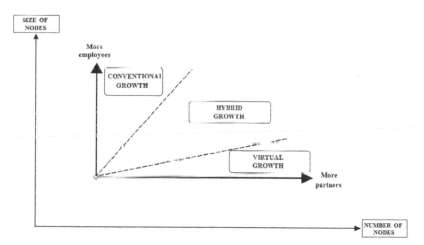

Figure 103:   Virtual and Conventional Growth of Networks

Very often configuring means *replacing* employment contracts by „interpreneurial" contracts. These „new deals" address exopreneurs, extrapreneurs (see also paragraph 7.2), freelancers, consultants, partners, agents, solutions providers or intermediaries who share both the opportunities and risks of the projects in which they are involved. Consequently, there are two ways of recruiting and two ways for virtual organizations manpower to grow (see fig. 103): *virtual growth* via recruiting new nodes (partners) of the interprise as well as *conventional growth* via recruiting new employees for existing nodes (partners). The conventional pattern also includes mergers and acquisitions. Since most interprises grow both ways, a decision has to be made to determine the optimal proportions of this hybrid growth pattern.

Specifics of recruitment for virtual organizations can also be illustrated by the *life cycle of teams* (see fig. 104). The „*forming*" stage covers configuration activities; orientation means the search for partners (e.g. from pools or communities), a major driver of transaction costs. The „*eroding*" stage does not stand for dissolution as in most traditional team approaches. Rather, it signifies the transition from a problem solving team to a pool. This pool serves as a platform for transferring knowledge („community of practice") and for maintaining social relationships (as in a club of alumni or an „old-boy network"). Pooling represents an efficient lever to reduce transaction costs of configuring new teams (out of „ex-"partners).

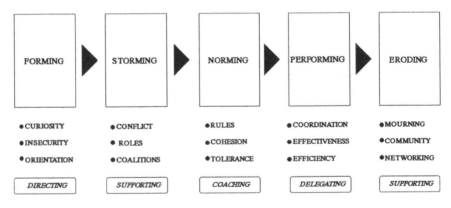

Figure 104:   Life Cycle of Virtual Teams

In virtual companies *virtual size* replaces physical size. Consequently, not everyone working for a virtual company is on its pay roll. As shown in fig. 105, the manpower in a virtual company comes from four different sources.

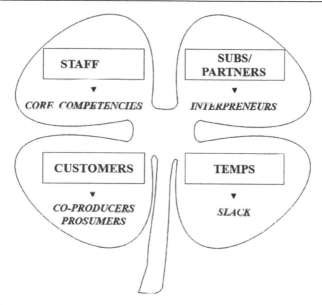

Figure 105:   Manpower of Virtual Companies

Subcontractors, partners and customers („co-producers" or „prosumers") are normally involved as „interpreneurs". They define the virtual manpower of the company. „Staff", comprising the hard core of highly involved intrapreneurs, establishes the „conventional" size of a company based on employment contracts. They also represent a part of the overall virtual size of the interprise. Subs and temps also exist in traditional companies as contingent workforce. In interprises, they form a by far higher percentage of the entire manpower than in traditional, flexible companies.

Professional recruitment is not only evaluated with respect to quality, quantity, time and location of the manpower acquired. Adequate configuration is also a question of the *optimal degree of association or affiliation*, especially within virtual companies. This optimization faces a *dilemma* between providing flexibility by loose association on the one hand, and warranting high integration by tight association on the other hand. In addition to classical employment, a wide variety of contracts, such as („body"-) leasing, "resourcing", borrowing, or interim management, to mention but a few, can be utilized to resolve this conflict. The art of recruiting manpower in virtual companies is the art of *fitting* the desired degrees of affiliation. That is, desired affiliation of the virtual company towards the manpower on the one hand, and the manpower towards the company, on the other hand (see fig. 106). Specific challenges are induced by "problems" in the workforce, such as "silver workers" incapable of keeping up with the pace of Internet business or with hyper-competition. Another challenge relates to stars (i.e. experts, content providers, internet start-ups, genuine entrepreneurs and others), who are indispensable to networks in building and sustaining competency. However, stars are very often reluctant to make an exclusive long-term commitment to a single virtual company.

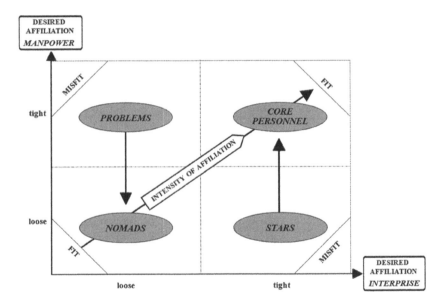

Figure 106: Optimal Degrees of Affiliation between Company and Workforce

As mentioned above, optimal recruitment for virtual companies has to be performed by *hybrid recruitment practices*. The required manpower is split in two segments. On the one hand, we have core personnel. In this segment, familiar staffing policies based upon close contracting warrant strategic flexibility of the company. On the other hand, there are non-core contributions from interpreneurs that are provided by loose contracting.

7.1.5 Motivating in Virtual Companies

For entrepreneurs, working in a flexible environment like a virtual company is *intrinsically* motivating: the built-in gratification of their jobs comes from *enriched* work (autonomy, no boss). For the interpreneur, being able to select one's partners – an option not normally available to intraprencurs - is an additional intrinsically motivating factor. This kind of flexibility enables "best of" configurations - a specific strength of virtual organizations.

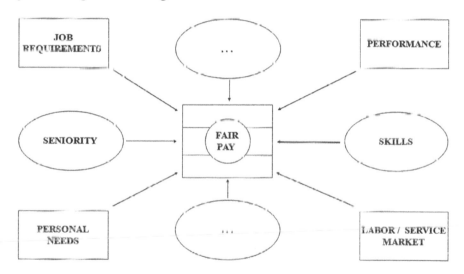

Figure 107: Determinants of Pay

Nevertheless, *extrinsic* motivation also matters to interpreneurs. While all the determinants of pay (seniority, job requirements, personal needs, skills etc.) specified in fig. 107 apply to employees in traditional companies, interpreneurs are paid primarily on a *performance base*, e.g. commission. This is normally a blend of *individual* performance and *project* performance. The level of payment does not (only) depend on supply and demand relations on labor markets (for specific professions), but (also) on markets for *services*. The respective services are „outsourced" from independent interpreneurs (IT support, consulting, logistics etc).

Modern instruments for retaining managers and professionals in the company, such as stock options to encourage (long-term) shareholder value-orientation, and similarly designed „golden handcuffs", cannot be applied to temporary partners, which represent the majority of interpreneurs.

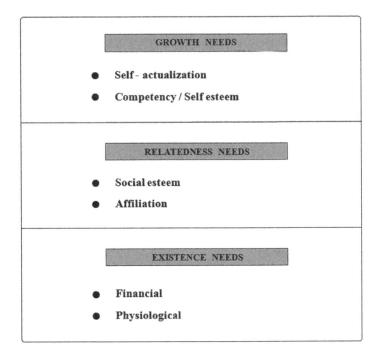

Figure 108:   Scope of Motives

Some of the motivation patterns used in virtual companies question familiar models of motivation, especially the *pyramidal models* of motives (see fig. 108). According to these pyramid models, growth needs (i.e. independence, self-actualization, ego needs, competence needs) are only activated if existence needs (material security) are satisfied. For many entrepreneurs, and certainly for the majority of interpreneurs (e.g. freelancers), this is not true: they strive for self-actualization in an environment that does not satisfy lower needs for financial security.

Modern tools for the performance assessment of managers operate on a multi-rating system: Assessment is not only the job of superiors (performance in terms of financial performance), but also of peers (colleagues), internal or external customers, and subordinates integrated in a so-called *360-degree feedback*. *Inter*preneurs are submitted to hybrid performance assessment based upon a *modified* 360-degree feedback, as illustrated in fig. 65. In contrast with traditional 360-degree feedback, „partners", not peers, assess performance. Partners expect interpreneurs to show supportive behavior in project teams. This often differs from the selfish behavior of an entrepreneur. Customer value is normally measured by fulfillment of service level agreements or by customer satisfaction feedback. The more employees become entrepreneurs, the higher the relevance of *competitive* reward systems, such as *awards*. I think of the „franchisee of the month" or the „supplier of the year" (e.g. Toyota's Global Contribution or Ford's Q1-awards). In traditional enterprises these awards serve as a substitute for non-existing markets and real competition. In interprises, awards supplement market performance-based rewards in terms of incentives.

7.1.6 Training and Development in Virtual Companies

Manpower training and development in virtual companies is the *privilege of core personnel*. For this segment of manpower, it represents a key issue in establishing and enhancing core competencies. Sophisticated programs offer on-, near- and off-the-job training opportunities. For non-core manpower, there are no formal training programs. Instead, recruitment is supposed to provide the required expertise by (re-)configuring the available manpower.

Although interprises are restrictive, when it comes to the training of individuals, they are open to *learning* on the organizational level. In general, organizational learning is accomplished by a blend of several *learning patterns* (see fig. 28): Combining learning by doing, by testing, in models and of models yields complex learning patterns, such as „broadband learning" and „ad hoc learning" (see fig. 109).

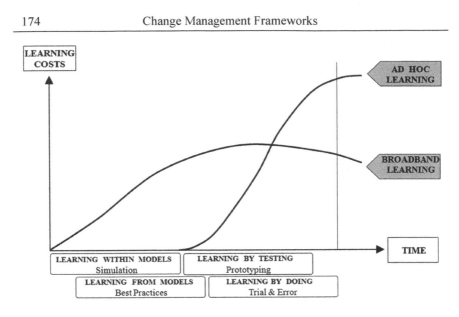

Figure 109:   Costs of Learning Patterns

Traditional companies have turned to the broadband pattern of learning, thus exploiting the advantages of benchmarking, simulation, testing and learning-by-doing, simultaneously. Virtual companies sometimes have a timeframe problem with respect to broadband learning. As a consequence, they are forced to learn in a launch-and-learn fashion. The two patterns differ with respect to the overall costs of the learning cycle. Broadband learning avoids error costs through extensive „proactive" learning processes. Ad hoc learning bypasses costly „offline" learning processes, but cannot avoid (opportunity-) error costs such as a lost order or even a lost customer.

As a rule, successful management requires a considerable number of *interpersonal skills*, in addition to technical and professional skills. In traditional companies, training in collaboration skills („how to cooperate in teams") and training in skills for competition („how to compete in markets") are two separate training arenas. Since network-shaped virtual companies are hybrids in terms of combining hierarchy and markets, they require „hybrid interpersonal skills" to cope with a hybrid social environment operating on *mixed rules* (for blended cooperation and competition). For these environments, the term „*coopetition*" has been coined (see also fig. 113 and paragraph 7.1.7). In interprises, training in interpersonal skills has to focus on the typical coopetitive environment. In other words, interpreneurs have to learn how to cooperate and to compete with the same institutions or persons in subsequent projects, or in different projects run simultaneously.

7.1.7 Organizing Virtual Companies: Network Organization

A considerable number of organizational practices in traditional enterprises can also be employed in interprises. This holds for the implementation of centers (business segments, divisions, business units, shared services, etc.), internal markets, holdings, ownership of business processes, teams, project organization and the like.

On a macro-organizational level, there are two directions that the transition towards a virtual company can take (see also fig. 116 and 117). For monolithic big businesses, the transition is from „*corporation to federation*", i.e. towards a network of more of less autonomous units. For small and medium sized enterprises in particular, virtualization is the transition from a loose, occasional market contracting to closer business relationships (*"partnership"*).

On a micro-organizational level, virtual organization is mirrored in virtual *teams* utilizing Internet technologies (e.g. Extranets) and a web 2.0 or web 1.0 software infrastructure. Furthermore, virtualization gives rise to „*virtual departments*": in a virtual HR department, staff members are not physically centralized in one building, but distributed all over the world, offering various internal services via call centers or customer interaction centers. Also events such as conferences or committee meetings are frequently virtual, sometimes hybrid in terms of some participants physically attending while others are attending via videoconference.

As mentioned above, virtual structures are just refinements and modifications of „modern" organizations, not radical innovations. Consequently, it would seem naive to describe virtual organizations as „centerless". This widespread misinterpretation can be eliminated by taking a closer look at the „standard" center structure of a company. Fig. 110 contains a confrontation of traditional and virtual structures.

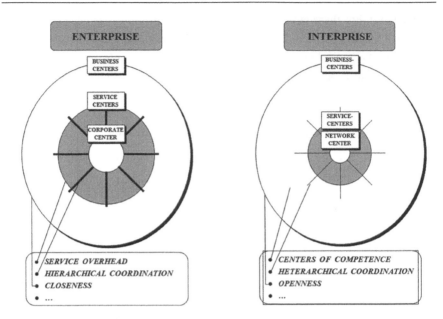

Figure 110:   Centers in Enterprises and Interprises

Business centers are ideal „home bases" for coping flexibly with segmented markets. In interprises, business centers do not only cover „internal" business units governed by a corporation, but also independent business partners („external" units). *Service centers* provide services primarily for business centers (i.e. they act as „internal" sources). As veritable entrepreneurs, they also deliver services to external customers (i.e. they act as non-captives). In enterprises services are provided by shared services whereas interprises frequently avoid this service overhead by establishing centers of competence: business centers also provide internal services for network members. The traditional corporate center is replaced by a *network center*. Both corporate and network centers perform a coordinative or integrative job. They differ, however, with respect to range (internal as opposed to external) and power base for coordination (hierarchy-based intervention as opposed to authority-based influence). A network center has the role of either a network broker or a focal enterprise (e.g. in franchising systems).

Almost all traditional companies have invested considerably in strategic alliances. Is the leadership role in interprises comparable, or even synonymous with that in *alliances*? The answer to this question is, 'no'. Alliance management is focused on a small number of handpicked partners. In interprises, organized relationship management is performed on *two* levels, and not only on the level of selected partners. On the *community management* level, the focus is on long-term relationships with a comparatively large number of potential or former business partners (take open-source communities as an example). This pool management can also support knowledge management. In particular, pools, designed as *communities of practice*, provide the required liaison device for retaining and transferring knowledge in virtual organizations. On the *commerce management level*, the focus is on configuring networks for specific projects in order to yield value for customers. Community management serves as a platform for commercial network management. The complementary relation between permanent pools and temporary nets indicates that the widespread distinction, „stable networks *or* dynamic networks" is misleading.

Process management in virtual companies is a perfect illustration of how (modified) *traditional and virtual* patterns of people management are combined. The philosophy of business process reengineering, „structure follows process follows strategy" (see fig. 129), is also valid in virtual companies. Optimized business processes are crucial to implementing strategies of diversification, concentration or hybrid competitive strategies, such as mass customization. The requirement, „structure follows process", is usually fulfilled by installing *ownership of customer processes*. Traditional structures for process ownership have to be modified in virtual companies, since process owners cannot exert hierarchical power over independent partners. In addition, processes such as billing, shipping (logistics), data processing and communicating (call centers) are very often *outsourced* from agencies (solution providers, Application Service Providers, etc.) which have these processes as their core competencies, and serve as the optimal process owners.

Within a value net framework (see also fig. 39) virtual growth of an interprise is not restricted to recruiting upstream partners (outsourcing from suppliers) and downstream partners (outsourcing from franchisees or even consumers). In addition to this interprising along the supply chain (e.g. good practices from Nike, adidas, Benetton and some others), also competitors and complementors (accessories, support services, …) are relevant candidates for an interprise (see fig. 111).

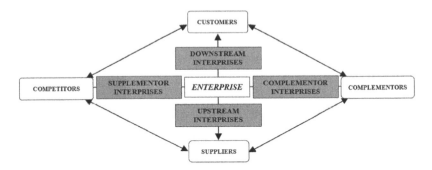

Figure 111:   Interprising in the Value Net Framework

All variants of network organizations are generally categorized as *hybrid* coordination forms (see fig.112).

This means that business relationships within a network vary between the extremes of hierarchy-based intra-firm coordination on the one hand, and market-based coordination through sales contracts on the other. The position of interprises (network organizations) in the continuum of governance structures is fuzzy: network organization covers closer forms of partnership contracts, strategic alliances or joint ventures, whenever more than two partners are involved.

Even if "network organization" serves primarily as an *umbrella label* for complex organizational forms "beyond market and hierarchy", several concept-specific characteristics can still be identified. These allow a network organization to be distinguished from adjoining organizational forms and thus prevent it from being "old wine poured into new bottles".

Every network organization has a specific *complexity*, which results from the number of network participants, and high interface and interaction density between the partners. This complexity distinguishes it from bilateral cooperation and from hierarchical forms of cooperation (e.g. a pyramid shaped supply chain), in which one focal organizational unit holds the reins and the remaining partners function merely as vicarious agents.

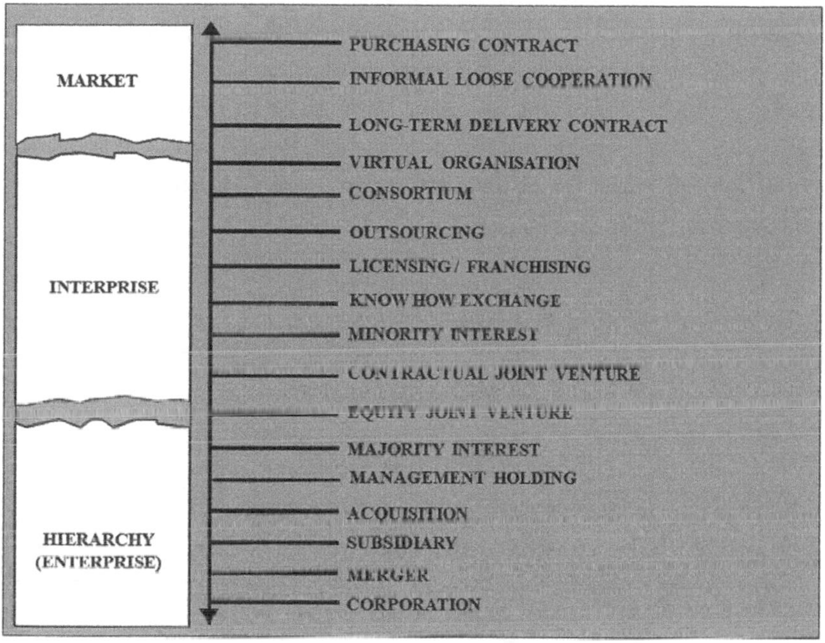

Figure 112:   Interprises in the Continuum of Organization Forms

The openness of networks constitutes another driver of complexity (see also fig. 110). Clear delimitation on the basis of *nodes* (network members) fails because of the *multiple association* of individual nodes with more than one network. Think of suppliers in the automotive industry (principally tier 1 and 2), who are integrated in the proprietary supply networks of several car makers. Furthermore, there are distinctly less official entry and exit barriers for (network) members than in conventional business organizations or traditional forms of cooperation. This results in a relatively high *fluctuation* among the members (see also fig. E 5). In networks, the coordination principles of the market and hierarchy overlap. Consequently, network members operate in accordance with *hybrids* and thus with rules that are constantly "charged".

The fact that networks a) do not completely eliminate competition among „partners", or b) do not forbid cooperation among competitors (e.g. tendering) is a major driver of complexity. A specific redundancy in the network configuration is responsible for the competition among network members: several nodes have similar competencies or corresponding performance profiles. Hence, networks do not constitute competition-free zones but obey the hybrid rules of so-called *coopetition*. This overlay of cooperation and competition leads to fuzziness in the distinction between foe and friend. Coopetition can be illustrated by the relationship between two automotive OEMs (see fig. 113).

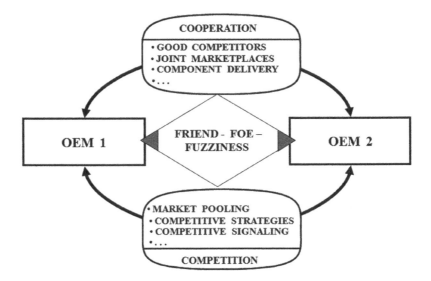

Figure 113:   Coopetition

Distinct hierarchies within networks also tend to be the exception. Numerous networks are therefore characterized not by a one-sided information asymmetry but by several *contrary* information asymmetries. In a distribution network, for example, the franchisor may have the better *overview* of the joint venture (branding, procurement markets) but it is the franchisee that has the better *insight* into the local market (the precondition for customer proximity). This contrary distribution of influence is termed heterarchy. Virtual companies made up of specialists are also heterarchical. A different partner dominates each branch of knowledge. All things considered, networks mainly comprise several shifting relationships of sub- and super-ordination. Hence, the explicit hegemony of a single node cannot be established.

As already mentioned briefly, virtual companies – like all networks – are made up of several layers, e.g. the commerce layer and the community level. The *commerce layer* refers to the commercial business networks. All network nodes function as value-adding partners, i.c. they are functional executives in a commercial value-adding process focused on the external customer market. The *community layer* refers to all activities that are officially organized to meet a network's internal requirements. Here we are dealing with internally focused processes of providing resources, and with relationship management. At this level, network nodes behave as members of a supply and relationship community. All the activities serve to build up the network's own resources capacity (e.g. knowledge, standards, competencies, reputation) and the relationship capacity (e.g. trust, reciprocity).

Informal connections, which exist in all social entities, are taken into account with a third *connection layer*. These emergent connections are not the intended result of organizational activities but are characterized by factual interactions and affiliations. Emergent action-reaction connections of this type are a result of cultural harmony, viral processes, external effects, sympathy as well as hidden agendas or intentions or having the same home region as other members ("clusters"), or they are the result of the proximity of locations

Another peculiarity of networks is that complexity within a network is not controlled by bureaucratic means but by network skills and self-organization. Networks are therefore not based on extensive written codes and organizational manuals but on soft integration forms such as trust, "linking pins", professional methodology for project management and so forth. The consequence of weak regulation is that organizational networks cannot be built or guided to a high degree. Rather, they evolve under their own momentum.

7.1.8 Network Culture in Virtual Companies

In the management community, *soft factors* have been considered as critical success factors for quite some time. Corporate culture (of traditional enterprises) describes a three-tiered concept covering visible elements (percepta) as well as hidden elements (concepta). As illustrated in fig.114, shared beliefs and values represent the core of a corporate culture because these „collective" attitudes, values and cognitive elements have immediate impact on the behavior of all members of the corporation.

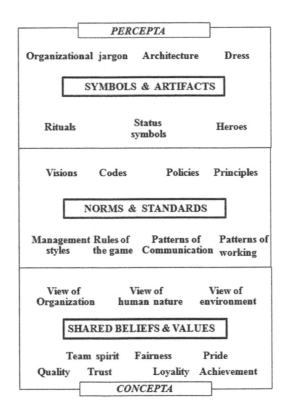

Figure 114:   Three-tiered Model of Culture

The three-tiered model also captures the essence of the culture of a virtual company or a network. *Modifications* are necessary, however, owing to the absence of physical features (buildings, uniforms, colors, etc.), i.e. the comparatively low content of symbols and artifacts. Cultures of virtual organizations also contain fewer documented norms and standards, such as handbooks, guidelines or formal dress codes. Consequently, the intangible hidden elements become more important: this holds for the emerging patterns of communication or leadership styles as well as of the shared views of how interprises work (self-organization, power, coalitions or sub-networks etc.), and what „trust" stands for in a temporarily configured, coopetitive organization.

More radical differences between the corporate culture of traditional enterprises and the network culture of interprises relate to the processes of „*building*" culture. Designing visions, handbooks, training new employees, referring to heroes and the history of the company and the like, are all traditional ways of building up a strong corporate culture. The majority of these instruments are „off limits" to interprises which – with the exception of franchising systems and other distribution networks - have no *shared or "common" history* or the common future of a „going concern". Consequently, new ways of establishing a network culture have to be explored. In particular, temporary project networks have to rely upon *importing* elements of existing culture(s) in their environment, i.e. from markets (e.g. rating systems, legal regulations), professional cultures (e.g. business ethics, codes of conduct), and possibly from the culture of specific industries, pools, clubs, clans and communities (e.g. norms of mutual support). This method of establishing a network culture seems to be time and cost- efficient. Unfortunately, it impairs the overall effectiveness of a culture: a traditional corporate culture enhances leadership activities with respect to *coordination, motivation, identification,* and *differentiation* (see fig. 115). In virtual companies, the network culture certainly facilitates coordination, thereby reducing transaction costs considerably. The benefits of a network culture with respect to motivation and identification are mediocre, when one considers the fact that exclusive membership in one interprise is the exception. Still, the mission of a virtual company exerts some motivational power. The most significant difference to *corporate* culture relates to differentiation, i.e. to the crucial question, „why are organizations different?" It is self-evident that an imported culture cannot serve as a powerful *differentiator*.

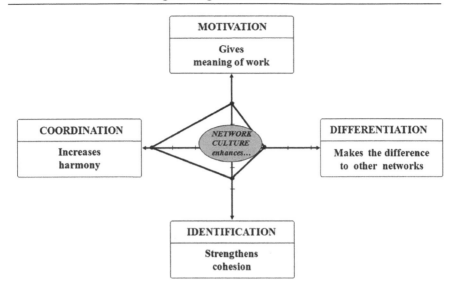

Figure 115:   Benefits of an Interprise Culture

7.1.9 Virtualization in the BR Framework

Networks owe their existence and prevalence to a variety of trends. These trends and mainstreams serve as powerful *facilitators for the implementation of virtual organizations*. Change managers should utilize them to overcome resistance, possibly even to establish commitment by emphasizing the advantages of networks: Networks result from the "social" nature of humans (networking), cultural conditions (clans as cultural communities), integrative developments in information technology (enabling by the Internet, facilitated by digital convergence), and from strategic considerations in virtual companies (interprises, see fig. 100). According to the "structure follows strategy" postulate, along with the governance structures also the conventional forms of *coordination*, i.e. hierarchy or market, are shifting towards the network model, thereby creating the so called "swollen middle". On the one hand, this takes place as an *erosion* (disintegration) of traditional corporate structures and on the other hand as a *consolidation* of market coordination structures into closer and durable business relationships (see fig. 116).

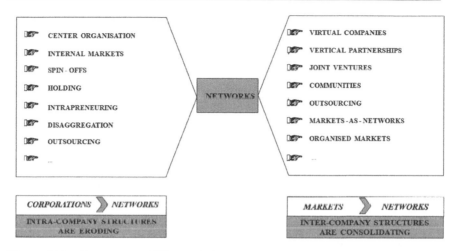

Figure 116:   Emergence of Network Structures via Erosion and Consolidation

The erosion takes place in three arenas: Towards *customer markets*, big units are broken down into autonomous and self-sufficient business units (divisions, business areas, profit centers) and if necessary, split into legally independent subsidiaries (spin-offs). In accordance with the motto "The corporation is dead, long live the federation!" centralized mainland structures undergo "cell division" and are disaggregated into decentralized island structures. The *value chain* of an enterprise is *reduced vertically* by outsourcing upstream or downstream to supplier and marketing business partners. Sometimes, relationships similar to marriage (lock-ins) emerge within such outsourcing of services. For example, Supply Chain Management with IT-outsourcing enterprises or with handpicked "purveyors to the court" within the scope of single sourcing. On the capital markets and labor markets, contractual relationships to shareholders and employees become less close. This leads principally to the erosion of conventional employment relationships. These are transformed into fixed-term employment contracts, part-time work, personnel leasing agreements and service contracts with subcontractors. Moreover, the physical integration of the workforce is reduced in many cases by the introduction of telework.

The erosion process comprises *two stages*, which make the most varied demands on change management (see fig. 117). The first stage of segmentation involves *cell division* and operations achieving economic self-sufficiency and legal independence. The aim of this spin-off process is to make former internal divisions and departments amenable to networks. The processes of detachment of divisions and employees, of cutting off the parental supply of resources as well as of confrontation with customers and competitors have to be supported by measures to cushion the impact of such a separation and measures to prepare for the new entrepreneurial status. At the second stage, the spin-offs affiliate with independent segments of other companies, e.g. former suppliers, competitors or allies. An important case of segmentation is centralizing distributed services (such as IT services) into some shared services and outsourcing the entire bundle of services as so called managed services. The processes of *forming* and *norming* such a network-shaped entity made up of many partners has to be supported in the *networking* phase. The blurred boundaries between the enterprises therefore clearly lead to a reduction (downsizing) as well as to an extension (extended enterprise) of the original association. New rules, for which change management has to prepare all the affected individuals, apply in the boundaryless organization.

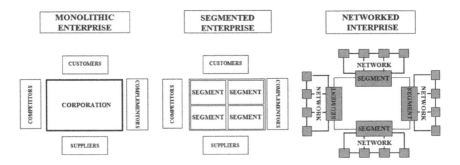

Figure 117:   Stages from Enterprise to Interprise

The shift from conventional employment forms, centric corporate structures, bilateral cooperation and market relationships (to more or less anonymous and thus exchangeable customers and suppliers) towards network structures is accompanied by a considerable increase in stress at interfaces and entrepreneurial stress amongst the affected workforce, thus provoking *strong resistance*. These barriers to success are manifested for instance in the relatively sluggish response to teleworking, an innovative mode of working from the 1970s. Resistance is greater than with other radical changes, such as a business reengineering project: in the end, more structural and leadership features are retained with the latter than with the transition to network structures.

Communication activities in the implementation process should focus on the advantages without ignoring the disadvantages of interpreneuring (entrepreneurship within the network). On the level of the affected employees and managers (targets), a distinct advantage is the intrinsic motivation potential of a self-determined activity. A disadvantage within a network organization, however, is that each network node is dependent upon other network nodes as a consequence of specialization. The emergence of strategy-driven networks is of particular practical relevance for implementation. Conventional organizational forms of intra-company coordination, of free-market customer-supplier coordination, and of bilateral alliances do not foster a sufficient organizational support for numerous competitive strategies (focusing on core competencies), innovation and diversification strategies, globalization etc. Relevant for both big business (corporations) and small business (SME) are the competitive advantages of interprises on the company level. Fig. 118 illustrates that the strategic profit of networks for corporations is flexibility whereas small and medium size companies profit from an increase in economies of scale as well as synergy (integration). Networks offer a hybrid strategic performance by balancing the strategic advantages of small and of big business.

As for *training activities*, the flexibility of a network depends essentially on the learning capacity of the network members which serves as generic barrier to failure in the BR framework. In this respect, older employees ("silver workers") represent a problem group when it comes to implementation. Here, „the young teach the old how to use the Internet"-models can provide some redress. Because modern network structures aim at efficient collaboration among specialists, there is hardly any demand for the development of expert skills. On the contrary: the available *multiple* competencies of many network members are superfluous and thus have to lie fallow because only the best skills are used in the network.

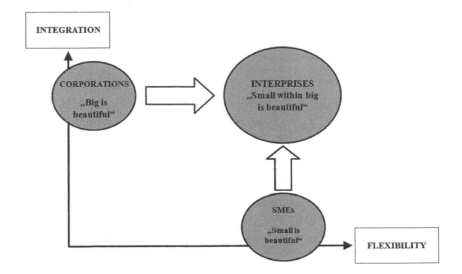

Figure 118:   Strategic Advantages of Interprises

Compensation for the disadvantages, which arise from taking over entrepreneurial risks, constitutes a key task of *motivation*. A trade-off in the form of an "employment guarantee" ("more entrepreneurial risks versus secure jobs ") is out of the question. What is possible, though, is an employment pact, in which the parent company awards contracts (e.g. warranted sales) to the spin-off in its initial phase.

Since the relationships and integration of employees are of prime importance for the success of the network, *new motivation and affiliation mechanisms* should be implemented in the transitional phase. This is about building up trust among the network members. Building up a *community based on trust* does however cause considerable difficulties. This is due, on the one hand, to the fact that conventional measures of building up trust (e.g. capital interlocking) would restrict the flexibility of the network configuration. On the other hand, a lot of time is required to build up specific bases of trust. Time is precisely what temporary network entities in particular do not have. It is essential therefore that in the implementation phase, a shared culture is *imported* using the cultural features already available on the community layer, especially shared professional features (from the professional management culture). These norms determine for instance whether enticement or bribes are classed as acceptable or forbidden business practices.

The lack of a concise *corporate culture* makes the transition to a network organization more difficult to manage. However, the lack of a culture does not necessarily make the implementation of network structures more difficult than the implementation of process management or Total Quality Management. Take corporations that have resulted from M&A processes for example: with them, a shared culture has proved all too often to be a phantom and not an actual reality capable of supporting implementation.

Altogether, go-with-the-flow patterns of implementation can help dismantle barriers to success of virtualization projects. Moreover, step by step-implementation (see fig. 117) and learning capabilities serve as barriers to failure. Another powerful potential is some entrepreneurial spirit in the existing manpower. This would create a mix of push entrepreneurship and pull entrepreneurship that could facilitate the implementation of virtual organizations tremendously.

7.2 Entrepreneurship, Intrapreneurship, and Interpreneurship

7.2.1 Scope of Entrepreneurial Models

The entrepreneurship framework is closely related to the virtualisation framework: virtualisation as the path from enterprises to interprises frequently overlaps with the transition from employees to entrepreneurs. Several innovative concepts of entrepreneurship have emerged hand in hand with the considerable increase in the number of entrepreneurs. The variety of the manifestations of entrepreneurs is constantly getting larger. Entrepreneurship is taking on different complexions: modern variants and classic prototypes appear side by side (see fig. 119). Consequently, the traditional perceptions no longer epitomize entrepreneurship as such. This observation applies to the traditional Schumpeter entrepreneur (distinguishing features: innovation, intrinsic motivation), as well as to owner-entrepreneurs (distinguishing features: small and medium size enterprise-based, patriarch in the family-owned business).

In the range of more or less innovative models of entrepreneurship there are several variants resulting from a combination of two – often seemingly conflicting – features. This *hybrid blending* often finds linguistic expression in neologisms or word combinations (see fig. 119).

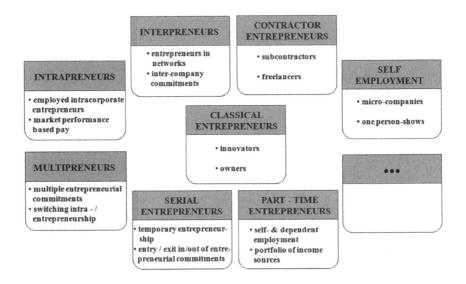

Figure 119:   Scope of Entrepreneurship

Intrapreneurs: These "intracorporate entrepreneurs" or "entrepreneurs within the company" are the result of management concepts which "bring the market into the enterprise" and thereby create relatively autonomous and self-sufficient „companies within the company" by transforming departments into *business centers* (e.g. profit centers). Executive personnel in terms of heads of subsidiaries, centers, spin offs, business and services units or ventures as well as opportunity managers become entrepreneurs who tune their relationships with external and internal customers according to market rules and who are remunerated on a profit-related basis, i.e. commissions, profit sharing and stock options.

Serial entrepreneurs: In contrast to the classic entrepreneur, whose life's work is represented by „his company", the serial entrepreneur enters into, and later pulls out of different entrepreneurial commitments. The withdrawal from an enterprise can be well-ordered, for instance, through an Initial Public Offering or the sale of a biotech start-up to a pharmaceutical heavy-weight. In this respect, it is normally a matter of a planned withdrawal and not a pullout forced by insolvency risks.

Multipreneurs: Multiple entrepreneurs of this type are not tied to a specific enterprise but are involved in several enterprises. This can be as an entrepreneurial partner (e.g. managing partner) or as an employee (intrapreneur). They therefore do not fit into the mould of classic career and development models.

Contractor-entrepreneurs: These subcontractors or freelancers work on their own account, for instance, in the transport services, distribution, consulting or infrastructure service industries. A vast group further forms the „new independents". These so-called „e-lancers" use the internet to offer specific services in software development or administration. In their line of entrepreneurial activity however, they are always dependent on a principal who keeps in direct touch with the customer. For the most part, they have no capital share nor any creative involvement in the business idea.

Everyone an entrepreneur: Some scenarios for the future of employment imagine a businessman in every employed person. This businessman offers his competence and expertise in a service market and not in the conventional job market. These concepts of „total entrepreneuring" (motto: entrepreneurship is for everybody) trade, for instance, under the label of „Me Inc." or „self-employment".

Part-time entrepreneurs: These hybrid entrepreneurs (sometimes also called "cappucino workers") draw their incomes from an independent enterprise, as well as from dependent employment. They do not therefore represent „thoroughbred" entrepreneurs, but have put together a balanced *portfolio* from several sources of income.

Interpreneurs: These "interprise entrepreneurs" do their business in networks (see paragraph 7.1). Besides high-tech also low-tech areas such as handicraft are a homebase for interpreneuring: there, network entrepreneurs offer all-round services within the scope of craftsmen's cooperations or general trade networks (e.g. for integrated facility management around real estate). Many spin-offs also operate as interpreneurs. They develop and run their business in a network inter-linked with the parent company and new partners. An interpreneur cannot, however, be equated with a „netrepreneur" or „netpreneur". This made-up word is aimed at entrepreneurs of the new economy, whose business takes place in the Internet (hence, „net"-preneur). However, many start-ups in the new economy run their business as interpreneurs. In this respect, interpreneuring constitutes a familiar business model for „dotcom start-ups", „click companies", „cyber companies" or „Yetties" („young, entrepreneurial, tech-based"). Besides freelancers or franchisees this category also contains extra- and exopreneurs. *Extrapreneurs* are individuals who leave their employment at an enterprise with the purpose of establishing a separate firm that complements the previous employer. *Exopreneurs* are cooperating with large organizations to establish new businesses. In contrast to intrapreneurship where innovation uses existing entrepreneurial resources within the organization, innovation is brought into the organization with the assistance of external entrepreneurial resources, for instance in an external venturing model between a pharmaceutical and a biotech company.

Apparently, the „new" types of entrepreneurs are dispersed over a very large terrain. Their natural habitats are not only small to medium-sized businesses in traditional industries or in the so-called New Economy. Rather, less distinctive variants of entrepreneurship are also found within industrial giants or on the „fringes" of these corporations. There, captives (intra-corporate suppliers with only intra-corporate customers) become non-captives (with business relationships to external customers). Parallel to this, the parent company turns from a monolithic corporation into a management holding (see fig. 116). With regard to various spin-offs and ventures listed on the stock exchange, corporations may also turn into primary financial-oriented investment holdings, from time to time seeing themselves as a *corporate venture capitalist*. Numerous industrial giants such as GE, AT&T, ABB, Bertelsmann, Siemens, VW or Bayer have chosen this path.

There is however a negative consequence of the inflation and innovation trends in entrepreneurship: it is becoming more and more difficult to define a consensual view of the entrepreneurial paragon. All politicians and visionaries, who all too thoughtlessly use entrepreneurship as a magic formula in their arguments, should bear this in mind. The outlined trends are actually leading to a problematic polarization with regard to the future prospects of entrepreneurship: *Total entrepreneurship* arises from the idea that, in the working environment of the future, everyone will operate as an independent entrepreneur. At the other end of the scale, modern concepts of entrepreneurship provoke the attitude that classic entrepreneurship no longer exists. The Schumpeter entrepreneur as well as owner-managers are becoming old hat. The scene is characterized by *pseudo-entrepreneurs* who do not meet the standards of genuine entrepreneurship. These include the pseudo-independents in the legal sense, and the de-facto pseudo-independents, for instance freelancers, subcontractors, and reluctant entrepreneurs. They do not choose self-employment voluntarily, they are pushed into entrepreneurship which quite often represents the only alternative to imminent unemployment.

The numerous *hybrid* models of entrepreneurship blend employment and entrepreneurship (intrapreneurs, part time entrepreneurs, multipreneurs) or embed entrepreneurship into a non-market governance (interpreneurs, exo- and extrapreneurs, contractor entrepreneurs). By applying the generic patterns of blending (coupling patterns, see fig. 44) to hybrid entrepreneurship, several variants can be generated: The *sectoral* blending is reflected in a portfolio of employment and entrepreneurship based jobs (see fig. 120). This portfolio covers the two dimensions of a) autonomy and b) security of income.

Employee jobs are characterized by low autonomy (being involved into a control-and-command system) but high security of income. Traditional entrepreneurship offers high autonomy with volatile income. Some species of subcontracting are precarious since they only provide low security and autonomy. An interpreneur job constitutes the "star" component in this portfolio due to comparatively high levels of autonomy and security. Actually, most interpreneurs' portfolios blend a) network businesses and b) solo businesses (as genuine entrepreneurs) thereby reducing the security level of the whole blend of jobs. Proportions of blending may differ significantly, for instance with affiliates on the internet who normally earn only a minor share of their total income from their part time job as intermediaries on the internet. *Serial* entrepreneurship is the result of sequential blending. Intrapreneurship and (some species of) interpreneurship represent bundle blending: the daily job activities of a profit center manager serve as a source of both contractual salary and residual entrepreneurial income.

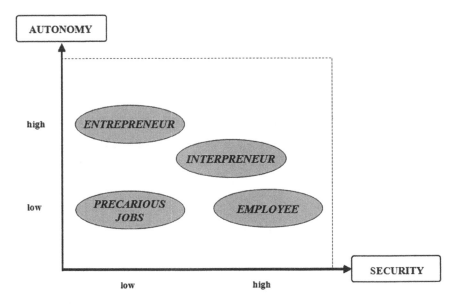

Figure 120:   Job Portfolio of Hybrid Entrepreneurship

7.2.2 Intra- und Interpreneurship in the BR Framework

Hybrid models of entrepreneurship constitute a specific challenge to change management. Management activities focus on the transition from an employee or manager status to an entrepreneur status. The managed transition is mostly driven by the *corporate strategies* of a parent company (see fig. 121): strategies of concentration (downsizing, focusing core competencies), revitalization (of unsatisfactorily performing existing businesses), and innovation "push" managers into intra-, inter-, exo-, extra- or entrepreneurship.

For the implementation of push entrepreneurship, all communication and motivation activities have to handle the ambivalent evaluation of hybrid entrepreneurship that derives from the generic nature of all hybrid concepts (see fig. 42). On the one hand, the conflict and chaos aspects of intra- and interpreneurship represent the inherent risks of this concept which will most likely trigger resistance, i.e. barriers to successful implementation. On the other hand, the compensation and synergy aspects represent opportunities which can be utilized as barriers to implementation failure or as ways of dismantling barriers to implementation success.

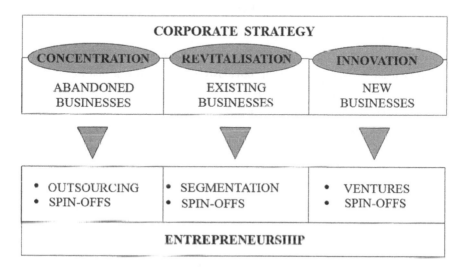

Figure 121:   Strategic Drivers of Push-Entrepreneurship

Dismantling barriers to implementation success: Some of the new *hybrid concepts* are classified as contradictions in themselves. this is true for the intrapreneur, i.e. the salaried entrepreneur. Because of his hybrid status, this concept is confronted with a fundamental criticism: the overlapping of market orientation and hierarchical subjugation is an unreasonable and intolerable inconsistency. Fundamental objections are also raised to neighboring hybrids, such as the contractor-entrepreneurs. Here, above all, entrepreneurial motivation is questioned. With no share in the business capital, and with no involvement in the business idea, a workable entrepreneurial commitment cannot develop. The upshot is that, with contractor-entrepreneurs, one is frequently dealing with a form of reluctant entrepreneurship. Such „push entrepreneurs" would – in complete contrast to

Schumpeter's „pull entrepreneurs" – rather work in salaried positions. The objection to part-time entrepreneurs is that human nature requires a fundamental decision between autonomy and security. An „as well as"-blending of self-employment and dependent employment (in analogy to hybrid "flexicurity") can, at best, be considered as a temporary solution. The motivational structure of individuals is geared in principle to an „either/or" decision.

In the case of *interpreneuring*, overcoming resistance of (reluctant) push entrepreneurs cannot be accomplished by relying on major trends and mainstreams. Although the network entrepreneur obviously combines two actual trends, he also appears to many as an ambiguous concept (see fig. 119) or as an ambivalent construction: at first glance, „network-based entrepreneurship" constitutes a welcome link between the *entrepreneurship trend*, which is so important for the revitalization of our economy, and the *network trend*, which facilitates an unbureaucratic and flexible combination of competencies beyond enterprise boundaries. Both trends are without doubt extremely plausible in themselves, and are classified as very relevant. However, the plausibility of individual trends does not guarantee that their „intersection" also works well. In fact, entrepreneurship and networking can obstruct each other: on the one hand, the desire for freedom of a typical entrepreneur restricts his readiness to make large cutbacks in his autonomy, only to meet the expectations of network partners. Some see another variety of pseudo independence in a network commitment, which degrades them to pseudo-entrepreneurs. On the other hand, there is the risk that only entrepreneurs in need of protection, who would otherwise not make it on their own, enter networks. Consequently, predominantly the hardship cases amongst entrepreneurs would hide behind the term „interpreneur".

Fortunately, communication and motivation activities can dismantle or even overcome some barriers by emphasizing the numerous *opportunities* of hybrid entrepreneurship. For interpreneurs an entrepreneurial activity is embedded in a network or an "interprise". Interpreneurs in terms of „entrepreneurs in networks", represent entrepreneurship which, in contrast to classic concepts, is characterized neither primarily by the entrepreneurial development of an individual person, nor by the collective entrepreneurial activity of a closely cooperating team (e.g. in a private limited company with several managing partners). Fundamental aspects of the business are borne rather by a group of independent companies who collaborate according to the principle of loose association: virtual enterprises, from multi-media cooperation and consulting partnerships via software development right through to virtual factories, represent part of everyday routine in many industries. Business logistics and distribution systems, from franchising to business partner programs, eco systems and business webs, are other natural habitats of interpreneurs. From the motivation point of view, the hybrid positioning of intra- und interpreneurs enables satisfying two basic needs (see fig. 108) in a more balanced way than entrepreneurship or employment can manage (see fig. 122).

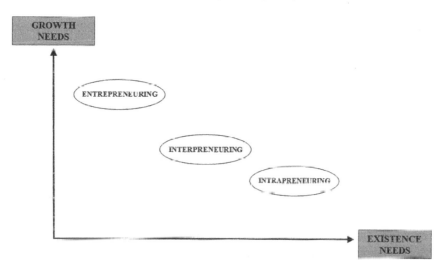

Figure 122:   Motivational Advantages of Hybrid Entrepreneurship

For hybrid entrepreneurs, *hybrid reward systems* help dismantle implementation barriers. This is illustrated in fig. 124 and 125 for intrapreneurs. Together with several market focused, structure focused and resource focused building blocks, hybrid reward systems constitute a critical component of a holistic concept of intrapreneurship (see fig. 123).

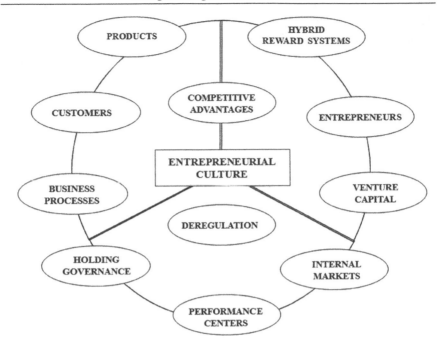

Figure 123:   Building Blocks of Intrapreneurship

Salaried entrepreneurs are rewarded by a blend of contractual income and residual income (performance based). Moreover, within residual *entrepreneurial rewards*, different "calibres" of performance indicators are blended: this blend supports both motivation and coordination of intrapreneurs. On the one hand, short-term, center-performance based incentives are most motivating, but also trigger egoistic and short-sighted activities. On the other hand, stock options and similar long-term, corporate-performance based incentives enhance coordination but have only a minor impact on motivation (see fig. 124).

Like all blending patterns, blended reward systems must be specified by *proportions*. This can be done by standard proportions (70:30 for all intrapreneurs) or customized to different categories of intrapreneurs (e.g. larger shares of entrepreneurial, market performance based remuneration for business division managers than for business team managers). Furthermore, to facilitate implementation via participation (see fig. 30 and 46), the customizing or personalization can be accomplished by self-customizing.

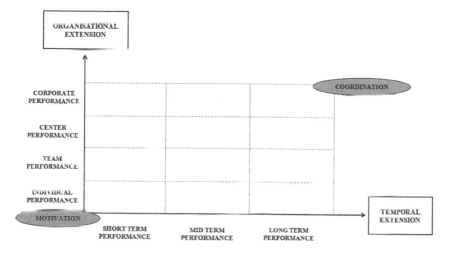

Figure 124:   Blended Performance Based Incentive System for Intrapreneurs

This corresponds to the logic of so called *cafeteria reward systems*. Fig. 125 compares two same size trays of two intrapreneurs (representing their total

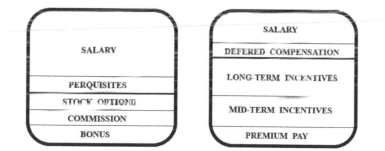

Figure 125:   Cafeteria Customization of Intrapreneurial Incentives

compensation), that are packed with two significantly different self-blended configurations of intrapreneurial rewards. Actually, the assumption of an identical size of total compensation does not apply to intrapreneurs whose incomes may vary according to their respective individual and center market performances.

More pro-arguments to be used in communication and motivation activities to facilitate the transition to interpreneurship can be found in the high-tech sector. There, *venture management* leads to network structures, which are run by independent venture capital companies or by corporate venture capital subsidiaries, and from time to time, also by networking agencies such as incubators. The venture organization combines the advantages of young *venture entities* (e.g. innovation and learning capacity) with the strengths of mature *sponsor entities* (e.g. experience, capital, network of connections). In this way, risk management for innovative business ideas can be better handled (see fig. 126).

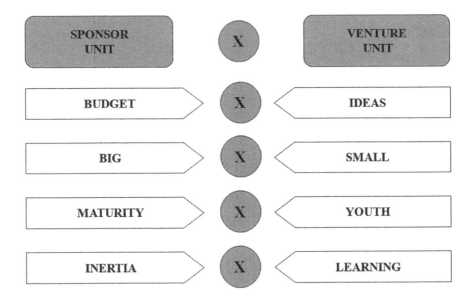

Figure 126:   Symbiotic-synergetic Interaction of Sponsor and Venture Units

Evidently, network entrepreneurship is more of a challenge than a panacea. Still, implementation activities can overcome the presumably antinomic blend of egocentric entrepreneurs on the one hand, and conformist networkers on the other hand: First, networks allow considerable scope for entrepreneurial *solo-business* (alongside the jointly run network business), according to the principle of loose association, and *interaction scope* for commitments in *other* networks (non-exclusivity, freedom of association). In principle, there is also room for the egoistic exploration of ideas in networks. As a rule, the network partner does not become a captive of a network. Furthermore, not all business-oriented activities have to take place in the network environment. The complete embedding in the network with the total loss of independence, the collectivization of individual ideas, and the abolition of private ownership is atypical. In addition, network organizations encourage and demand self-sufficiency of their members. A reputation and a minimum self-sufficiency are the standard criteria for acceptance to business partnerships. The problem of hardships is clearly defused through this natural selection mechanism. In addition, it must be made clear, that entrepreneurs are not primarily competitors, nor are they dogmatic network adversaries. As a rule, they support and operate various networks and communities of interest, for instance collective buying according to cooperative principles, and relationship networks, for instance as networking on the personal level (e.g. alumni clubs) or at the organizational level to promote interests (e.g. lobbyism).

Moreover, entrepreneurs have a feel for the complexity of real business. This is frequently the result of having to supply customers with an all inclusive offer, as is typical for the solutions and systems-selling businesses. However, even an all-rounder cannot always bring this off. The high demands on the specificity of knowledge, together with specialization in competencies, see to it that disseminated knowledge has to be brought together by an appropriate organization model for cooperation amongst *complementors*. The pressure to integrate in a network is especially heightened when small and young entrepreneurs want to branch out into complex business transactions. The network organization is suitable for all these requirements because competencies can be incorporated in the network in a flexible, time and cost efficient way.

Employees as well as intrapreneurs may be persuaded to join the bandwagon of network entrepreneurship. The intrinsic motivation also results from the network success formula „Small within big is beautiful!" (see fig. 118). Yet, they also react to the perceptible pressures to network. They know that there is often no attractive alternative to network business: the status of a components supplier or subcontractor is undesirable; market positions in mass markets for highly standardized services are very difficult to defend. Often the alternative is even simply „net-work" or „not-work".

Implementation success is furthermore facilitated by sophisticated *stepwise implementation* (see fig. 24 and 77). Instead of a radical "big bang-transformation" of employees into entrepreneurs, a step by step migration causes less resistance. Segmentation of a monolithic corporation into business segments (see fig. 117) turns employees into intrapreneurs, a transition that also can be incrementally designed when employees climb a career ladder of entrepreneurship by a consecutive management of a revenue center, a profit center and finally an investment center. The stage of intrapreneuring is followed by interpreneuring. The starting point is intra-corporate networking in a federation of business centers. The process of spinning-off the parent company can be dosed by gradually reducing the affiliation to the parent (with respect to capital, resources, and shared services) until the status of entrepreneurship is reached, i.e. the business relationships to the former parent company do not differ from any other business relationship (networked interprise).

Building up barriers to failure: The most effective way of preventing failure is establishing an entrepreneurial spirit and culture. Together with entrepreneurial skills (bargaining, controlling, marketing, customer and competitor intelligence, etc.) they serve as a dynamic capability (see fig. 19). Thereby, the strategically *pushed* entrepreneurship (see fig. 121) can be assisted by some *pull* entrepreneurship. The blending of pull and push characterizes management buy outs (buy ins) or employee buy outs. An important barrier to failure built into the implementation process is a *return option*. This does not only mean testing entrepreneurship at a pilot step (see fig. 23 and 28). Moreover, it allows reversing the centrifugal process of spinning-off into a centripetal process of strengthening the ties between the spin-off and the (ex) parent company. Such a re-entry option is helpful in case the spin-off turns out to lack competitiveness.

7.3 Business Reengineering

7.3.1 Radicality and Risk

Among the current change management frameworks, great attention has been paid to "Business Reengineering", "Business Process Reengineering" or in short, "Reengineering". This observation is especially true for the consulting scene from which the reengineering concept originated. Like overhead management in the 1970s, reengineering has been applied in specific variants by nearly all large consulting firms. This also holds for client companies where the approach has been implemented in many large-scale projects that have been more or less explicitly declared as reengineering programs (e.g. "Time Optimized Processes" at Siemens, "Business Procedure Reengineering" at BP or "Customer Relationship Management" at IBM). Management academe has also got around to having a good look – albeit somewhat critically at this approach. The impressive resonance of reengineering among the experts can be put down to the following factors:

Reengineering is a concept propagated by management gurus and consulting firms, and professionally marketed via best sellers and journals (e.g. the Business Process Management Journal). The approach was developed at a time, when structural problems in many industries and companies in the West reached a peak. Reengineering represents a western alternative to Japanese concepts, in which various implementation barriers became apparent as a result of cultural incompatibility. The key components of the reengineering approach represent a contrast to Lean Management, Total Quality Management and other preceding concepts. Consequently, many target groups see reengineering as a genuine innovation.

Change by way of a reengineering project should result above all in quantum leaps in almost all performance indicators: from customer satisfaction and throughput time, time to market, reduction of inventories, process costs right through to increases in profit. The change process involves a reconfiguration of the business portfolio of a business segment, changes in the competitive advantages of individual business segments, in business processes, in the relationships to customers, to suppliers and to employees. As a rule, there are extensive personnel replacements in the course of optimizing business processes.

Against this background, the radical nature of the approach constitutes the characteristic feature of reengineering. Radicality is reflected in the transformation of the company, in breakthrough strategies as well as in radical change management. The radical nature of change management is manifested in the contents of the induced changes as well as in the *change process*, i.e. in the path that is taken and therefore in the way that the concept is implemented: the aim of reengineering is to bring about change in huge leaps, the results of which clearly exceed the incremental continuous improvement process changes and even the 10-20% improvement levels typical of traditional overhead management. The approach knows no taboos. Rather, all the facets of an enterprise can undergo a change within a zero-based approach, as if one were designing the enterprise from scratch. For many experts information technology is not only a critical success factor but is also a driving force. Dramatic improvements can only be attained by using ERP and CRM software, cloud computing, business intelligence and networks.

The change process is initiated top down and also pushed top down. Self-regulating forces only play a role within teams that are installed specifically for process optimization. In contrast to evolutionary learning processes, reengineering projects should be implemented quickly, e.g. within a year. Advocates of the concept assume that the readiness and capacity to change cannot be sustained over a longer period of time.

Over the past years, another characteristic of reengineering became evident: there is an extraordinarily high risk of failure and discontinuation - around 50-75%. These dramatic figures reveal that "risk" is just as much a characteristic feature of reengineering, as is its radical nature. Unsuccessful reengineering projects cause considerable and sometimes irreversible insecurity, tension, conflicts and loss of value. Notably from a balanced resilience point of view, such risks of financial and cultural damage have to be taken into account.

There have been various attempts to reduce business reengineering to a short formula. One prominent example is the 4R scheme, whereby reengineering always entails renewing (innovation through learning organizations), reframing (change in attitude as a basis for organizational change), restructuring (customer-oriented, IT-supported processes), revitalization (developing new business segments). Different versions of this R-scheme are in circulation in the reengineering community, sometimes broadened by relocating and other modules. More relevant than these patterns is a look at the tools of reengineering.

7.3.2 Tools of Reengineering

The tools of reengineering can be divided into two categories. The first category of performance management tools concerns the "what" of change, i.e. the areas of reorganization, information technology (workflow, groupware, corporate portals, inter-organizational information systems, etc.), performance-based reward systems etc. The second category comprises tools for change management, i.e. for the "how" of the change process (see fig. 21).

Tools for process management

Reengineering concepts apply to all sectors of management, from strategy to organization and personnel, right through to IT-systems. As a rule, the core area is the organizational sector. There, the aim is to change from the isolated optimization of value-adding activities (marketing, development, purchasing, etc.) to the optimization of cross-functional value-adding processes which is reflected in the term "Business Process Reengineering (BPR)". Within a so called "house" of business processes management, core and support processes are differentiated. Reengineering is supposed to particularly optimize the *core processes* of the enterprise. Fig. 127 comprises the five generic processes with a focus on the external customer.

The list of standard core processes – or key, main or mega-processes - includes product development, order fulfillment, logistics, business planning, customer acquisition and other processes that are critical for competitiveness.

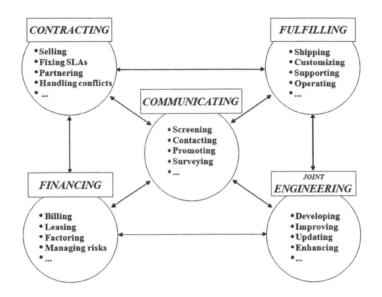

Figure 127:   Scope of Customer Processes

In a way, process reengineering leads to the structure being turned from a *vertical* to a *horizontal* organization (see fig. 128).

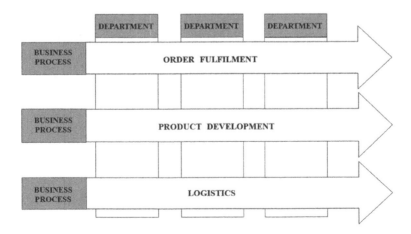

Figure 128:   From the Vertical to the Horizontal Organization

Now and again, a crowding-out „process substitutes structure" is erroneously assumed here. In actual fact, the result is the implementation of a process-oriented structure or in short, a *process organization*: from a change management perspective, reengineering means the shift from a "process follows structure"-pattern to a *"structure follows process"-pattern* of organizational design (see fig. 129),

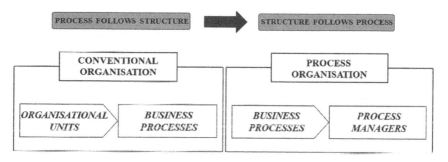

Figure 129:   Process Focused Pattern Shift in Organizational Design

Process managers – operating on an IT infrastructure - have to be assigned to the defined processes (see fig. 130). The process organization is thus embedded into the

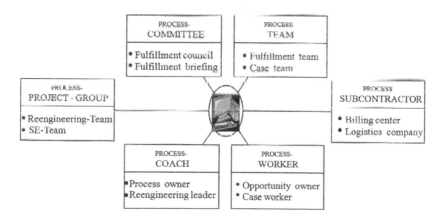

Figure 130:   Organizational Units with Responsibility for Processes

organizational structure. Prevalent examples of individual process managers are process mentors (part-time process owners) or full-time process owners (case workers, along the lines of "position owner = process owner"). Group responsibility for processes is assumed by fulfilment councils or committees, fulfilment teams or case teams.

Responsibility for some business processes is outsourced to subcontractors. *Business process outsourcing* (BPO) is frequently applied to tax counseling, legal processes, auditing, and more processes outside the core business, such as billing, logistics, vendor managed inventory, managed IT services, and call center services.

In order to understand the complexity of business process management, we have to consider that there is no such thing as „the" core process, e.g. one single form of order fulfilment. Reengineering is always about *variants* or *versions* of a business process (see fig. 131).

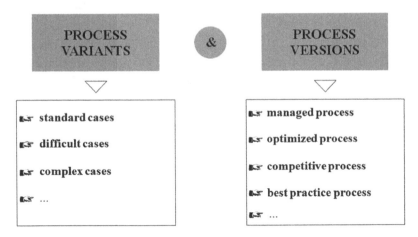

Figure 131:   Business Process Variants and Versions

At least two process *variants* can be distinguished within the order fulfilment process. A widespread differentiation exists between standard and special orders. The various types of orders are further differentiated, for example, into batch processing, customized processing or made-to-order processing. Process *versions* are defined by the degree of maturity of the process design. The degree of maturity is expressed in a special rating for the process in question similar to school grades, or is expressed by terms of maturity models (see fig. 70).

Process orientation triggers other changes that need to be dealt with in reengineering:

Organization: The distribution of the responsibility for processes is associated with a flattening of the hierarchical structure of the organization. The radicality of reengineering is also vividly demonstrated by the fact that the traditional organization chart is turned on its head: it is not the bosses who occupy the top of the pyramid, but the employees who interact closely with the customers. The flattening of the hierarchy as a coordination instrument has to be compensated by the simultaneous establishment of self-coordination instruments. This requires empowerment in terms of a relocation of certain competencies to the employees.

Strategy: Business reengineering means radically questioning existing business definitions and business portfolios. This can lead to fundamentally changed business models, e.g. when an energy supply company turns into an energy services company. Business definitions are often based on the three business types of mass business ("out of the rack"), class business ("one of a kind") and mass customization (see fig. D 2). Parallel to this, the business portfolio is optimised between concentration on core competencies on the one hand and diversification of businesses on the other hand. Analogous considerations have to be made to disaggregate the value chain, e.g. via outsourcing.

Personnel: Here, skilling offensives and recruiting measures to ensure the necessary competence for the business processes constitute key issues, i.e. training in methodical skills (IT training, problem-solving techniques, etc) and holistic ways of thinking and working. As a supporting measure, reward systems to establish intrapreneurship have to be developed.

Systems: There are several tools within the scope of activity-based management that can be used to support process optimization. By activity-based costing systems some of the weaknesses of conventional costing systems in the management of overheads can be overcome. Since process-costing is more suited to the improvement of existing business processes, the radical "redesign" of processes better relies on process-benchmarking in which there is an orientation towards (worldwide) best practices in process control. A very broad range of tools can be used for IT-supported process modeling, documentation, analyses, visualization and simulation.

Tools for Change Management

Besides the process management tools outlined above, this second category comprises the entire arsenal of transformation management measures. A special procedural model acts serves as a framework for the approach and is conceived mainly as a phase scheme (see fig. 132). The phase scheme describes the activities specific to a phase, available tools, necessary skills and organizational responsibilities, and above all, the suitable project organization for a reengineering plan.

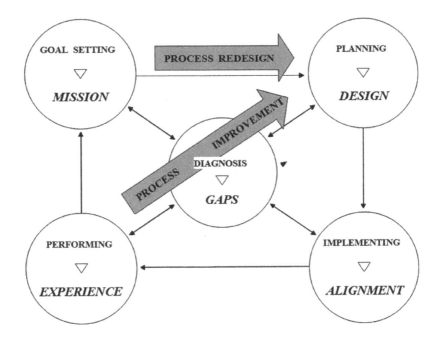

Figure 132:   Phases of Process Reengineering

The goal-setting phase involves establishing the requirements of a process. This goes beyond just formulating a process vision ("visioning", e.g. to become the most customer-friendly company) and means that the process has to be embedded in the respective competitive strategy (e.g. price and/or time advantages), thereby defining the *mission* of the process. All the variables for process identification and specification (e.g. customer benefits, costs, robustness, process stakeholders) have to be deployed in measuring procedures (e.g. customer satisfaction index, service level, response times, process costs).

Process optimization takes place in the design phase. Whenever new process missions are derived from business strategies this means process *redesign*. In the case of an already implemented process, this means *improvement*, streamlining or standardizing. Ideas for optimization stem, for example, from process simulations, benchmarking information as well as from complaints and suggestions systems. A fit has to be achieved in the implementation phase, i.e. compatibility and alignment between the optimized process model and the context. To this aim, specific measures have to be taken to (re-) align the IT infrastructure, controlling system, attitude, qualifications, and - whenever necessary – headcount. The realization phase provides the long-term test for the reformed process. Here, experience is gathered according to the "learning by doing" principle.

Like all phase schemes, the execution of the reengineering phase scheme is not strictly sequential and linear. More often than not, it involves loops, feed forwards and feedbacks. To this aim, diagnostic processes are carried out between the phases outlined above. Evaluations, audits, monitoring, benchmarking, as well as swot-analyses, cross impact and gap analyses are carried out in these diagnostic phases. According to the results of these diagnostic processes, certain phases have to be executed again. Another question that needs to be answered, is how the two basic forms of process optimization, i.e. radical redesign and incremental improvement can be blended. Simultaneous coupling could prove fatal in terms of a learning dilemma. Here, we would be perfecting a process whose premises we question. For this reason, only sequential coupling can be considered. Advocates of reengineering are unanimous in their support for the "first radical process innovation, then step-by-step improvement" pattern.

7.3.3 Development Stages of Business Process Reengineering

The implementing challenge related to business reengineering depends on what category of process management constitutes the concept to be implemented. Reengineering covers an entire family of different concepts. Different chronological stages of process orientation can be identified in the handling of business processes. Somehow they represent different "generations" of reengineering (see fig. 133).

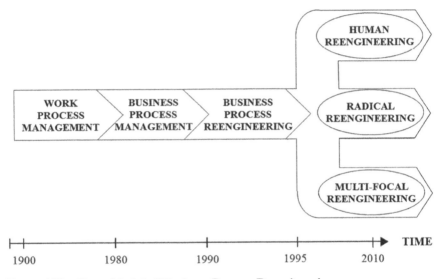

Figure 133:   Stage Model of Business Process Reengineering

The history of business reengineering can be roughly divided into three eras. In the *first* stage of process optimization, all precursors of business process reengineering are located. This includes optimizing work processes, on the one hand, covering operational manufacturing and logistics processes (e.g. Continuous Flow Management, Just-in-Time systems). Here, technical optimization takes priority over customer orientation. On the other hand, the reengineering approach has its roots in the business process improvement trend of the early 1980s. The objects of this business process improvement trend are medium-range sub-processes, e.g. promotional campaigns, ordering procedures, recruitment, etc.

The *second* stage, core process reengineering, entails radical optimization of extensive business processes. In contrast to business process improvement, business processes are redesigned from scratch ("process innovations"), as illustrated in fig. 134. Instead of mass production (for inventory), we have, for example in the automotive industry, made-to-order production (batch size = 1), which the individual customer can initiate via a sales center or via Internet.

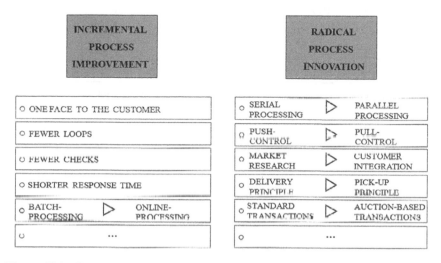

Figure 134: Incremental Process Improvement versus Radical Process Redesign

Radical process redesign results in simultaneous instead of sequential engineering as well as in pulled instead of pushed flow processes. Many a process innovation is enabled by digital infrastructures: this holds for customer intelligence that is not accomplished by market research (e.g. customer panels, focus groups and surveys) but by analyzing customer activities on the web (e.g. click stream analysis, data mining). Likewise global auction sales substitute standard transactions in commodity procurement. In e-business the customer is normally self serving (pick-up principle) supported by search engines and portals, but not by traditional information delivery.

The *third* stage of development is characterized by holistic reengineering. "Total Reengineering" of this type (e.g. focused on "Total Cost of Ownership") extends cross-company to the entire supply chain and is not restricted to intra-company processes. Control lies mostly in the hands of a focal enterprise (e.g. a PC-, apparel-, or sports equipment-company, a franchisor). These brand-owning companies demand and support process optimization of all members of a development-, production- and distribution-network. X-engineering constitutes an approach for some *incremental* cross-company business reengineering (see fig. 135).

Figure 135:   Building Blocks of X-engineering

A *radical* model of supply chain reengineering relies on a *process organizational design* (see fig. 129). Whereas X-engineering and the majority of existing supply chain management models (such as supplier relationship management or efficient consumer response) work on the "process follows structure"-pattern in terms of a) fixing the boundaries of enterprises involved in the value creating system first and b) subsequently optimizing cross-enterprise business processes, the radical reengineering approach works the other way round: value creating processes are defined first and only thereafter the allocation of processes (or process segments) to different organizational units is determined. Implementation activities mainly accommodate the context, i.e. the existing supply chain, to the optimized processes by out- and in-sourcing, forward and backward integration (or disintegration) as well as networking (e.g. contractual joint ventures). Fig. 136 illustrates this radical inter-company reengineering by comparing two function diagrams. They visualize the transition from *centralized* to *decentralized* (outsourced) business process responsibility in a value net model, consisting of an OEM, a systems supplier and a service complementor. Primarily the planning and the executing functions in the business processes are outsourced, some process responsibility is shared between two players. The focal OEM remains the coordinator of the respective product-service system.

COMPANIES / PROCESSES	OEM	SYSTEMS SUPPLIER	COMPLEMENTOR
ORDER FULFILMENT	P,C,E	-	-
PRODUCT DEVELOPMENT	P,C	E	-
LOGISTICS	P,C	-	E
AFTER MARKET	P,C,E	-	-

	OEM	SYSTEMS SUPPLIER	COMPLEMENTOR
ORDER FULFILMENT	P,C,E	-	E
PRODUCT DEVELOPMENT	P,C	P,E	-
LOGISTICS	C	-	P,E
AFTER MARKET	C	-	P,E

P = PLANNING   C = COORDINATION   E = EXECUTION

Figure 136: Inter-company Business Process Reengineering

Moreover, efforts are made to improve the handling of the *interfaces between core processes*, e.g. between product development and order fulfilment (see fig. 137). Sometimes the interfaces are considered as bridging processes, e.g. the technical change management process and the ramp-up process.

At present, no dominant trends can be identified in the holistic reengineering stage (see fig. 133). Totality is expressed, on the one hand, in an increased radicality of the approach. Here prototyping is applied to shorten periods of transition. This means that an initial, still "immature" process concept leaves the design phase very early on, and is then tested mainly in the realization phase by trial and error. On the other hand, tendencies towards *multi-focal* reengineering stand out. Unlike supply chain management, the value net approach is not characterized by one focus of value adding processes, i.e. the customer, but by multiple foci. In addition to customer-focused business processes here investment is made in competence-focused processes to enhance resources (from supplier-focused supply management to employee-focused human resources management through to investor-focused shareholder value management), as well as in competition-focused processes in innovative business areas (e.g. for the sake of diminishing competitive disadvantages, extending and defending a competitive advantage).

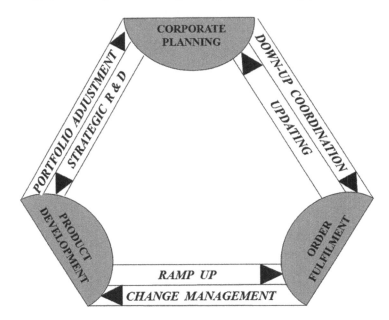

Figure 137:   Interface of Core Business Processes

Finally, attempts are made at *human* reengineering, i.e. greater consideration for the individual and other process-relevant "soft factors" (e.g. building up trust).

7.3.4 Business Process Reengineering in the BR Framework

Dismantling barriers to implementation success: radical approaches to change such as Business Reengineering provoke huge resistance. Resistance is intensified by the close relationship between reengineering and "notorious" cost cutting programs such as overhead cost management, e.g. zero-base budgeting or overhead-value analysis. To aggravate matters further, reengineering represents reform brought about by the initiative of top management and thus possibly only allows for pseudo-participation on the part of the affected employees. Against this background, resistance means not only lethargy but also active opposition (see fig. 14). This is motivated by the need for security and the protection of vested rights, which the affected employees consider threatened by the radical change and "demolition" activities that reengineering entails.

In order to reduce resistance, communication and motivation activities should emphasize the intrinsic advantages of reengineering. The particular attractiveness of business reengineering derives from the fact that several, generally considered conflicting goals, can be simultaneously reached via process orientation (see fig. 138).

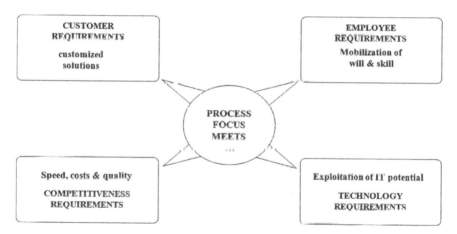

Figure 138: Convergence of Diverging Requirements through Process Orientation

It is *customers* who benefit from this "goal harmony", in that they can be provided with customized goods and services. *Employees* with comprehensive process responsibility are motivated and qualified by the intrinsic motivational potential of the enlargement and enrichment of their jobs, and the associated empowerment.

Reengineered companies can better differentiate from *competitors* by being faster in developing new products and processing orders. Finally, process-oriented organizational forms facilitate the better use of the potential of information and communication *technologies*, e.g. Internet technologies, workflow or simulation software (e.g. for the digital factory).

Nevertheless, communication activities must not keep quiet about or exclude the *weaknesses* and *risks* of business reengineering. Some of the risks reside in the reengineering concept itself. Perfected customer orientation, where each individual customer is treated as a small market ("segment-of-one market segmentation" or "1:1-marketing") easily leads to customer inflation which overstretches the potential for handling complexity. Remedial action can be taken by way of the complexity-reducing strategies of mass customization. Setting up a process organization without first defining business, and segmenting business into business units or divisions is also quite risky. A vacuum in business specifications usually makes it impossible to focus on customer groups or on competitive advantages. It is not always possible to compensate for vague business specifications by developing process variants at a later stage (see fig. 131). Overestimating information technology has often proved to be a weakness. Information technology should only be an "enabler" or a "facilitator" for more effective and more efficient processes. If, however, it is deployed as the prevailing "driver" of the restructuring process, the potential for improvement is reduced considerably.

Another risk arises from a miscalculation of the actual attainable degree of harmony (see fig. 138). Not all trade-offs between several goals or conflicts between process stakeholders can be reconciled via process orientation. Areas of conflict emerge between customer interests and investor interests. Faster order-processing means that customers are provided with the ordered services as promptly as possible. But they are also presented with the bill at the same time in order to reduce the interest loss on the part of the supplying firm. Conversely, it is in the customer's interests that damage or loss be settled as swiftly as possible which is not necessarily in the interests of the insurance company. Similar areas of conflict are found in value (date) practices of banks when calling payments on customer accounts.

Conflicts can also arise between the interests of employees and those of the company. In principle, there is the danger that the reengineering concept is interpreted according to Tayloristic principles. This occurs mainly when process orientation is used as an opportunity to regulate employee behavior *via process guidelines – in addition to result-oriented performance controls and resource-*oriented budget controls. The resulting overdose is manifested in inflated organizational manuals, in the de-motivation of employees and their reactance (see fig. 83).

These barriers to transformation are taken into account in the concept – as expounded – by means of in-built change management via sophisticated models for a project organization. These models aim at safeguarding power and process promotion by means of several caretakers, such as reengineering leaders, reengineering "tsars", process owners and process managers.

Another way to dismantle barriers to implementation is the reduction of complexity so as to meet the high change requirements without relinquishing the demand for revolutionary transformation. Process managers, for example, are installed step-by-step. First, part-time process owners are installed. After a trial period, full-time process managers are installed owners within the primary organization.

Because several processes have to be optimized within a reengineering project, an optimal combination of these various initiatives has to be found. In a radical approach, the core processes would be the first to be restructured because the highest profitability (i.e. the biggest performance leaps) would be expected from such a move. A more cautious approach – as was typical for the earlier eras of business process management – would concentrate on local processes with modest scope because there, redesign can be effected more quickly and less problematically. If one wants to produce early, albeit only local success, and at the same time achieve global quantum leaps in the long term, then a mix of "process sites" according to the portfolio principle can be used (see fig. 78). A process portfolio is characterized by a balanced mixture of manageable projects to optimize local sub-processes and mega-projects to optimize global core processes. Here, balance – in keeping with the portfolio principle – means that experience, a motivating sense of achievement, and cost-savings from the successful optimization of sub-processes can be transferred to difficult core process projects.

Building-up barriers to failure: Holistic thinking and problem solving as well as awareness of interdependencies and interfaces represent capabilities that may prevent the failure of business process reengineering. In a world of specialization however, they do not serve as a reliable basis. Against this background approximations of a process organization are more relevant in case it turns out to be not viable to implement the perfect process organization. Fig. 139 outlines the

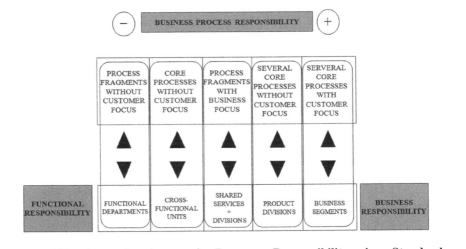

Figure 139: Approximations of Process Responsibility in Standard Organizational Structures

ingredients of business process responsibility that conventional organizational forms such as the functional (F-form) and the divisional form (M-form) contain: these - sometimes rudimentary - process elements are already implemented. So, a *step-by-step transition from functional to divisional forms* serve as a way of approaching a veritable process organization. For instance, quality, security and environmental management and other cross-functional units imply process responsibility, although not focused on the expectations of the customer. In fact, managers of business segments (geographic divisions, solutions businesses, key accounts, etc.) are simultaneously responsible for all business processes. However, this most likely creates an overload constellation. Still, they provide more customer focus than product division managers who are not capable of offering product-service-solutions to meet problems of customer segments or individual customers.

7.4 Knowledge Management

7.4.1 Relevance of Organizational Knowledge

Products and services are turning more and more into intelligent goods. This may be computer software and hardware, smart mobile phones, biotechnological products, nanotechnology-based "cyborgs", communication satellites, but also buildings, vehicles, kitchen appliances, sports shoes, and toys with embedded electronic components. Moreover, these products are developed, improved or produced by knowledge workers (and not primarily by "hardware") who are utilizing intelligent technology for developing and manufacturing. Intelligent services, on the one hand, accompany intelligent products, as far as planning, developing, implementation, etc. of these products are concerned. On the other hand, they supplement existing forms of services, frequently as an upgrade of these services (e.g. online updating of car electronics). All of these developments are enabled by the use of a *knowledge base*. With the trend towards a knowledge society, knowledge is becoming more important than the traditional assets (labor, raw material, etc.). Knowledge management also represents the core of many *resource-based* and most *competency-based strategies*. From the perspective of asset management, knowledge management is principally about intellectual assets and intellectual capital.

Not only individuals, but also groups, companies, public administrations, networks, communities, and societies have their own knowledge base. Explicit organizational knowledge is archived in systems, which are independent of individuals. These systems cover operating procedures, routines, traditions, specific data banks, patents, the organizational culture, etc. Encyclopedias capture collective knowledge, e.g. in science or society. A well-known digital encyclopedia is Wikipedia. On the company level, for instance "intelpedia" (Intel) and "bluepedia" (IBM) are archiving firm relevant knowledge.

7.4.2 Categories of Knowledge

Functional scope: The *know-how*, *know-why*, and *know-what* distinction signals that different categories of knowledge constitute the standard objects of management.

Dictionary knowledge ("What?") is organizational knowledge that a) defines und b) describes things and events. Explications clarify specific terms, e.g. mass customization. Taxonomies deliver system for handling a set of interrelated notions, e.g. transformational, transactional, and charismatic leadership. Data banks contain a plethora of information about the state of various entities, such as data collected in fact sheets, annual reports, best practices, rankings, survey results, to name only a few.

Axiomatic knowledge ("Why?") is basic knowledge about the reasons for specific incidents or developments. Cause-and-effect models (if-then-statements), that connect conditions (antecedents) to consequences, help to understand patterns and regularities.

Teleological, technological or pragmatic knowledge ("How?") represents knowledge for solving problems and for developing strategies. They answer questions like "What should be done to succeed?" They serve as a foundation for technical and social engineering as well as organizational design. Methods (statistics, presentation, arithmetic, etc.) constitute a subset of know-how in terms of meta-technologies which have other categories of knowledge (data, models, methods) as operands.

These archetypes of knowledge are very often combined to modules ("chunks"). So, *explanatory* knowledge is a combination of what-knowledge (antecedents), why-knowledge (if-then-statement) and some method for reaching conclusions from assumptions (know-how).

Information content: Content is related to formal features such as (differences in the) extension, vagueness, detailing, operationalization or precision (specification) of knowledge. Extension fosters efficiency of knowledge management since the same item can be applied to a multitude of contexts. This especially holds for "nomological" scientific knowledge.

Accessibility: The difference between "explicit" and "tacit" knowledge is reflected in the statement "we know more than we can tell". *Explicit* knowledge is documented and represented in letters, numbers, drawings or diagrams. It is therefore not linked to a specific person but generally available in documents, papers, files, models, and reports. This kind of knowledge is easily transferable and can be expressed in formal speech. It can also be stored, processed and transferred by information and communication technology. Tacit or *implicit* knowledge is based on experiences, perceptions and implicit theories (attribution, personality, intelligence, etc.). It is stored in mental models of its owner – individual or collective - and linked to this specific person or cultural community. This kind of knowledge is difficult to formulate and transfer. It can be found in cognitive rules, which individuals use to perceive, interpret and select information, as well as in individual and organizational schemes and beliefs. The traditional view that explicit knowledge represents just the tip of the iceberg of our total knowledge may have to be revised considering the bulk of explicit knowledge available on the Internet.

Validity: Knowledge does not only contain corroborated or true elements (e.g. facts). Also conjectural elements (e.g. predictions, rumors, weak signals) or heuristics (e.g. rules of thumb, approximations, improvisation as opposed to algorithms) constitute a valuable asset. In a dynamic view, this distinction sometimes reflects the maturity lifecycle of knowledge. A key job of knowledge quality management is to increase the quality level. With respect to tacit knowledge, this categorization corresponds to the competence level of different persons, differentiating between beginners (novices), advanced and experts (masters) in a certain field.

7.4.3 Complementary Management Areas

Knowledge management is part of the management areas that deal with *intangibles*, such as culture, intellectual property, reputation, business relationships, competencies, and human capital. There are several management areas that handle resources which have an affinity to "knowledge": fig. 140 suggests that primarily the core objects of *information* management, *idea* management, *innovation* management and *learning* intersect with knowledge.

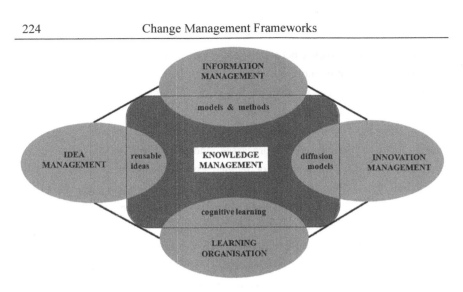

Figure 140:   Complementary Management Areas

Information: Information covers data, models, and methods that are needed to underpin decisions. Models and methods represent the reusable and generic resource elements in an information system whereas many data are subject to obsolescence. Furthermore, models a) determine what data are relevant and b) help organize data in order to prevent an information overload.

Ideas: They constitute solutions for specific problems, e.g. products that meet customer requirements, "apps" or practices that make processes more efficient. Whenever ideas have not just one single application, but can be multiply applied, they become part of a knowledge base.

Innovations: They represent those ideas that are a) novel (e.g. patents) and b) can be marketed (e.g. sold, licensed). Knowledge in terms of diffusion models to investigate market performance is part of the innovation model.

One common denominator of generating knowledge, ideas, information, and innovations is the installation of *groups*. Fig. 141 outlines the scope of groups that are (primarily) used to create ideas (problem-specific information) or knowledge (generic information). The reach of involved members (as well as the extension range of application of the respective output) increases from the left to the right. The core contribution of coordination committees is knowledge transfer between groups, both within one category and between two categories of groups.

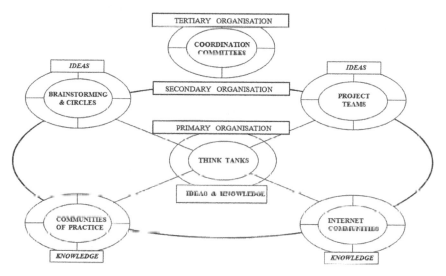

Figure 141:   Scope of "Intelligent" Groups

Learning: With individuals as well as social entities, learning describes the acquisition of new ways to cope with problems or the extinction of ineffective and/ or inefficient behavior. So called *cognitive* learning processes – as opposed to operant conditioning or learning by repetition (learning curves) - imply knowledge acquisition.

There are different *levels* of learning within social entities. Besides the learning process at the individual level, learning processes take place at team level, the level of the organization as a whole, and at an inter-organization level.

Learning at the individual level: There are several phases of the learning process in cognitive models of individual learning. First of all new information is identified within the environment that is then analyzed and evaluated. If new behavior is required, it has to be developed and tested in the environment. If effective, this behavior will be retained and repeated.

Learning in teams: This type of social learning requires the ability and willingness for open dialogue and critical discussion. Individual knowledge is first communicated, then it is compared and interpreted mutually. This can take place, for instance, via an internal feedback process or a common understanding of the team mission. Team learning is supposed to give team members the opportunity to acquire new skills and knowledge through social facilitation.

Organizational learning: The sum of the knowledge of all individuals within a company is not equal to the knowledge of the organization as a whole. Organizations learn by storing knowledge in an organizational knowledge base. This means that the knowledge of the members remains within the company even after these members have left. Organizational learning not only helps to create core competencies but also to scrutinize these competencies.

Inter-organizational learning: Emergent inter-organizational learning is accomplished by observing, intelligence or learning from models. Organized learning between organizations happens via strategic alliances, joint ventures or through networks with customers, suppliers and complementors (e.g. in eco-systems or clusters). It can also take place in benchmarking communities or within Internet communities, in which case, not only does the community or network learn as a whole but also every member of the community, network or cooperation at the node level. Inter-organizational learning is promoted by several knowledge paradigms such as open innovation, co-generated content, collaboration, wisdom of crowds, and swarm intelligence. Corresponding to the distinction between conventional and virtual size (see fig. 101), all models of open knowledge management replace "proprietary knowledge" (conventional size) by the virtual size of a knowledge base, i.e. available knowledge.

There is a close connection between organizational learning and the organizational knowledge base: cognitive organizational learning is defined as the way the knowledge base of an organization is changed and developed. Fig. 142 illustrates the building blocks of a *learning organization*.

The learning structures focused in fig. 142 are part of the infrastructures for knowledge management (see paragraph 7.4.5).

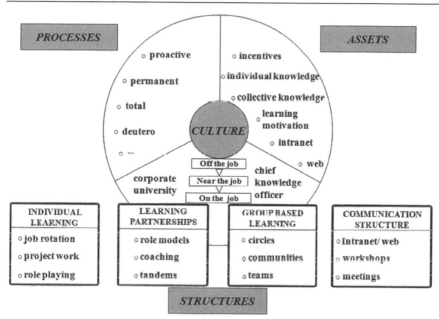

Figure 142:   Elements of a Learning Organization

7.4.4 Core Processes of Knowledge Management

Several "core processes" of knowledge management deal with the different categories of knowledge (see fig. 143). Like all processes of handling (intangible) resources they cover *generating, utilizing* and *sourcing* knowledge. All processes are modeled in two significantly different ways: The *allocation approach* considers knowledge as an *asset* and deals with functional transformation, assignment or dedication processes which cause *production* costs. "Sourcing" means absorbing existing knowledge. This inter-entity allocation is accomplished by translocating ("importing") existing knowledge from external into internal knowledge. The *association approach* considers knowledge as a right of a social entity to handle some intellectual property. Property rights include modifying, benefiting from, and selling knowledge as well as excluding others from this asset (e.g. by patenting). Knowledge management is based on business relationships in terms of contract-based transactions and of pooling of knowledge that are embedded in legal regulations of handling intellectual property (e.g. patent and anti-plagiarism laws) within or between social entities. Costs of knowledge management also contain *transaction* costs (contracting costs). Whereas the allocation approach ignores property rights and consequently does not differentiate between a private and a public domain, the association approach considers some external effects such as imitation (learning from models) or pooling of open source knowledge as free riding that questions the essence of property rights.

SECTOR Knowledge management APPROACH	Knowledge GENERATION	Knowledge UTILIZATION	Knowledge SOURCING
ALLOCATION	Knowledge DEVELOPMENT/ MAINTENANCE	Knowledge APPLICATION	Knowledge ABSORPTION
ASSOCIATION	Knowledge CO-CREATION	Knowledge SHARING	Knowledge ACQUISITION

Figure 143:   Core Processes of Knowledge Management

Sourcing knowledge: Whenever analyses show that internal knowledge alone is not sufficient and that the required know-how cannot be developed within the company, then additional knowledge needs to be procured from external knowledge holders, other companies, stakeholders (e.g. customer knowledge), knowledge brokers and knowledge products (e.g. the "cloud"). Monitoring market processes (e.g. the activities of technology leaders) is also an important source of external knowledge in order to discover best practices, not only in search of ideas, but also patterns. As mentioned above, there is a mainstream to extend the reach of available sources: from individuals to groups and from companies to networks.

In the association approach, sourcing means contract-based acquisition of property rights, e.g. via transferring, swapping or licensing knowledge (including knowledge ingredients of products, e.g. "Intel inside"). Simultaneously, this approach advocates a regulatory infrastructure to protect intellectual property in conjunction with sanctions for non-compliant behavior.

Both the allocation and the association approach provide measures of *knowledge retention* to prevent knowledge drain, e.g. to protect source code or blueprints against outsmarting, espionage, and plagiarism (e.g. via reverse engineering). In the case of *implicit* knowledge this may imply the retention of personnel (knowledge holders) to avoid some "brain drain". In the allocation approach the focus is on protecting the content (IT-security, concealment, firewalls, etc.), whereas the association approach manages knowledge security by patenting or non disclosure agreements.

Sometimes, knowledge constitutes not only the object of sourcing, but also of transferring or selling. These business processes beyond resource management define the business model of knowledge companies (e.g. engineering services) and an occasional option for other companies that sell licenses.

Utilising knowledge: All components of knowledge management have to be oriented towards the efficient use of individual and collective knowledge bases. In the allocation approach, utilization means applying knowledge to task fulfilment. This normally requires some customizing of knowledge to the respective context of application. Fig. 144 illustrates the logic of application by a tree metaphor: three categories of technological knowledge (trunk) are jointly applied in two areas (branches), each of which contains several products (twigs). The logic of application can also be depicted by an arborescence (directed graph), e.g. a gozinto graph.

In the association approach, utilization means contract-based distribution and sharing of knowledge by several clients: within an organization, isolated or locally available information has to be made available to the entire organization. The question is who should know what, to what extent, for which price, and how the processes of distribution can be managed with minimal transaction costs. An infrastructure for knowledge distribution facilitates sharing processes.

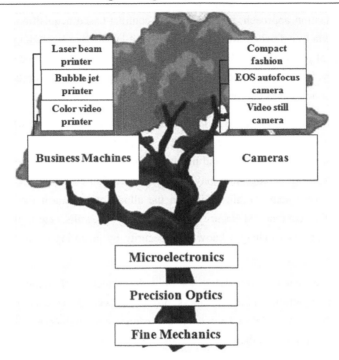

Figure 144:   Logic of Knowledge Application (Example)

Generating knowledge: In addition to the outsourcing of knowledge, *developing* and *creating* knowledge is another way of providing knowledge and competencies within a social entity. Whether knowledge should be generated or outsourced, constitutes a strategic make-or-buy decision. There is a plethora of tools and methods for developing and validating knowledge, ranging from new ways of learning (e.g. deutero learning, see fig. 29) to creativity enhancing techniques, analogies, deductive and inductive reasoning to empirical surveys and testing. Within the association approach, interaction, communication, transparency and integration are the key factors for collective knowledge development also called *co-creation, co-generating* or *collaboration*. The existing knowledge base has to be *maintained* over its lifecycle: Knowledge can get lost through personnel fluctuations, or it can become obsolete. There are three major processes of maintaining knowledge: selection, storing and updating. In the selection phase, the valuable knowledge content is identified. The valuable knowledge needs to be stored within the organization in an individual, collective or electronic memory. Since decisions based on old or incorrect information (deviating from standard scientific knowledge for instance) can result in high costs, the knowledge base needs to be constantly updated.

Knowledge can also be generated by *converting* types of knowledge, especially implicit and explicit knowledge. There are four modes of knowledge conversion (see fig. 145). *Socialization* is the process of transferring the implicit (tacit) knowledge of

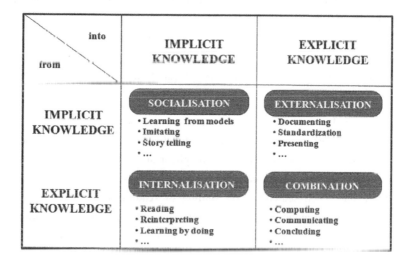

Figure 145:   Modes of Knowledge Conversion

one social entity so that it becomes the implicit knowledge of another entity. *Externalization* is when tacit knowledge becomes explicit knowledge, *internalization* the inverse process. A common way of generating knowledge is to *combine* several components of explicit knowledge so that it becomes new explicit knowledge.

Socialization: Through socialization, experiences are shared resulting in technical skills and shared mental models. Young apprentices can acquire technical skills from senior employees via observation, imitation and application. The cognitive dimension of tacit knowledge can be established through informal off-site meetings and sometimes educative story-telling. Many factors influence how employees share their knowledge within an organization, the most important being the culture of the company. An open communication culture, supported and visibly adopted by the management, is an optimal basis for socialization. Typical examples include the integration of a new team member in the mental and working patterns of a group or combining two different intangible assets in M&A processes.

Externalization: Externalization is the conversion of implicit knowledge into explicit knowledge e.g. by documenting it (for instance in templates). With externalization, participants scrutinize each other's cognitive systems of rules, metaphors, hypotheses, concepts, models and analogies. Externalization is important because externalized knowledge can be distributed, located and made available to others more easily.

Internalization: Internalization means explicit knowledge is converted into tacit knowledge. This process is closely related to "learning by doing", and involves individuals or groups learning cognitive or physical routines or rules which have been explicitly formulated beforehand. This is a process which almost everybody does every day when searching for, finding or reading something in the work context. But reading alone does not automatically convert explicit knowledge into tacit knowledge: understanding, application, assimilation and learning are also necessary.

Combination: Exchanging and combining several explicit sources of knowledge can create new explicit knowledge. This can happen via different media, such as documents, meetings, the telephone, conversations, computerized communication networks or calculations. Combination occurs, for example, when knowledge that was generated by externalization becomes available to other members of the organization. They add the new explicit knowledge to their own explicit knowledge or modify their explicit knowledge because of the new information.

The outlined core processes of intervention are embedded in *diagnostic* processes. They determine the gap between the available and the required knowledge. This gap information enables both the retrospective monitoring of the performance of interventions and the prospective determination of demand for interventions in knowledge management. The existing knowledge base has to be analyzed both on an inventory level (assessing) and on a monetary level (evaluating).

Assessing knowledge· Many companies, especially multinational groups, suffer from poor internal transparency and a glut of information. This results in inefficiency and idle potential. An appropriate level of transparency of existing internal and external knowledge is necessary. The capacities within the organization have to be identified. This means the knowledge of individuals, especially experts, as well as the collective knowledge of teams or the organization as a whole. Tools, which can be used for this task, include internal best practices, yellow pages, knowledge maps, etc. Knowledge in the environment outside the company (e.g. the knowledge of external experts and networks), also has to be located. Benchmarking is one way of creating external transparency.

Evaluating knowledge: The majority of traditional evaluation approaches are not focused on intellectual (intangible) assets, but on physical assets and physical output. However, they are not sufficient to evaluate the organizational knowledge base. To measure the success of knowledge management, e.g. the transformation of knowledge into the performance of individuals and organizations, two groups of tools are available: deductive summary approaches and inductive analytical approaches. *Deductive* summary approaches start by estimating the difference between the market value and the book value of an organization. The resulting indicators, such as the market value/book value-relation, Tobin's q or the Calculated Intangible Value, represent the intangible assets in monetary form. But they do not – or at least, not completely – explain the difference between market value and book value, and are thus not wholly satisfactory. *Inductive* analytical approaches describe and assess the individual elements of the organizational knowledge base. Examples of this type of approach include the Intangible Assets Monitor, Intellectual Capital Navigator and the Balanced Scorecard.

7.4.5 Knowledge Management Infrastructure

Knowledge management activities and interactions need an infrastructure. This is made up of five sectors (see fig. 146). The *technocratic* sector covers standards and rules (codes, policies, performance indicators, etc.). The *informational* sector comprises tools, methods and IT, i.e. hardware, software, digital content and networks. Roles and coordination forms in knowledge management are defined in the *structural* sector. The *people* sector focuses on reward systems for the appropriate use of knowledge. These four sectors are overlaid by a *cultural* infrastructure that contains the internalized and shared values, attitudes and mental models of knowledge management.

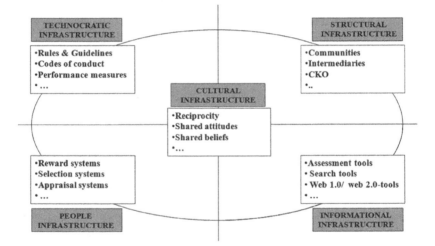

Figure 146:   Infrastructure of Knowledge Management

Informational Infrastructure: In addition to the generic methods of generating knowledge, this sector contains specific tools conceived to support the core processes of knowledge management. The *assessment* of knowledge in a social entity is facilitated by several tools:

Knowledge Maps are defined as graphic catalogs of knowledge holders, knowledge stocks, knowledge structures, knowledge applications or stages of knowledge development. This instrument has no knowledge content itself, but indicates the path(s) to the desired knowledge and facilitates rapid location of relevant knowledge. Knowledge maps can come in the form of cognitive maps, yellow pages (index of experts) or smartly structured databases.

Knowledge holder maps show the sphere(s) and extent of knowledge that each knowledge holder possesses. They exist in the form of knowledge topographies, yellow pages, knowledge sources maps, competency maps or pointer systems. Knowledge sources maps show which individuals - within a team, the organization or the environment - have relevant knowledge for a specific task.

Knowledge stock maps show where and how a specific item of knowledge is stored and how it can be reached. It can make a big difference to the user whether the desired information is stored in a file, on paper or in the mind of an expert. Therefore, these maps also provide information about the ways of processing the stored knowledge.

Knowledge structure maps contain the methods of concept mapping, clustering, schematizing, and relational mapping. Structuring knowledge involves clustering topics and indicating the relationships between them. Knowledge of the same content, which is usually stored at different places within the organization, is grouped together. These maps, also called knowledge structure diagrams or topic maps, have a huge potential and enable large amounts of unstructured documents to become available through a knowledge structure. The knowledge structure diagram can be used to create an organizational memory system.

Assessing, generating, maintaining, utilizing, and sourcing of knowledge is extensively supported by *digital tools*. So, the assessment and retrieval relies on sophisticated search engines. Web 1.0-tools like portals, chats, video conferences, forums, and CSCW-systems as well as interactive e-learning (e.g. virtual classrooms) facilitate the exchange of knowledge. However, the roles of authors (producers) and of users of a specific content are still strictly separated. Digital sharing systems serve as a platform on a company's intranet (e.g. ShareNet for best practice sharing at Siemens) or in the cloud (e.g. Microsoft's SharePoint). More effectively, web 2.0-tools, especially wikis, social networks, jam-events, and blogs enable (not only dialogue, but) collaboration, in other words: all involved actors jointly act as "prod-users" of (co-generated) content.

Structural Infrastructure: When creating a knowledge base, it is essential that somebody is responsible for its success. Various role concepts have been developed for specific responsibilities within knowledge management.

The *Chief Knowledge Officer* (CKO) is responsible for managing knowledge within the organization. He is responsible for the knowledge infrastructure and thus, also for the organizational knowledge base. He has to design, control and develop the knowledge base of the organization. "Knowledge islands" within the organization have to be identified and rendered useful. The CKO helps managers to derive knowledge goals from organizational goals and has to demonstrate the desired knowledge culture in his daily work. The Information Quality Officer is subordinate to the chief knowledge officer. His task is to conceive instructions for dealing with information, i.e. the creation of internal paper documents, such as presentations, reports, etc. These documents are all part of the organizational knowledge base. Instructions regarding the design and content of a digital knowledge base, i.e. platforms, portals, blogs, etc. are of particular interest. The information quality officer is also responsible for the quality of the knowledge stored in this knowledge base.

Intermediaries serve as bridging devices between heterogeneous and distributed actors participating in a knowledge management system. This holds both for *informal* intermediaries such as knowledge gatekeepers or boundary spanners and for *official* authorized intermediaries. The task of a *knowledge broker* is to mediate between knowledge holders and knowledge users. He also has to eliminate barriers to knowledge use and improve transparency within the organizational knowledge base. In innovation management *venture capitalists* do not only provide money, but *smart* money, i.e. money plus knowledge relevant for implementing business ideas. In venture management, brokers bridge the gap between ventures and sponsors (see fig. 126). Another characteristic job for intermediaries is operating communities, especially benchmarking communities and internet communities. *Cybermediaries* like yet2com, exnovate, ninesigma, and innocentive connect supply and demand for knowledge and ideas. Mostly within companies, *communities of practice* constitute an important facility of knowledge management. Fig. 147 illustrates the typical roles of the participants of a community-of-practice organization at an automotive company.

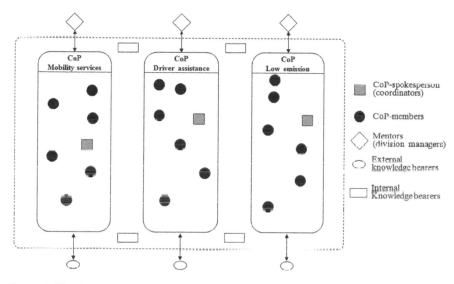

Figure 147:   Communities of Practice

People infrastructure: Reward systems are required to motivate organization members to contribute knowledge to the knowledge base and to use this knowledge pool in their everyday business. Motivation can be extrinsic or intrinsic. *Extrinsic* rewards can only be used successfully at the beginning of a knowledge initiative. Behavior resulting from extrinsic rewards will disappear if the incentives are withdrawn (because the organization is unable or unwilling to afford them any longer). *Intrinsic* motivation increases when employees realize that they can benefit from knowledge sharing, e.g. if it makes their daily jobs easier. This form of motivation is a critical factor in knowledge processes, such as knowledge development and knowledge sharing, a lesson learned from open source communities (e.g. Linux). For the transfer of tacit knowledge in particular, extrinsic rewards will not work. Tacit knowledge is not measurable and several people are involved in its transfer. It is impossible, therefore, to measure individual efforts when conceiving a reward.

Learning in groups or teams (e.g. in communities of practice, internet communities), also requires specific reward systems to combat motivational lethargy within the team. Motivational lethargy includes "social loafing", which occurs when no personal benefits can be perceived or there is no personal responsibility for the results; "free riding" because of the prevailing view that there is no connection between individual performance and team success, and the "sucker effect", which is based on the assumption that other partners are taking advantage of one's willingness to cooperate.

In addition to rewards, other aspects can help boost motivation to learn, e.g. the creation of member profiles (like in social networks), support in the form of moderators with clearly defined tasks (e.g. for brainstorming groups), and transparency within the system. Evaluation systems in the form of points systems (scoring systems) have to be developed so that the contributions of the individual participants within a knowledge management system can be measured. In a points system members receive, for example, bonus points (e.g. air miles) for every item of knowledge they share (content points). When a certain number of points have been amassed, the member has the honor of appearing at the top of a "hit list" and a reward could be in the offing, e.g. public praise. To uphold quality and prevent community members from receiving bonus points for irrelevant knowledge, other users of the system can assess every item of knowledge. The assessor receives points just like the assessed does, provided that his/her knowledge item has done better than average, otherwise points are deducted.

To support the natural efforts of a member in making his/her mark, a hit list can be instituted in which the actual scores and the member's ranking as a valuable knowledge contributor are shown („In the system's hit list, you are in fourth place with 450 points"). To preclude misuse, the system's administrators should be allowed to deduct points.

Other typical elements of a community-based learning system include fun (when using the knowledge management system, e.g. via quizzes, anecdotes, amusing incidents, jokes and comics), variety (through the richness of media), choice (of several media, learning channels, etc.), social interaction (contact opportunities), error tolerance (a learning environment without „demoralizing punishment"), measurement (performance indicator oriented towards personal improvement), feedback (so that suggestions for improvement(s) can be considered and the necessary steps taken at the first signs of a loss of motivation), challenge in assignments, and recognition (of progress in the learning process from the system, peers or supervisors).

Technocratic infrastructure: Planning and controlling of knowledge management covers performance measurement systems (e.g. performance indicators), rules, codes of conduct, guidelines, and policies for designing the core processes of knowledge management. This relates to fixing criteria for make-or-buy decisions (e.g. sourcing costs, confidentiality) and guidelines for blogging, criteria for admission to communities (e.g. selection of participants) and access to data. In case of a competitive generation of knowledge via tendering and awards, more rules have to be fixed to warrant a fair competition. In addition, this sector contains all regulations to protect intellectual property, both laws and internal compliance systems (see fig. 150).

Cultural infrastructure: Like culture in general (see fig. 114), the knowledge management culture comprises shared values (e.g. attitudes, reciprocity) and beliefs (apart from symbols like community mascots and logos). Fig. 148 contrasts two opposite *attitudes towards learning*. Only a positive error-tolerant attitude can deliver an appropriate infrastructure for knowledge management.

Another core component of a cultural infrastructure is shared *beliefs*, e.g. concerning the ways of *validating* knowledge. Fig. 149 outlines the scope of somehow antithetic validation paradigms. A culture in terms of collectively shared beliefs requires that a choice is made which of the three paradigms is accepted within a knowledge community. When knowledge systems with different underlying validation paradigms - like controlling and marketing subcultures or engineering versus management subcultures – meet, a culture clash will arise. This lack of infrastructure will cause considerable costs of conflict management and coordination.

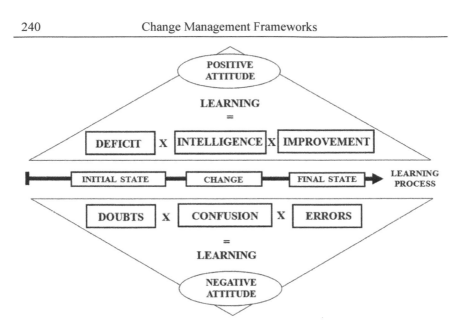

Figure 148: Attitudes as Elements of a Learning Culture

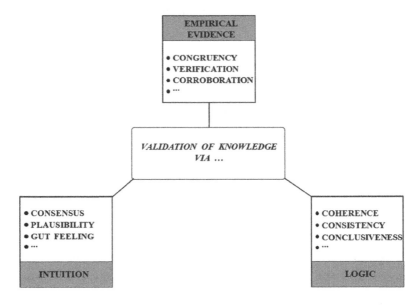

Figure 149: Validation Paradigms as Elements of a Knowledge Culture

An overall infrastructure requires an *alignment* of the five infrastructural sectors in fig. 146. This alignment is reflected in bilateral or multilateral patterns of complementary configuration: communities rely on IT-platforms (as enablers), platforms need governance (e.g. operators, codes of conduct), performance measures determine (the amount of) rewards. Sometimes the integration of different sectors is accomplished in a *portfolio* mode. Fig. 150 illustrates the portfolio mix of a soft tool (Chinese walls) and a hard tool (firewalls) for knowledge protection. Chinese walls originate from the governance sectors, i.e. structural and technocratic sectors, whereas firewalls are positioned in the informational sector. A portfolio mix is effective since the two devices for obtaining security differ considerably with respect to two performance criteria: *effectiveness of security* on the one hand and *feasibility* on the other hand. So, firewalls can only protect digitalized knowledge, Chinese walls cannot be strictly administered, since their effectiveness depends extensively on compliant behavior.

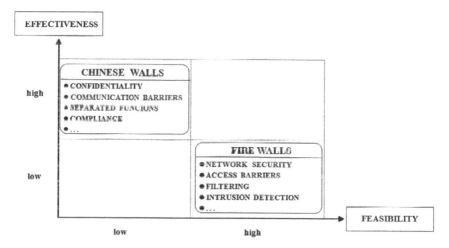

Figure 150:   Portfolio-Based Security Infrastructure

7.4.6 Knowledge Management in the BR Framework

Implementation of a knowledge management system should not be confused with fostering the generation, utilizing and sourcing of knowledge in a context characterized by a *lack* of knowledge-focused activities. In fact, implementation deals rather with an *abundance* of separated activities of knowledge handling. So the implementation job is primarily building bridges between knowledge islands. "Failure" in this case denotes a state of disintegration or "fragmentation", i.e. existing knowledge that is not available to users who need this knowledge. A specific variety of failure is *one-sided* (unbalanced) *absorption* when agents with significantly different absorptive capacities interact. From a management point of view, all integration efforts must meet efficiency requirements by following cost-benefit considerations. Whenever the costs of producing and transferring knowledge overcompensates the benefits, integration does not make sense. Since benefits of knowledge management are more difficult to estimate than its costs, tackling efficiency barriers (see fig. 17) represents a typical challenge to the implementation of knowledge management. In other words, the frequently propagated paradigm shift from proprietary to collective knowledge is not a convincing argument for communication and motivation activities in implementing as long as this shift is not underpinned by cost-benefit-reasoning. Likewise, a salient barrier to open knowledge management, the notorious not-invented here-syndrome, does not necessarily express a culture of demarcation, arrogance ("we are the best!") or splendid isolation. It may be economically justified by high (transaction) costs caused by the need to scrutinize and validate imported knowledge. Conversely, outsourcing may be preferable whenever the total costs of buying knowledge are lower than those of developing the required knowledge ("reinventing the wheel"). This resembles more a "less costly found elsewhere"-pattern than the mainstream "proudly found elsewhere"-pattern. Even the transition from the proprietary to the open paradigm of knowledge management may be triggered by a cost-benefit rationale: on the one hand, the protection of intellectual property causes high costs, notably when the virtualization of organizations is accompanied by difficulties to factually deny access to certain actors (vulnerability as the dark side of openness). On the other hand, the value of intellectual property is systematically diminished by shortened half-life periods of knowledge.

Consequently, implementing knowledge management constitutes a considerable challenge for change management. A number of *barriers to success* are involved. Knowledge management, as a long-term resource project, is an alien element in a streamlined organization oriented towards short-term success: projects that do not yield direct profits ("billable hours") are in a difficult position as "internal" projects, and thus have low priority. Aspects of comfort also constitute a barrier to the acceptance of knowledge management systems, especially when the sharing systems lack user-friendliness. Added to these, are well-worn habits in dealings with knowledge that act as obstacles to "liberal" dealings with knowledge (open sharing). Think of the use of knowledge as an individual competitive advantage ("knowledge as power", information asymmetry), and the most varied reasons for secrecy ranging from personal protection (e.g. protection of personal data), the protection of competitively relevant knowledge (e.g. degrees of confidentiality for selective access) right through to the protection of third parties (e.g. discretion with regard to customer data, non-disclosure of benchmarking information and banking secrecy). Moreover, spatial virtualization (see fig. 92) may obstruct proximity, an important basis for communication and likewise for knowledge transfer. Spatial separation of more than 30 meters may lead to a significant reduction in the intensity of communication. Suitable remedies could include the physical concentration of project teams along the lines of the "project house"-model or the installation of development centers (e.g. Mercedes-Benz Technology Center). Unfortunately these models decimate the reach of available knowledge sources. Hierarchy constitutes another barrier for knowledge sharing, not only across hierarchy levels, but also between line units and staff units within a line-staff-structure.

Dismantling barriers to implementation success: Infrastructures (see fig. 146) are a powerful device to dismantle efficiency barriers. Producer-friendly IT-infrastructures facilitate the documenting of knowledge which in turn facilitates knowledge retrieval, sharing and transfer. Smart search engines reduce the costs of "hunting for and gathering of" existing knowledge. Team-orientated remuneration components would also be suitable for motivating employees to exchange knowledge because they support the aim of collective success. Positive motivational impulses can also be generated by access to extensive information and by employee participation, for instance enabled by web 2.0-infrastructures. Several structural arrangements help make transfer of *implicit* knowledge more efficient. Fig. 151 outlines three options of using *linking pins* for intra-organizational linking. In addition, e.g. resident engineers enable inter-organizational linking.

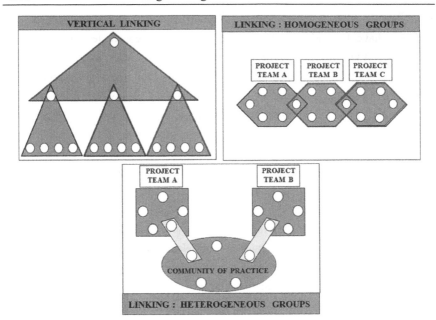

Figure 151:   Linking Pins for Transferring Implicit Knowledge

As efficient structural infrastructures for transferring explicit knowledge, decentralized networking instead of centralized coordination committees promise to be more effective (see fig. 141). Networking helps to break down (emergent) walls between social entities in a knowledge management organization. The "throw it over the wall"-pattern constitutes an inefficient and ineffective way of knowledge transfer und sharing. These walls not only separate individuals or departments, but also groups (see fig. 141). Moreover, they separate knowledge producers and knowledge users. Fig. 152 illustrates a three step model of networking amongst producers and users. Starting point is a (digital) *knowledge market* where an intermediary or cybermediary connects the demand and supply side consisting of non-cooperating producers and users of knowledge. Step 2 is characterized by *two cooperative networks,* one on each side of the market. Step 3 creates a *knowledge community* with members who co-generate knowledge, in other words who act as knowledge producers (authors, creators) and users simultaneously.

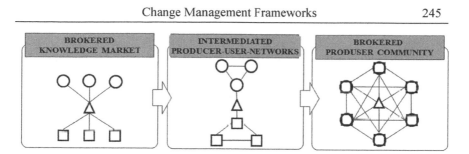

Figure 152:   Networking for Transferring Explicit Knowledge

Building-up barriers to implementation failure: Apparently, relational assets – such as trust - may prevent failure, both in terms of effectiveness (a fragmented instead of an integrated knowledge base) and efficiency (e.g. high costs of scrutinizing imported knowledge or protecting proprietary knowledge). Moreover, failure in terms of a disintegrated, fragmented knowledge base can be realistically battled by promoting dynamic capabilities such as curiosity and absorptive capacity. The underlying openness relies on an awareness of mutual interdependence, which is also inherent in heterarchical as opposed to hierarchical structures. Equally important is a shared notion of *reciprocity*. The prevalent notion of reciprocity in terms of a balanced give-and-take-interaction between two social entities (e.g. two individuals, two companies, two communities) turns out to be of limited value for knowledge management because normally more than two actors are involved. More relevant – but at the same time more challenging - than these bilateral reciprocities on a micro-unit level or a macro-unit level is a cross-level micro-macro reciprocity. Fig. 153 outlines the typical transactions between a knowledge community and a community member.

To implement this species of reciprocity, a knowledge turnover account is kept for each member of the community. When a user puts content or appraisals into the system, the corresponding revenue is credited to his account. Access to content incurs charges that are deducted from a user's account. The value of an item increases with its popularity: the better the appraisal of the content - the more frequently a certain item is accessed, and the higher it is assessed - the more expensive it becomes. There are methodological affinities to the evaluation of websites based on Web analytics (number of visitors, average visit duration, number of "likes", etc.). Revenues from the sale of content are allocated to the authors. Thus, a knowledge market develops in which content is traded according to supply and demand. The dynamic nature of the market should raise the motivation of the "prod-users" and increase the quality of the content.

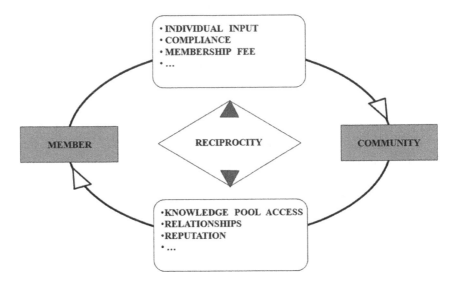

Figure 153: Reciprocity Model for Knowledge Communities

Last but not least, a resilient implementation management must foster an awareness of typical *pitfalls* in knowledge management. Even a reciprocity based community management cannot prevent that some community members profit more from the community process than others, for instance due to a superior endowment with absorptive capacity. In other words: compliance to the rules of open knowledge management does not democratize knowledge management in terms of equal opportunities. In fact, competitive *disadvantage* may be the paradoxical outcome of an open knowledge handling in rule-controlled communities.

7.5 Multi-Channel Business

7.5.1 Managing Changes in the Channel Portfolio

As a rule, marketing activities use several channels to reach (downstream) customers or (upstream) suppliers. A *multi-channel* approach to business entails (manufacturer-run) stores, franchisees, business partners, wholesalers and retailers ("brick channel"), mail order ("flip channel"), TV, affiliates, and online- or e-business ("click channel"). Change processes in multi-channel business deal with modifications of a) the *number* of channels and b) the *relevance* of channels. As for relevance, there is a focus on the steadily increasing importance of the click-channel, i.e. *e-commerce or e-business*. Consequently, the major arenas for change management in a multi-channel context are 1) implementing the online-channel (see paragraph 7.5.2) and 2) aligning the new e-business with existing channels (see paragraph 7.5.3).

E-business represents a major trend in management, with an impact comparable to supply chain management, the servitization of the industrial economy, sustainability or globalization. In IT-management e-business can be compared to trends such as Enterprise Resource Planning or cloud computing. E-business primarily stands for Internet-enabled business. The enabling process is based upon the application of Internet technologies (e.g. Extranets, web 1.0 and 2.0) and related standards (HTTP, HTML, XML, etc.). The enabling process spans several *levels* (see fig. 154). The non-interactive information level serves as a platform for three levels of web-enabled interactions.

Information: The Internet can be utilized as a powerful source of information for business purposes. A vast number of users worldwide have uncomplicated, "democratic", and low-cost access to a plethora of data on the World Wide Web. For vendors, business on the Internet requires (at least) a website, listing in various electronic yellow pages and social networks as well as linking (to other websites, AdWords, banners) to enable traditional one-to- many advertising. Customers surf to find the desired information. Surfing is supported by numerous services (portals, search engines, product configurators, tracking and tracing-systems, etc.) that help to improve the transparency of the respective markets.

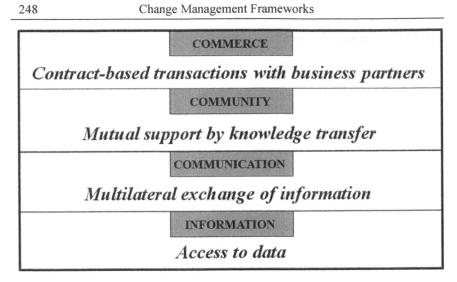

Figure 154:   Levels of Internet-enabled Business

Communication: Using the Internet as a device for communication enables a simple level of interaction. This may be accomplished by e-mail based services (e.g. electronic customer interaction centers for customer questions and complaints, newsletters, micro-blogging) and can attain the more sophisticated level of business portals, customer communities, bidding in digital auctions, or social networks. Linking Internet users facilitates communication with potential business partners worldwide.

Community: Furthermore the Internet can be used to exchange knowledge, in a Business-to-Business- (B2B), a Business-to-Consumer- (B2C) and a Peer-to-Peer (P2P)-context. Among "registered" community members – such as participants in open-source projects (e.g. Linux) or social networks - the multilateral exchange of complex information is time- and cost-efficiently accomplished by an Internet platform that meets the security demands of the community members. Thus, the community platform fosters idea management (e.g. crowdsourcing) and collaboration on the Web.

Commerce: The core business functionality of the Internet is enabling transactions, i.e. contracting, sometimes fulfillment (e.g. virtual products) and billing via the

Internet. To support these business processes, (i.e. to coordinate in order to match supply with customer demand), market places, electronic signatures or internet-specific payment systems (micropayment, cybercash etc.), and other infrastructure components have been designed and implemented. The commerce level is embedded into the community level where product related knowledge is generated, shared and transferred.

All interaction levels in e-business cover both loose and close forms of interaction. The label "web-based *collaboration*" is normally applied to *closer* forms of interaction. From the viewpoint of a company, e-business supports both *extra*-company interaction with customers (e-commerce) and suppliers (e-procurement) and other stakeholders, and *intra*-company interactions, within intra-corporate project teams or transactions on internal markets. So, e-commerce as opposed to e-business, covers just one facet of electronic business, i.e. selling products via Internet.

In order to provide detailed answers to questions such as "What is particular about e-business?" and "How does e-business differ from traditional business?" the building blocks of e-business as a management system have to be outlined (see fig. 155).

E-strategy is concerned with specific business models such as distributing digital products (e.g. software, e-books) on the Internet channel. E-business affects almost all business processes. This holds for customer integration via community models, customer-to-customer processes (e.g. production processes that are initiated "on demand"), and other changes in the sequence of activities, such as the switch from the print-distribute pattern to the distribute-print pattern. Very often e-business reinforces complex forms of competitive strategies, especially hybrid strategies like *mass customization*. In fact, e-business enables an upgrading of mass customization. In contrast to the merely *product-focused* mass customization, the upgrade (*mass personalization*, see fig. 156) covers *all four marketing "Ps"*. With products, internet-based mass personalization supports self-customizing by the help of configurators and downloadable body scanners. In the pricing sector, dynamic pricing, personalized free-fee-combinations (so called freemium strategy) or rewards for affiliates can be efficiently handled. Moreover, e-business offers a choice of distribution channels also including new Internet-based intermediaries. Finally, promotion couples standard messages with personalized media, location based contents (i.e. tracing services owing to GPS-positioning) and P2P-interactions (i.e. viral marketing, strengthening or weakening the credibility of advertising messages).

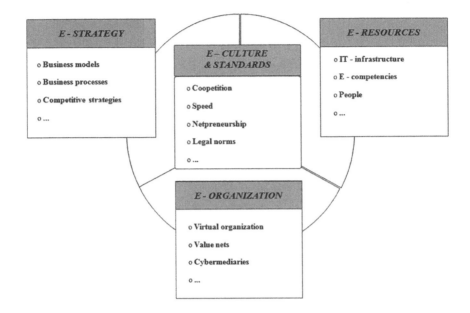

Figure 155:   Building Blocks of E-business

E-resources include IT-infrastructure and HR-infrastructure. The human resources infrastructure for e-business is not merely about e-competencies, i.e. handling the Internet, new media and the complexity of e-business (volatility, hyper-competition, etc.). It also requires people acting as entrepreneurs (some of them as netpreneurs) rather than as traditional employees or managers (see paragraph 7.2). As a rule, different generations of manpower (e.g. digital natives versus silver workers) have different level of e-competency. The lack of e-skills causes a considerable demand for training activities in the process of implementing e-business.

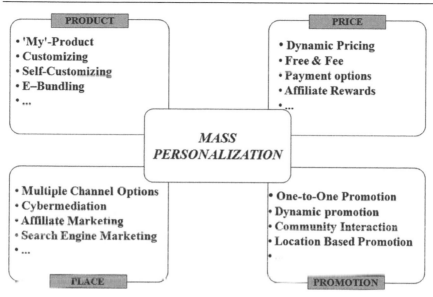

Figure 156: Internet-enabled Mass Personalisation Strategy

E-organization is closely associated with virtual organization and virtual companies (see paragraph 7.1). E-business relies on all three dimensions of virtuality, i.e. the temporal, spatial and inter-organizational dimensions. The way these three dimensions are mixed differentiates two (not mutually exclusive) "archetypes" of virtual organization, i.e. virtual companies as electronic companies and virtual companies as network organizations. E-business is often carried out by asynchronous work of experts (e.g. companies, departments, centers of competence, e-lancers) distributed all over the globe and coordinated by loose contracts for specific projects. The value net (see fig. 65) serves as a framework for these value-creating e-processes. The network relationships within the value net cover cooperation and competition, e.g. alliances, digital markets, and new contracts (new labor relations with freelancers and subcontractors that bypass labor unions, etc.). For coordination purposes new species of intermediaries are involved on all levels of web-enabled business (see paragraph 7.4.5). These so-called cybermediaries (search engines, operators of digital market places, portals, infomediaries, value added resellers, trusted third parties etc.) replace and/or complement traditional intermediaries, such as distributors, wholesalers or retailers.

E-culture and standards represent both soft and hard standards as a mandatory infrastructure for cost- and time-efficient e-business. The philosophy of the Internet economy relies on a spirit of entrepreneurship with a dominance of self actualization (in relation to security), on ubiquitous forms of fuzzy relationships (called "coopetition") beyond the traditional cooperation or competition paradigms as well as on the acceptance of e-business complexity (speed of innovation, short product life cycles etc. and the underlying paradigm of emergence instead of control). Probably the most controversial item of e-business culture is trust, both among partners and in the technological infrastructure. Last but not least, "hard" standards, i.e. legal norms for Internet-security (digital signature, laws concerning hackers, cyber-terrorism, protection of intellectual property, etc.) represent an important part of the infrastructure.

7.5.2 Implementing E-Business

Communication, training and motivation activities should focus the *performance aspects* of e-business. Besides impressive success stories there are also mediocre or even bad practices, due to slow and retarded diffusion, roller coaster ups and downs (so called hype curve) and shake out-processes (new economy). Apparently, the life cycle of e-business is not shaped according to a steady diffusion expansion pattern, but more to a rise and fall-pattern. Consequently, performance in e-business ranges from hits (owing to "killer applications") to flops with many question marks in between, primarily businesses which have not reached their break-even point yet. In e-business, performance ranges from *excellence* (bonanza profitability) to *existence* (just reaching the break-even point) to *exit* (having to leave the market, e.g. the so called dotgones).

The process of implementing e-business follows a life cycle pattern (see fig. 20). It entails *diffusion* on the one hand and two particularly challenging stages of implementation, viz. confusion and erosion, on the other hand. *Confusion* is due to technical problems, rivalry of several standards, the need to unlearn habits, doubts, perceived security problems, lack of pioneering spirit, missing standards, to mention but a few. *Erosion* occurs, whenever old habits prevail (e.g. not using the Internet, but the phone as a familiar communication device), security risks have a deterring effect or more efficient technologies emerge (e.g. M-Commerce).

Consequently, a balanced approach to communication and motivation is required: implementation activities have to combine opportunity management (referring to best practices) and risk management, i.e. learning from failure stories by proactive and reactive handling of various risks. In a BR framework, performance-focused implementation activities must primarily take care of barriers to success as well as barriers to failure. Most elucidating is implementation towards customers. Determinants of customer acceptance are often captured in a list of several "co..."-factors, comprising cost, commerce, content, community, convenience, connectivity etc., which emphasize the advantages of e-business in comparison to traditional "brick-commerce" (see fig. 157).

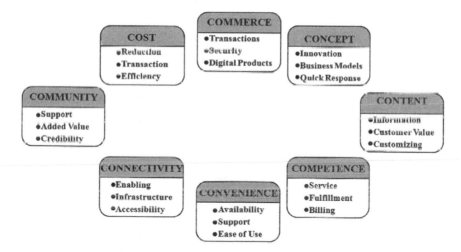

Figure 157: Determinants of E-business Acceptance by Customers

Cost stands for cost-efficiency through low transaction costs as well as time efficiency through the reduction of logistical processes (inventory, transport). However, this reasoning must not ignore the high costs of return logistics, a risk connected to the fact that products offered on the Internet cannot be thoroughly inspected by customers. *Commerce* stresses profitability of the business, as opposed to mere enhancement of customer satisfaction. Profitability requires reengineering of all - and not just some - business processes (including Internet payment systems). *Content, competence* and *community* are primarily related to effectiveness in terms of high quality products and services (such as up-to-date, personalized newspapers, tracking services, apps, etc.), and knowledge exchange (advice, tips, background information, mutual support, etc.). *Convenience* ("just 8 clicks to buy a new car") and *connectivity* provide both efficiency (speed) and effectiveness (access to peers). However, the inherent inconvenience of customer self-service (e.g. search and validation operations) has to be taken account of.

Dismantling barriers to success: What keeps e-business from becoming an excellently and rapidly accepted business and keeps its performance on the existence-level? The major cause is constituted by deficits in infrastructure that have a restrictive and retardatory impact, in other words act as barriers to success:Gaps in *technological infrastructure* are typical examples of barriers to success: Take for example security risks or the lack of voice-detection software which could contribute significantly to the convenience of e-business. *Logistics*, (i.e. physical processes) are the bottlenecks of a high-speed e-business (see fig. 127). They prevent e-business from having a significant competitive advantage over traditional business. A negative impact is also caused by the lack of widely accepted *standards*, problems caused by *culture clashes* in brick and click-alliances as well as non-existing complementary *organizational structures* (decentralized network structures, certified new intermediaries, etc.). *Diseconomies* of the Internet (e.g. information overflow causing reluctance towards Internet use) also have a restrictive effect. Despite assistance from call centers, almost all e-business relies on self serving activities of the customer. This triggers a demand for motivational interventions which must offer some compensation for the inconvenience of self serving, mainly by attractive pricing of services and products (e.g. reduced fees for online-banking).

Building-up barriers to failure: Major implementation risks originate from a) gaps in *legal infrastructures* for online-commerce, such as unsolved problems of protecting intellectual property in a world of uncontrolled downloading and b) lack of protection against the IT-risks of phishing, identity theft, cyber-fraud, hacking, and cyber-terrorism. The *investment in security* relies on numerous services provided by IT-complementors, such as trusted third parties, providers of business continuity systems, intrusion detection systems, disaster recovery, and certification agencies. Another barrier of failure is *slack resources.* Financial slack may be generated via cross-subsidizing from existing cash cow businesses, i.e. from established channels. With respect to intellectual resources such as experience and knowledge, an existing "flip channel" turns out to be even more supportive than a brick channel. *Risk sharing* can be accomplished by co-entrepreneurial "pay on output"-contracts among partners in value nets. So, risks can be carried on the shoulders of several complementors, e.g. game consoles manufacturers *and* games developers instead of exclusively by the provider of a platform product (i.e. game consoles). Like in other technologically challenging markets, the strategy of an early follower (see fig. 87) is less risky than a leader strategy because learning not only from good, but also from bad practices (errors of change leaders) is provided more or less "free of charge". *Diversification* of channels delivers a multi-channel menu.

This holds both for the implementation of e-business (mainstream moving "click complements brick") and for the opposite direction "brick complements click", i.e. for dotcoms (e.g. online-banks and notebook distributors) expanding their channel portfolio into offline business. *Competency based diversification* represent a powerful dynamic capability: a generic competency (like syndication, virtual reality technology, customer-centric consulting, "understanding customers' business", etc.) serves as a base for diversification, allowing access to new customers and/ or new products, in other words a broad range of applications. Finally, the amount of impending damage can be reduced via *step-by-step- implementation* (see fig. 24). So, certain products may be offered on the B2B market first and on the B2C market afterwards whenever B2B is supposed to harbor lead users. Unfortunately best practices for such implementation roadmaps are rare: with respect to digital marketplaces for instance, most companies exploit the opportunities of proprietary, third party- and cooperatively operated markets simultaneously (see fig. 158).

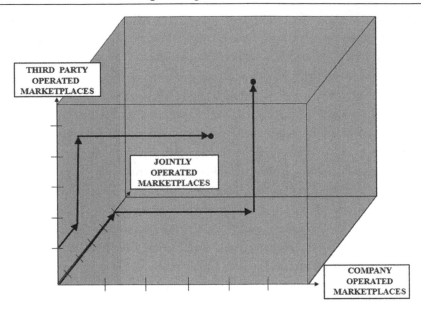

THIRD PARTY
OPERATED
MARKETPLACES

JOINTLY
OPERATED
MARKETPLACES

COMPANY
OPERATED
MARKETPLACES

Figure 158: Step-by-step Implementation of Digital Market Places

However, there is no guideline for a step-by-step exploration that would recommend where to enter and how to continue in the terrain of digital marketplaces.

7.5.3 Alignment in Multi-Channel Business

Another challenge to the implementation of e-business is the alignment of old and new channels. This alignment in a multi-channel system is usually characterized as handling channel *competition*. Viewed through the eyes of an implementation manager, the competition model directs attention to the losers of this process, mostly brick channels. This view is misleading in at least two ways: First, due to the focus on multitude (see fig. 3) other complexity facets of a channel system are neglected. This primarily concerns the *diversity* of channels which creates *hybrid channel system*. There are various species of hybridity in channel systems apart from the brick-click diversity: In so called *dual (or plural) forms* for instance, distribution via franchising and manufacturer-owned stores is combined, mostly in a sectoral architecture, i.e. metropolitan mega-stores blended with smaller franchise stores.

This signals that architectures of (hybrid) multi-channel systems impact the level of competition, another aspect ignored by the mainstream competition view. The respective architecture of a hybrid channel system does not only affect the intensity of competition, but also its overall performance, e.g. due to synergy (see fig. 42). In fact, the entire scope of hybrid architectures can be applied to hybrid channel systems (see fig. 44): In addition to the afore-mentioned *sectoral* coupling, there is a *sequential* coupling, e.g. whenever pure clicks (also) go offline. A *subsidiary* coupling entails the click channel as a default (due to attractive fees and pricing for the customer) and the brick channel as an exception. *Menu* architectures provide a maximum freedom of choice for customers, albeit with a maximum of infrastructure costs for the company. Last by not least, brick and click channels converge into an *amalgam* architecture. This is partly the result of a unilateral assimilation of digital elements (click) to the richness of real-world components (brick), e.g. by multimedia, replacing 2D with 3D representations or using personalized avatars. Moreover, physical and digital channels converge in augmented reality, in business sometime also characterized as "no-line commerce", whenever customers use their digital devices (even) in a physical shop situation to collect additional information (e.g. best price-information) about the product that is physically right in front of them.

All things considered, the alignment of brick and click channels rather follows the complex *coopetition paradigm* than some oversimplified competition paradigm (see fig. 159).

Channel coopetition not only concusses the black-and-white differentiation between friends and foes, but also between winners and losers of implementing e-business. So, the widespread view that intermediaries are the victims of e-commerce revolution suffers from superficiality. In fact, some intermediaries from the brick era actually are victims, i.e. there revenues and margins shrink due to a *disintermediation* process.

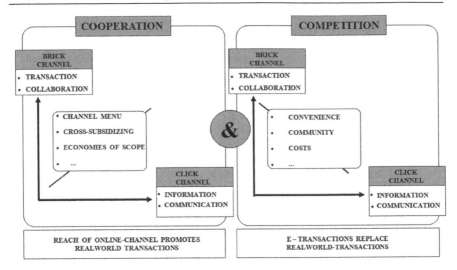

Figure 159:   Coopetition between Brick- and Click-Channels

However, at the same time a *re-intermediation* tales place which turns some new intermediaries into winners of e-business (see fig. 160).

Figure 160:   Intermediaries as Losers and Winners of E-business

The demand for a differentiated handling of intermediaries in change processes can be exemplified in the publishing area. The Internet has augmented the number and diversity of actors involved into the distribution of "books" considerably (see fig. 161).

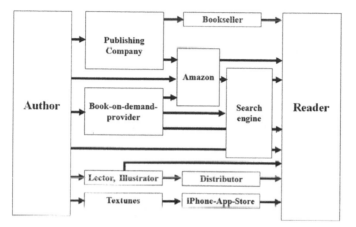

Figure 161: Scope of Intermediaries in Publishing

How intermediaries are affected by e-business also depends on their institutional integration. Especially the media industry practices diversification comprising digital and print media. Consequently, traditional intermediaries become part of an intra-corporate portfolio of media. In this case, the parent company determines to what extend digital and print media are winners or losers of e-business.

Appendices

A Servitization

Servitization denotes the change from "manufacturing products" to "providing services", accomplished by the same companies that address the same customers. This change process perfectly illustrates all the different aspects of *change complexity*: It covers a multitude of change objects, a tremendous variety in terms of a paradigm shift, the ambiguity of the new paradigm and uncertainties in as well as unsteadiness of the transition process.

On the company level, the challenge of servitization for several industrial branches in the economy is reflected in a *culture change* (see fig. A 1). All elements of a corporate culture have to undergo a considerable change (see also fig. 114).

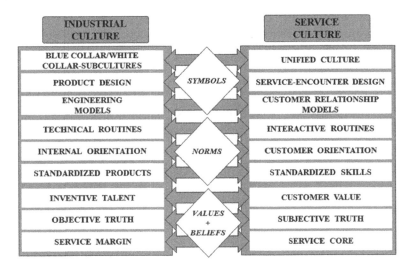

Figure A-1: Transition from Industrial Culture to Service Culture

At the level of individuals, servitization is not only a matter of new skills (e.g. empathy, understanding the typical problems and processes in customers' organizations), but also of motivation. Particularly the employees who have immediate contact to customers are facing a demanding *role conflict* (see fig. A 2).

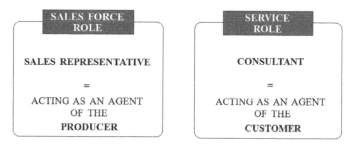

Figure A-2: Role Conflict Caused by Servitization

With servitization, the *performance indicators* for all individuals acting as "faces to the customer" such as revenue on the one hand and customer satisfaction on the other hand are often conflicting. The extreme version of this conflict in the power industry reads: "consulting a customer may enable power savings and consequently reduce power outlet", or in the machinery industry, "providing solutions to customers as a broker may lead to recommendations of competitors' products".

The servitization mainstream does not give an unambiguous orientation. Actually, it covers a *moderate* and a *radical* architecture of product-service systems (see fig. A 3).

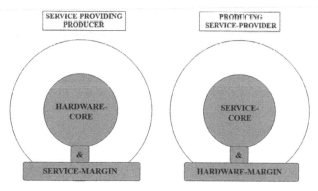

Figure A-3: Moderate versus Radical Architectures of Product-Service-Systems

Change managers operating within the *moderate* architecture primarily have to train social skills (empathy, integration of customers, etc.) that complement existing technical and management skills for product development, manufacturing and distribution (see fig. A 4). These skills are mandatory for selling services that either supplement products or support the user of these products during the overall lifecycle of the product.

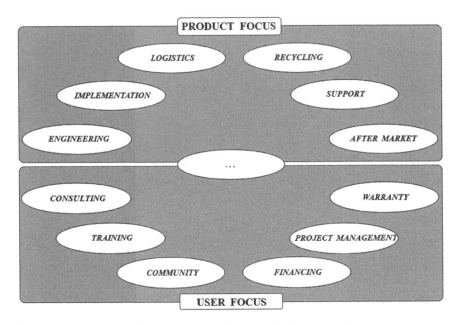

Figure A-4: Scope of Complementary Services for Industrial Products

In contrast, the *radical* version impacts all sectors of a company and represents a genuine corporate change (see fig. 2). The immense demand for change activities results from slogans that characterize the fundamental strategic reorientation of a "manufacturing company" that wants to turn into a *"producing service-provider"* (see fig. A 5).

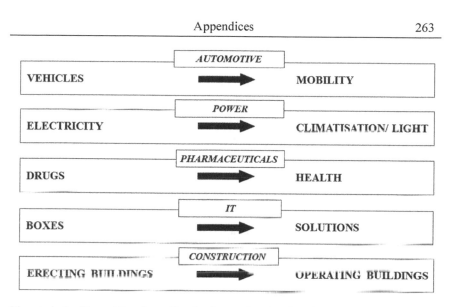

Figure A-5:   Transition from Producing to Service Providing

Sometimes, different markets require different models of servitization which means that both models have to be implemented side by side within one company. Moderate and radical versions can be also viewed as two subsequent steps in a two step-model of implementing "sophisticated" servitization. Moreover, in a dynamic view, going back from radical to moderate is also a relevant path of implementation: This to-and-fro process (see also fig. 26) is predominantly triggered by two trends: 1) self service (e.g. self customizing) helps reduce the costs of servitization significantly. 2) The reluctance of customers towards self service is overcome by offering a user-friendly digital infrastructure, e.g. self-service technologies, community platforms, configurators, and manuals - and not just an attractive pricing of products. All things considered, this strategy relies on substituting services by smart (electronic) devices. This leads to a generic trade-off between the two business mainstreams of servitization and digitalization.

B Projectification

Projectification denotes the increasing relevance of a project-based execution of business activities coupled with the decreasing relevance of a department-based handling of these processes. In contrast to repetitive routine *jobs*, projects deal with *tasks* in terms of novel or rarely appearing "missions" that have to be executed within a given timeframe. Projects are taken care of by project teams: they represent temporary units which are metaphorically characterized as *tents* (or academically as *secondary* organization). Contrary to that, repetitive jobs are dealt with in permanently installed units, so called *palaces* (e.g. centers of excellence, departments, profit-centers as building blocks of the *primary* organization). Projectification is the result of a shift in the portfolio of activities *from jobs to tasks*. This is caused by innovative ventures or by replacing standardized offerings with customized and personalized solutions (e.g. 1:1 Marketing). To adapt organizational structures to this shift, the primary organization is downgraded whereas the secondary organization is upgraded and empowered (see fig. B 1).

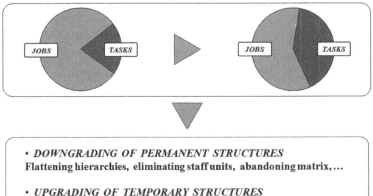

Figure B-1: **The Relevance Shift from Permanent to Temporary Organizational Structures**

Projectification as a change process follows an ambiguous vision entailing a *moderate version* ("project management") and a *radical version* ("management of projects") of relevance shift (see fig. B 2). Empowerment of projects and depowerment of primary structures serve as the common denominator of both visions.

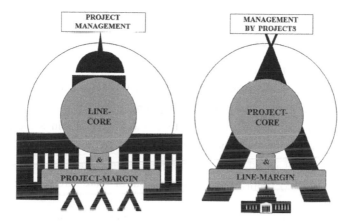

Figure B-2:   Moderate and Radical Visions of Projectification

The empowerment of projects within the *moderate version of projectification* strengthens both the autonomy and the autarky of projects (see fig. B 3).

Figure B-3:   Two-way-Empowerment of Projects

The enrichment of *autonomy* is mainly accomplished by delegating competencies from the steering committee to the project managers, e.g. options of recruiting project manpower or ways of using project budgets. The *autarky* of a project is strengthened by allocating resources (i.e. experts, IT-infrastructure, testing devices) in the project base, i.e. translocating them from a shared resource pool to an on-board equipment exclusively dedicated to project purposes (see also fig. 38).

Both ways of project empowerment also affect the power distribution between line organization and project organization. This is primarily reflected in a shift from line-dominated species of project organization (e.g. line-integrated as well as staff project organization) to project-dominated structures (see fig. B 4). In a project matrix organization the asymmetry of power is changed in favor of projects. This can be accomplished by so called heavy weight project managers. High levels of both autonomy and autarky characterize the autonomous or "pure" project organization.

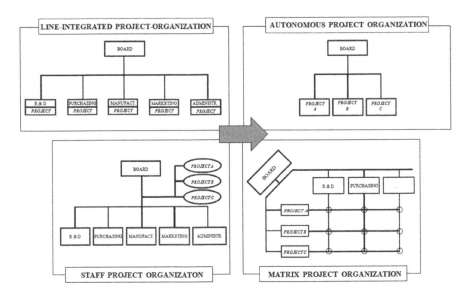

Figure B-4:   The Effects of Project Empowerment on Project Integration

The *radical version of projectification* primarily affects all business processes focusing on external customers: management by projects means that sales activities are pulled by the customer (not pushed by marketing departments) and that they deliver customized solutions instead of standardized offerings.

The acceptance of projectification requires communication, qualification, motivation, and organization activities. A specific challenge to change *communication* is provoked by the fact that project work is team based. On the one hand, acceptance of team work is facilitated by a team ideology on the societal level (captured in slogans like "Nobody is perfect but a team can be!") that stresses the advantages of team work. On the other hand, there is also considerable skepticism with respect to team work as fig. B 5 suggests.

sucker effect	can result when some group members reduce their involvement in response to a group member they perceive to be more enthusiastic or capable
free riding	a common criticism of all forms of group work, that it can allow some members to carry the workload, while others do not contribute but may still gain the same rewards
perceived loafing	one or more group members are perceived as contributing less than they could to the group
social inhibition	the presence of others while performing leads to a declining performance
group think	a deterioration of mental efficiency, reality testing, and moral judgment in a group that results from an excessive desire to reach group consensus
group polarization	group judgements tend to be more extreme
rich get richer effect	group members with high ability and motivation take over key roles in order to benefit themselves
risky shift	group decisions tend to be more risky than decisions made by individuals
shirking	restraining individual performance

Figure B-5: Disadvantages of Team Work: Adverse Effects

Communication activities must not ignore this dark side of project work. Rather, communication managers should address these flaws in a balanced approach to the advantages and the disadvantages of team work (see fig. B 6).

Moreover, implementation managers should be aware of the fact that there are *losers* of projectification as a result of processes of depowerment. Consequently, line managers have to be compensated for their loss to overcome their resistance to an empowered project management.

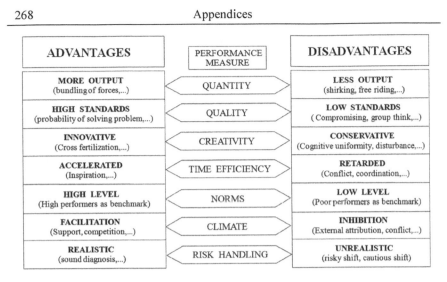

Figure B-6:   Advantages and Disadvantages of Project Team work

C Mergers & Acquisitions

The transformation of two companies into a new company belongs to the classical terrains of change management. Longitudinal studies show peaks in the frequency distribution of Merger & Acquisition (M&A)-deals over time. This indicates imitation behavior, which turns M&A into a fashion-like phenomenon. The essence of change management related to M&A is inter-organizational *integration*. The *efficiency* of these alignment processes is measured by integration costs and duration of integration processes. The *effectiveness* of M&A-processes is normally assessed by the obtained synergy (according to the 2+2=5 formula). From a change management point of view, synergy is dependent on a) how a new post-merger identity can be created (e.g. Novartis) and b) how the pre-merger identities of the respective companies (e.g. Sandoz and Ciba Geigy) can be preserved. With respect to existing "old" cultures and a new corporate culture, fig. C 1 outlines that acquisition projects do not automatically yield both benefits.

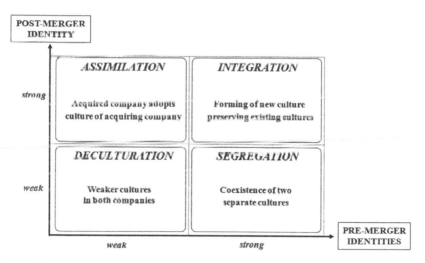

Figure C-1: Culture-focused Effectiveness of Acquisition Management

Integration activities in a M&A-context must cover five generic sectors of the merging companies (see fig. C. 2). In order to reduce the complexity of the change project, the sectors can be attended to in a step-by-step process.

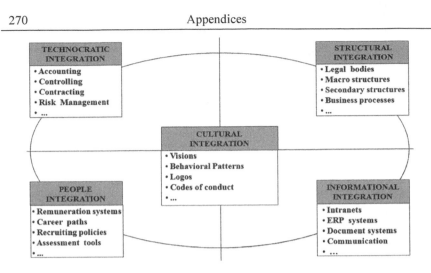

Figure C-2:   Sectors of M&A-Integration Management

The standard framework of change management related to M&A-processes is *post merger integration (PMI)*. Fig. C 3 clarifies that this *reactive* pattern of handling inter-organizational alignment does not cover all relevant approaches to integration management. There is also a *proactive* approach to integration management (see also fig. 19).

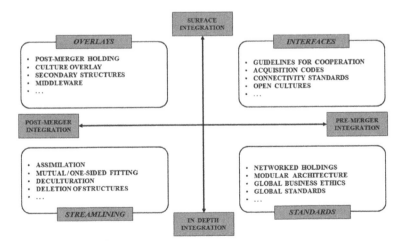

Figure C-3:   Frameworks and Domains of M&A Integration Management

By definition, processes of *pre-merger* integration cannot be focused on a specified object of acquisition. Rather they create some M&A *readiness*, which will serve as a facilitator of (various possible) M&A-projects. Via pre-merger integration, companies are better prepared for M&A: They have for instance a *segmented* architecture (see also fig. 117) which facilitates an inter-company reconfiguration of business segments which is (metaphorically) accomplished just by relocating "lego bricks". The pre- as well as post-merger integration is accomplished either without significant modifications of the respective companies (*surface integration*) or by rearranging cultures, structures, controlling systems, legal entities, databases, logos, or even "demolishing" existing legal units, cultures, etc (*in-depth integration*). Surface integration preserves most features of both companies, i.e. leaves them unchanged and accomplishes integration reactively by some integrative *overlays* or proactively by implementing bridging *interfaces* between the two more or less unmodified entities. These interfaces are warranting coordination, interoperability, and compatibility.

The aspired *efficiency* level for post- and pre-merger integration management is determined by cost-benefit-reasoning.

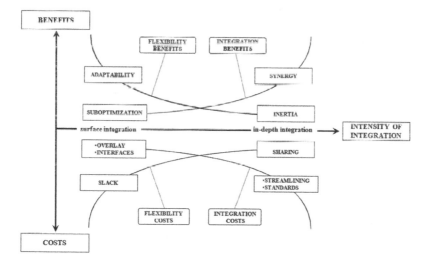

Figure C-4: Performance Measurement of Merger Integration Management

Fig. C 4 substantiates that "total integration" does not serve as a viable orientation for integration activities: a maximum integration does not only disregard the costs of integration. It also ignores the trade-off between integration and flexibility. Highly integrated big companies may suffer from inflexibility in terms of retarded instead of quick responsiveness or lack of innovativeness.

Implementation efforts in the context of M&A projects are facing specific challenges. The failure risk of M&A-projects is exemplified in fig. C. 5 (see also fig. 20). The attainment of synergy, a major driver of M&A-deals, is postponed because of the costs of integration activities. In this confusion period, a negative synergy (2+2=3) has to be dealt with since costs of integration overcompensates benefits. For many a M&A-project the lack of synergy turns out to be a failure factor: failure is not only caused by negative reactions (e.g. withdrawal) of shareholders but also by the fact that PMI-phases are characterized by an *internal* focus in the newly established company. The lack of an external focus (e.g. competitor reactions) is responsible for vulnerability and may eventually cause a decline of market performance which is (paradoxically) triggered by the M&A-project.

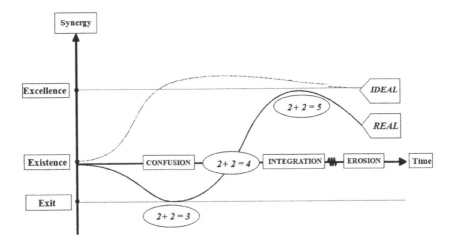

Figure C-5: Dynamics of Integration Performance in M&A Projects

Another challenge to M&A-related change management also appears in the shape of a paradox (see fig. C 6). M&A-projects question the benefits of strong corporate cultures. Despite their obvious advantages for *intra-corporate* cohesion (see also fig. 115), they may cause *inertia* due to their conservative character: most components of a corporate culture were created in the early lifecycle of an organization, which may make them obsolete. Furthermore, strong cultures often *impede* inter-organizational cooperation and cultural integration (see fig. C. 2). Any stringent differentiation from the rest of the world makes cultural integration almost impossible. Failure of M&A- endeavors due to cultural discrepancies can only be avoided by a) a one-sided assimilation to a dominant culture (see fig. C 1) or by b) restricting integration efforts to surface integration (see fig. C 3).

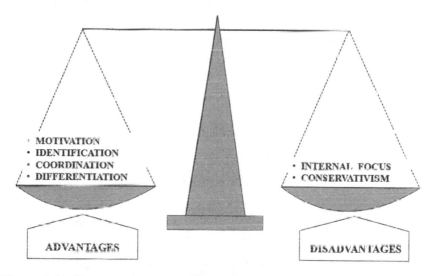

Figure C-6: Strong Corporate Cultures as Barriers to M&A Success

D Implementing Hybrids

Hybrid management frameworks constitute one of the major mainstreams in management. This megatrend has a twofold effect on change management: on the one hand it is reflected in numerous *blended* approaches to the management of change, such as guided evolution, planned change, planned path emergence, logical incrementalism, the mix of electronic and face-to-face tools or the BxB-framework (see paragraph 1.3). On the other hand implementation activities must cope with a plethora of *hybrid concepts* that have to be aligned with the existing context. Quite often, combined hybrid concepts (e.g. hybrid channel systems, see paragraph 7.5) replace simple "straight" concepts (e.g. a brick-channel focused distribution). With respect to governance structures, this shift from the straight concepts, i.e. market or hierarchy to hybrids (i.e. cooperation, networks; see fig. 112) has been characterized as the "swollen middle" of the market-hierarchy-continuum. Fig. D 1 exemplifies the wide range of hybrid frameworks relevant for change management.

Figure D-1: Scope of Hybrids in Management

With respect to the *implementation of hybrid management concepts* the crucial question reads: Is it *more* or is it *less* challenging to implement hybrid concepts in comparison to implementing "simple" straight concepts? From a BR-framework point of view, "challenge" refers to the hardship of a) dismantling barriers to success (e.g. resistance towards hybrids) and b) building-up barriers to failure (e.g. return option to simple concepts).

The "less challenge"-view

There are several powerful arguments signaling that barriers to resistance are more easily surmounted or even avoided: first, hybrids represent *compromises* which per se do not only satisfy the expectations of one involved stakeholder but of several stakeholders. Secondly, one component of the hybrid (e.g. one channel) is already implemented, as a rule. Consequently the *workload* for implementation managers is actually smaller than the complex hybrid concept itself suggests. Thirdly, hybrids cause less *resistance* since they do not cause "creative destruction", do not require radical unlearning (see fig. 22) nor do they radically depower involved parties, e.g. by eliminating established organizational units or closing plants. Finally, the propagated creed of promoters of hybrid frameworks, captured in the *"best-of-both-worlds*-slogan", may not only reduce resistance but even trigger enthusiasm, in other words furnish an excellent level of acceptance (see fig. 15). The acceptance of the matrix organization in the 1970s, both from academia and practitioners, perfectly exemplifies this attitude of "embracing hybrids".

Hybrid competitive strategies that simultaneously provide cost advantages from mass products ("out of the rack") as well as differentiation from class offerings ("one of a kind") serve as perfect illustrations of the available options to implement a hybrid concept. Fig. D 2 exemplifies this by the different paths of implementing *mass customization* (MC). All paths aspire to blend the rather antithetic "class" and "mass" functionalities. Implementation means either adding a customer focus to the existing cost focus whenever a mass manufacturer (of commodities, standardized products and services) or a discounter wants to reach the strategic MC-position starting from a M-position. Vice versa, the MC-position is approached via adding a cost focus to an existing customer focus whenever providers of class products and services (e.g. project businesses, turnkey facilities, consultancies) want to enrich their C-position by cost-focused processes of production and distribution (e.g. replacing individual call center services with standard FAQ-lists). The challenges for implementation managers differ significantly: so a M-to-MC- implementation has to cope with the challenges of *servitization* (see appendix A) whereas a C-to-MC-implementation must deal with resistance triggered by the *industrialization* of the service economy, e.g. building craft or catering.

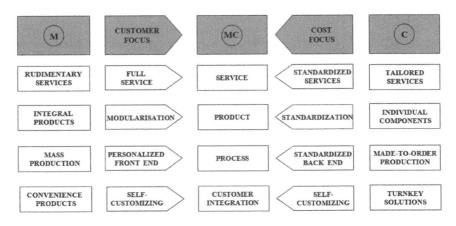

Figure D-2: Implementing Mass Customization

According to the structure-follows-strategy paradigm, a hybrid structure like a product-region matrix is also capable of supporting hybrid competitive strategies such as *glocalization*, the simultaneous utilization of competitive advantages from localization (products customized to local specifics) and globalization (standard "world products"). Fig. D 3 illustrates the hybrid blending of two advantages that normally represent either-or options for strategists, who are inclined to focus either *differentiation* (via localization) or *cost leadership* (via globalization). From a marketing mix point of view, the transition from multinational or global strategies to glocalization requires activities comparable to implementing mass customization as long as the focus is merely on products (and services): so, glocalized media products and services (e.g. newspapers or TV channels with a worldwide reach) are composed out of generic worldwide content and specific regional contents. Likewise, glocalized movies are the result of the dubbing of the movies into several local languages. In addition, the remaining 3 Ps (place, promotion and price) have to be glocalized, e.g. with respect to local logistics, language (English, "Globish", national), celebrities, events, just to name a few. For internet business, some lessons learned in mass personalization (see fig. 156) can be transferred to the marketing for glocalization.

For change managers, glocalization is not restricted to changing competitive strategies. Moreover, *recruiting strategies* have to be aligned to competitive strategies, e.g. from polycentric or geocentric strategies to a hybrid glocalized recruitment. Most likely, the corporate culture will also be an object of change management, possibly geared to the vision of a so called transnational company.

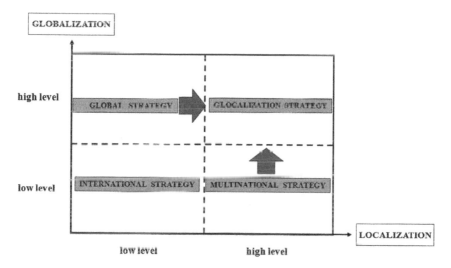

Figure D-3: Paths to Glocalization Strategy

Another exemplification of the simplified implementation of hybrids is *ambidexterity*, i.e. a company's ability to *exploit* new opportunities in existing businesses and *explore* opportunities in emergent new businesses at the same time. The distinction between *mechanistic structures* and *organic structures* reflects the grave diversity between exploitation and exploration (see fig. D 4). There are several options for implementing organic components into a mechanistic context. For instance, this can be accomplished by installing organically operating venture units or by an organic overlay (e.g. project teams and similar "tents"). The efforts of dismantling success barriers, i.e. resistance from the established "palaces", will have to yield comprises as for the distribution of power between the organic and the mechanistic layers. Establishing mechanistic components into a project-based organic structure is accomplished by service providers, i.e. departments that provide IT, training, or coaching services for organic project work.

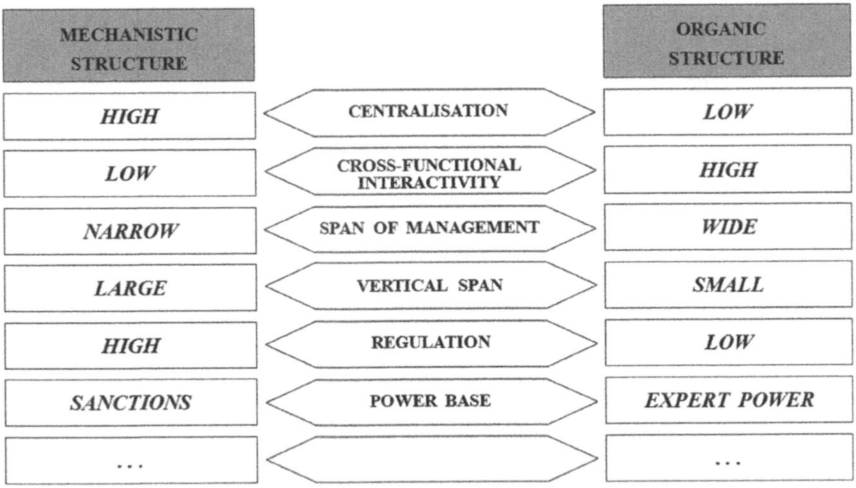

MECHANISTIC STRUCTURE		ORGANIC STRUCTURE
HIGH	CENTRALISATION	LOW
LOW	CROSS-FUNCTIONAL INTERACTIVITY	HIGH
NARROW	SPAN OF MANAGEMENT	WIDE
LARGE	VERTICAL SPAN	SMALL
HIGH	REGULATION	LOW
SANCTIONS	POWER BASE	EXPERT POWER
. . .		. . .

Figure D-4:   Diversity of Organic-Mechanic Structures

The "more challenge"-view

On the other hand, the "dark sides" of hybrids (see fig. 42) make their implementation more strenuous than implementing "straight" concepts. Apparently, hybrids such as matrix structures cause higher manpower costs than one-dimensional entities. Moreover, the tension between the antithetic components causes considerable conflict which triggers high costs of coordination (i.e. the inefficiency of hybrids) as well as impairs motivation and creativity (i.e. the ineffectiveness of hybrids). Furthermore, hybrids go along with specific emergent dynamics due to the innate tension which causes a considerable fragility of the compromise. The explanation of emergent dynamics requires co-evolutionary models. With hybrids, dynamics mainly concerns the endogenous variations of a) component diversity, b) blending patterns (see fig. 44) and c) component proportions.

On the one hand, *diversity* is reduced by processes of *assimilation*. Intrapreneurship, a species of hybrid entrepreneurship, combines an employee component with an entrepreneur component (see paragraph 7.2). The employee part may be assimilated to entrepreneurship whenever employees are paid according to performance (instead of requirements) in terms of the quality and quantity of the results they deliver. Such a performance-based payment approximates typical entrepreneurial payment systems that reward revenues, profits or return on investment. On the other hand, *dissimilation* increases diversity: with intrapreneurship a two-class constellation in the company's manpower would exist if only the shareholders of the company (e.g. partners, owners of stock options) are paid as intrapreneurs, whereas (even) heads of business units and the remaining manpower would receive a requirement-based pay. Dynamics of *blending patterns* (see fig.44) occur either as a shift towards tight coupling (e.g. amalgam patterns or menu patterns) or towards loose coupling (e.g. sequential or sectoral patterns): so, mechanistic and organic structures may dissociate and become two separate "reservations" within the company or they may converge in a melting pot. Dynamics of hybrids is also reflected in changing *proportions*, especially in an increasing symmetry or asymmetry between the blended components. In a hybrid channel system for instance, the click component may become dominant. In contrast, blended learning may tend to a symmetrical blend when the duration of face-to-face episodes equals the duration of e-episodes.

The most radical increase in the workload of implementation managers derives from fundamental skepticism vis-a-vis hybrids. With respect to hybrid competitive strategies (such as mass customization) the "stuck in the middle"-warning may trigger a rejection of hybrid concepts: The message of all stuck-in-the-middle-reasoning is that the performance of hybrids is inferior to that of straight approaches. Consequently, critics advocate a back-to-the-roots approach, such as abandoning the two-dimensional matrix by going back to a one-dimensional divisional structure. So, radical de-hybridization-dynamics most likely ends up in a pendulum (swinging from hard to soft factors) based on *straight* frameworks (see fig. 7) as opposed to *hybrid* frameworks.

Coopetition represents an excellent illustration of implementation challenges due to the hybrid make-up of the respective concepts. Organized cooperation and competition are frequently coupled in a sequential blending (see fig. D 5). There are two blending options: 1) the (familiar) pre-competitive cooperation (e.g. risk sharing and economies of badge engineering amongst competitors) and 2) the pre-cooperative competition (or post-competitive cooperation) whenever the best and the second best bidder at the end of a tender procedure are requested to cooperate because the expectations of the principal with regard to quality and security can only be fulfilled by merging the capacities and capabilities of the two competitors (a process sometimes also called "second sourcing"). This sequential blending may have a thoroughly negative impact because a) *no genuine cooperation* will be practiced with the prospect of subsequent competition nor will there come about a *genuine competition* when a post-competitive cooperation seems likely. In other words, the hybrid concept represents something like a "neither-nor"-mix that is inferior to the performances of both of the blended components: metaphorically speaking, the generated "steam" (pseudo cooperation and competition respectively) is worth less than both of its components "water" or "fire".

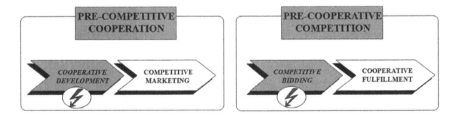

Figure D-5:   Disadvantages of Sequential Coopetition

Apparently, there is no generally valid answer to the question "Is it *more* or is it *less* challenging to implement hybrid concepts?" The lesson learned from the "less" and "more" cases outlined above is that the specific *blending patterns* have a crucial impact both on the benefits, i.e. acceptance of the hybrid, and on the costs of implementation activities. So, lose coupling in terms of a sectoral blending goes along with *minor conflicts and costs*. Fig. D 6 exemplifies that ambidextrous structures can be implemented more easily when exploration and exploitation have separate caretakers, e.g. divisional R&D departments for exploitation and venture units for exploration.

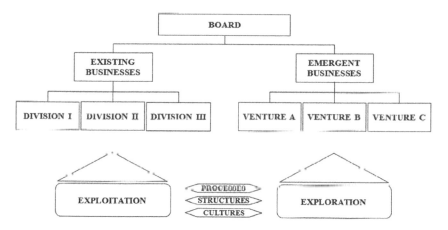

Figure D-6: Sectoral Blending for Ambidexterity

Whereas sectoral architectures separate mechanistic and organic structures, the two structures intersect when tighter patterns of blending are applied. This is the case with subsidiary blending, i.e. with an organic project overlay of a mechanistic structure (that is in charge of coping with routine problems). Likewise, glocalization is facilitated by geographically sectoral architectures, i.e. with a divide of geographic markets to be operated in a globalized fashion and others to be operated in a localized way. In contrast, amalgam blending patterns normally turn out to be most challenging for change managers. An amalgam architecture for intrapreneurship expects intrapreneurs to run their business centers simultaneously according to mechanistic and organic principles: organic principles should be applied to product development and mechanistic principles to order fulfillment. Unfortunately, whenever order fulfillment is accomplished in a management by projects-fashion, the binary distinction between mechanistic and organic has to be replaced with a continuum of more or less organic and mechanistic respectively. Furthermore, deliberately installed hybrid architectures undergo emergent changes.

So, a product-region matrix organization implemented to support glocalization may evolve into a *network organization* (see fig. D 7). For instance, this transition is caused by establishing of geographical centers of excellence in the wake of a so called lead country approach. Geographically distributed units take over services and coordination competencies that used to be allocated at the headquarters level. Headquarters focuses on coordination and changes from a hierarchically operating corporate center in to a heterarchically coordinating federal center (see also fig. 110).

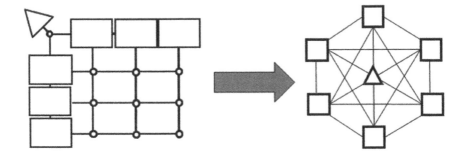

Figure D-7:   Transition from Matrix to Network Structures for Glocalisation

E Errors in Implementation

Risks caused by inadequate behaviors of change managers are either *errors*, i.e. misuse of the Change Management Body Of Knowledge (CMBOK), *pitfalls*, i.e. unexpected surprises for overly involved change managers and *misconduct* such as cheating or free riding which impair the relationships amongst the players in the CMVN. Four categories of errors may have a negative effect on performance (see paragraph 6.3.1): *Type I- and type II-errors* in therapy and *type III- and type IV-errors* in diagnosis. Erroneous diagnostics are often responsible for inadequate therapy.

One generic source of errors is the *inadequate handling of complexity*, either in terms of *under*rating the factual complexity or sometimes also by *over*rating it. The following exemplifications of misjudgments are clustered according to the four dimensions of complexity, i.e. multiplicity, diversity, ambiguity, and dynamics (see fig. 3). Due to the proliferation among the four dimensions, misjudgments of multiplicity are also reflected in erroneous ratings of the remaining three dimensions.

Underrated multiplicity: Attempts to reduce complexity by focusing on the one presumably critical determinant of change project performance may trigger activities resulting in an unsatisfactory performance. In servitization projects (see appendix A), this error may be triggered whenever only one barrier to servitization, e.g. high manpower costs of providing services, is tackled. In fact there are several barriers which have a relevant impact on performance (see fig. E1)

In general, complexity is oftentimes underrated when menus of alternative options are composed of *two extreme options only*, such as first-order and second-order change, digital and face-to-face tools or market and hierarchy. These dichotomous "black or white"-taxonomies ignore interpolated options that are located on a continuum, e.g. the market-hierarchy, the virtuality-reality or the emergent-engineered continuum. Sometimes, interpolated options, e.g. networks or augmented reality, are generated via blending. The multiplicity of options on a continuum facilitates the search for compromises, provided change managers are aware of this species of complexity.

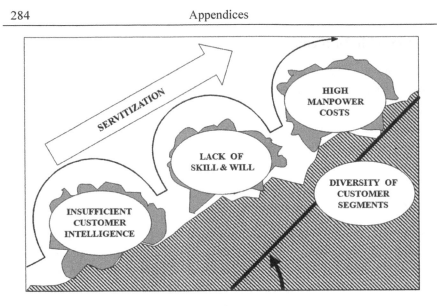

Figure E-1:   Multiple Barriers to Servitization

Another typical error is operating on simple *chain*-models instead of *complex* network models. Chain models of communication or of supply underestimate the density of interfaces and sometimes also the number of involved actors. This has already been clarified with respect to the complexity of a project organization for change management projects when introducing the Change Leadership Value Net replacing the supply chain-approach. Fig. E 2 illustrates the overall scope of factors that advocate a *transition from chain to net modelling*: recycling (closed loop), "leapfrogging" in the supply chain (long-distance in addition to short-distance relationships), concurrent instead of sequential patterns plus the coupling of two or more supply chains in a value net constitute real-world complexities that cannot be appropriately be taken care of in chain models.

Network models analyze relations between nodes by *triads*, i.e. immediate relations between three actors. This signals that all *dyad*-based models underrate the complexity of relationships. So, change champions have to think in triads when dealing with their target groups. In the CMVN, they operate as a "platform" that addresses (several) customers as well as (several) complementors simultaneously: in

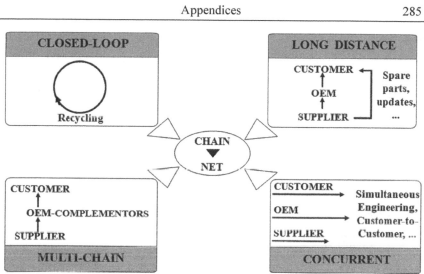

Figure E-2:   From Chain Modelling to Net Modelling

this change triad of change champion, customers and complementors, the customer decides whether some service provider (trainer, mediator, trusted third party, and so forth) offers complementary services or not. Vice versa, the complementor co-determines customer satisfaction. In other words, change champions do not only have to optimize their dyadic customer relationships, but their triadic *complemented customer relationships.*

Furthermore, *evolutionary* models, e.g. the Darwinian variation-selection-retention model (see fig. 33) rely on an oversimplified rationale since they do not explicitly take account of *co-evolution*, i.e. the mutual adaption of two populations. In the Change Leadership Value Net, the two populations of change managers and of complementors co-evolve with respect to their offerings for customers and principals whenever these offerings are not formally aligned by agreements but rather by mutual observation of customer relationship management and service development activities.

Underrated diversity: Quite often this deficit is the result of insufficient *differentiation*. Virtualization serves as a perfect portrayal of underrating the diversity in change processes. A major driver of virtualization is outsourcing (see paragraph 7.1). Quite often, *outsourcing* and *off-shoring* (or near-shoring) are not differentiated although these two transition processes go along with different opportunities and risks: change triggered by outsourcing deals with overcoming boundaries between companies (e.g. lack of trust, NIH-syndrome), off-shoring induced change with boundaries "between countries", for instance in terms of local content or governance regulations. Fig. E 3 delivers the differentiation necessary to determine the workload of implementation processes: domestic outsourcing delivers the advantages of inter-organizational specialization without having to tackle international diversity. Vice versa intra-corporate off-shoring avoids the workload of redesigning inter-organizational business processes between two companies.

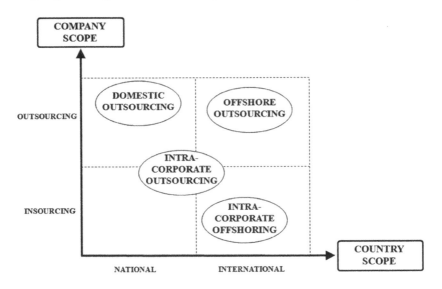

Figure E-3:   The Outsourcing-Offshoring Interface

An even more relevant cause for underestimating diversity is *dilemmas*. For instance, many models for measuring the performance of change processes refer to "the" performance without separating short-term and long-term performance (see fig. E 4). Consequently, they ignore an imminent *dilemma between the two performance orientations*: change management initiatives normally impair short-term performance (as a result of confusion, see fig. 20) for the sake of a better long-term performance (e.g. sustainable performance). Vice versa, short-term quick hits – often the result of postponing unpleasant measures to reduce resistance (see fig. 94) or utilizing placebos (see fig. 89) – may downgrade the prospects of long-term performance. As demonstrated, *portfolio-based* approaches serve as an antidote against both myopic short-term orientation and hyperopic long-term orientation (see fig. 78): they deliver short-term success without neglecting sustainability. Likewise, slack - e.g. in terms of "20%-rules" encouraging people to save a share of their working time for "business as unusual" such as change and innovation – support a balanced performance orientation.

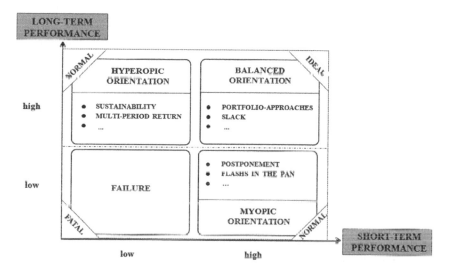

**Figure E-4:   Interdependencies   between   Short-term   and   Long-term
                Performance**

Quite often, the diversity of members in a Change Leadership Value Net is underrated, even if the basic diversity entailed in the four-cluster configuration (suppliers, customers, complementors and competitors) is considered. Especially the value contributed by *trusted third parties* (see fig. 39 and 58) may be questioned. However, this additional species of members is needed as a means in the battle against the risk of *adverse selection* of CLVN-members, predominantly service providers and service complementors. Adverse selection is provoked whenever some characteristics of member candidates and their service offerings are hidden to buyers. Project managers following the signaling activities of service providers have no choice but to assume, that all service providers offer the same quality level although there are actually above and below average offerings. Providers of bad quality services may even deliberately hide this characteristic of their offerings. Providers of premium services will ask for higher prices to cover their quality assurance costs. Since buyers decide on the assumption of an average quality from *all* of the providers, they are not willing to pay higher prices. This will eventually eliminate the premium providers from the market. In order to avoid adverse selection, in other words, in order to avoid that - contrary to the Darwinian selection process - not the fittest will survive, objective signaling by (trusted) *third parties* – such as certificates from associations of project management or consulting – is required. However, this will increase both the multiplicity and diversity of the configuration of CLVNs.

Underrated ambiguity: As far as a well-defined orientation of change managers is concerned, this problem has already been addressed with regard to projectification and servitization: the visions behind these two mainstreams are ambiguous in terms of relying on a *radical* or a *moderate* paradigm. More ambiguity derives from ambiguous wording: "global" on the one hand, means "worldwide" signaling a *high* complexity of business due to geography. On the other hand, "global" in "global strategies" means "standardized" which attributes more or less *zero* relevance to geography. Likewise the patterns for coupling shared services and managed services are ambiguous: sometimes they are considered as alternative options of sourcing, sometimes they are sequentially linked in a two-step outsourcing process with shared services as an antecedent of outsourcing (see fig. 44).

Quite frequently, *inappropriate means to reduce or eliminate ambiguity* are applied, for instance when determining the boundaries of an organizational entity: virtualisation is reflected in blurring boundaries of interprises as opposed to enterprises. This becomes even more evident in a multi-layer model of organizational networks where the demarcation of insiders and outsiders gets more and more difficult when moving from the commerce layer via the community layer to the connection layer. Whenever a stringent delineation is applied, change managers run the risk of neglecting organizational units that factually impact the change project. Awareness of this risk can be better established by a demarcation model that does not operate on strict separation, but on a fluent demarcation (see fig. E 5): within this approach, enterprises (hierarchical corporations as well as heterarchical federations of business centers) can be more easily separated from each other than interprises, e.g. strategic alliances and networks.

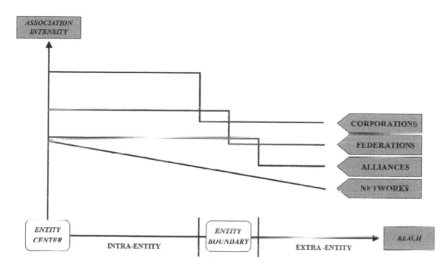

Figure E-5:   Blurring Boundaries of Organizational Entities

Ignoring change management specific *paradoxes* constitutes a major reason for underrating the ambiguity of outcomes. Some paradoxes are inherent in change concepts: e-business for instance, reduces physical activities in the initial phases of business processes (e.g. ordering) but paradoxically they often increase in the terminal phases (e.g. returns logistics). Some paradoxes characterize generic management processes: Adding manpower to a late project paradoxically does not accelerate but delay the project in question (Brooks's law, see also fig. 13). Efforts to fight chaos by regulation may trigger more chaos owing to reactance (see fig. 83). Moreover, intensive investment in intelligence may be paradoxically detrimental to the capability of acting and making decisions. This *paralysis by analysis-paradox* (see fig. E 6) particularly affects change processes because of the plethora of change-related *uncertainties* such as rumors and speculations. They are most likely reflected in an overload of weak signals and contradictory information when second opinions deviate significantly from existing opinions. Instead of delivering an informational substantiation of decisions, the investment in intelligence hinders decision making and intervention. Moreover, the paradox implicitly justifies intuitive intervention that forbears from thorough intelligence. However, pleas for intuitive change management are not thoroughly convincing, since there is no objective method to monitor and agree upon intuitive ways of decision making (see fig. 149).

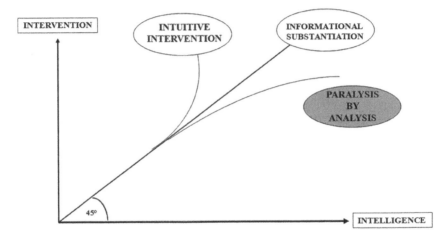

Figure E-6:   The Paralysis by Analysis-Paradox

Underrated dynamics: A path-dependency approach to change management interprets change as a combination of path breaking and path creation (see fig. E 7). Sometimes, the model suggests that the transition period between an old and a new equilibrium (in other words: de-locking and re-locking) constitutes a continuous replacement or migration process. When applying such "switch models", the factual complexity of the transition process gets underrated. Radical changes more likely tend to a long lasting diversity, i.e. instability and confusion (see fig. 20). Fig. E 7 exemplifies furthermore that this diversity may lead to actual new paths that are *inconsistent* with the planned path.

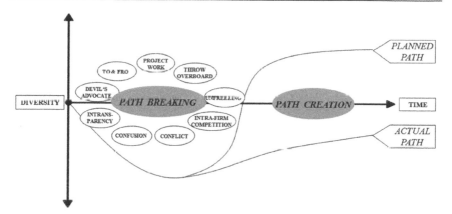

Figure E-7:   Duration and Outcomes of Path Breaking Processes

The dynamics of *blended* concepts, e.g. brick & click companies, coopetition, guided evolution, matrix, ambidexterity, and glocalization (see fig. D 1), are systematically underrated, because there is no comprehensive approach to capture both the *endogenous* and *exogenous dynamics* in the overall lifecycle of these composed concepts. *Exogenous* dynamics refers to the generation and degeneration of hybrids in terms of hybridization, i.e. the transition a) from straight concepts into hybrid concepts (e.g. divisional structures into matrix structures) and vice versa de-hybridization, i.e. b) from hybrid concepts into straight concepts (e.g. matrix structures into divisional structures). *Endogenous* dynamics denotes the co-evolutionary changes within hybrid concepts, viz. the dynamics of a) component diversity (assimilation or dissimilation), b) blending patterns (see fig. 44) and c) component proportions (see appendix D). Consequently, dynamic models of hybrid concepts differ from generic dynamic models (such as path dependence). Fig. E 8 outlines the contours of a path dependency model for matrix structures. Instead of a stringent diversity reducing lock-in, the lifecycle of matrix and other hybrid structures is characterized by *continuous endogenous dynamics*, for instance due to modifications from a "palace" matrix (permanent hybrid structure) to a "tent" matrix (temporary hybrid structure). As opposed to change in terms of a sequential coupling of functional and divisional structures, matrix is based on a parallel coupling of the two organizational archetypes, which creates something like a "swollen path".

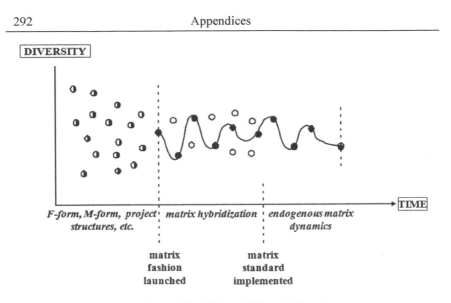

Figure E-8: Path Dependency Modelling of Matrix Structures

Even more complexity goes along when we try to assess the *future scenarios* generated by breaking the "matrix path". Fig. E 9 illustrates the diversity of a) endogenous matrix dynamics (modifications) and b) exogenous matrix dynamics in terms of post-matrix scenarios, i.e. moderate alternatives (surrogates) as well as radical alternatives (substitutes). Matrix *modifications* on the one hand intend to reduce matrix complexity. This is accomplished by leaning the matrix (few organizational units involved cause less complexity in a two-line control system), influence matrices (asymmetrical distribution of power between the two matrix lines) or temporarily instead of permanently installed matrix structures. On the other hand, a three-dimensional product-region-function matrix increases the structural complexity. Matrix *surrogates* are two-dimensional, such as mixed teams (with members from departments and divisions) or sponsorship systems (a senior manager works part-time as caretaker for markets or products in addition to his job as head of a functional department). However, they do not establish a two-line control system the way matrices do. Networks deliver the interface complexity of matrix structures

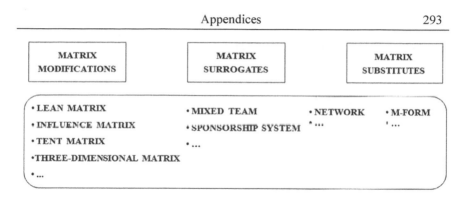

Figure E-9: Scenarios of Matrix Development

but replace the hierarchical by a heterarchical make-up. The typical *substitutes* for two-dimensional matrix structures are one-dimensional M-forms. Frequently, the development path of companies covers the three stages F-form, matrix and M-form: for this population, hybridization appears to be an interlude or even detour between two (heterogeneous) non-hybrid structures.

F   Glossary of Fundamental Terms

360-degree feedback
Multi-rating system with normally four raters, i.e. superiors, subordinates, customers and peers (or partners).

Autarky
When an organizational unit has its dedicated resources (know-how, manpower, facilities etc.) and is thereby self sufficient.

Autonomy
When an organizational unit is vested with decision-making powers.

Balanced Scorecard
Performance measurement and management framework based on the balanced blending of financial and non-financial performance measures.

Benchmarking
Comparing one's own enterprise with external models ("best practices"), to derive measures to improve performance, processes and resources.

Business center
Organizational unit within a corporation running a specific business with external customers (e.g. division, spin-off, venture, line of business).

Business Reengineering
Fundamental rethinking of existing strategies, processes and structures, and a radical, top-down controlled renovation of business processes towards more customer orientation with a simultaneous reduction in costs and speedier services.

Business unit
Organizational unit (eg division), whose activities are focused on one output object that defines a business area (eg product, service, customer, region).

Cafeteria system
Reward system allowing employees to configure an individualized combination of rewards within the limits of their respective total compensation (mostly applied to fringe benefits).

Center
Either a coordinative organizational unit (e.g. corporate center, center of competence) or an entrepreneurial organizational unit (e.g. business center).

Centers of competence (Centers of excellence)
Organizational units which provide a special expertise (e.g. in information technology) for the entire corporation in addition to their day-to-day business and serve as a single intracorporate source for this competence.

Change Manager
A person, group or organization, that deliberately actuates and controls specific processes of change within the framework of change schemes. The change manager helps to identify an organization's targets and to work out change strategies. When implementing the processes, contact with the involved parties is maintained.

Coaching
When an internal or external adviser is put in charge of individuals or a team with the aim of enhancing productivity and motivation. A coach provides individualized (tailored) support. The principle is that the individuals or teams take complete responsibility for themselves.

Community of practice
Thematic groups established to support the transfer of knowledge within, sometimes also between companies.

Competence
In the organizational sense, competence stands for authority, licence, right of disposal, and is the expression of the autonomy of an organizational unit. When applied to resources, competence stands for a special ability of a person, a group or an enterprise, and is the expression of the self-sufficiency of this organizational unit.

Complementor
Provider of complementary products and services.

Congruence principle
States that, a balance of rights and duties must be ensured for every organizational unit.

Coopetition
Hybrid interaction concept comprising cooperation as well as competition (e.g. cooperative R&D and competitive marketing).

Coordination units
Organizational units, whose main task is to coordinate other units.

Corporate center
Coordinative headquarters of a corporation (e.g. a holding).

Corporate Culture
Generic term for all the shared underlying assumptions, values and norms of the members in an organization, which are manifested in specific verbal and non-verbal expressions, interactions and symbols such as, rituals, legends, role models, language rules and dress codes.

Degree of organization
Describes the stringency, detail, uniformity and permanence of organizational regulations, as well as their documentation in organization manuals.

Delegation
Is when different responsibilities are exercised separately via several positions. The transition from centralised decision-making to delegation means that the asymmetry in power amongst the organizational units is diminished.

Differentiation, organizational
covers the distribution of tasks or work (duties, burdens, responsibilities) as well as the distribution of organizational responsibilities (rights, authority, power, influence opportunities). The outcome of differentiation is a complex of organizational units which are determined by their duties and rights.

Division of authority
Distribution of formal influence and power amongst several organizational units.

Division of labour
Distribution of tasks amongst several organizational units based on the classic principle of specialisation in specific activities. This principle is applied to business processes as well as to technical processes (eg workshops as functional units in production).

Dual organization
Combination of primary and overlaying secondary organizations, in which the same set of employees deal with different types of tasks under different organizational working conditions. For example, regular tasks within the hierarchical structure of line activity, and extra-duty assignments in team work that is hierarchy-free and de-coupled from everyday business.

Empowerment
The transfer of decision-making powers to employees or teams in the lower levels of the hierarchy, as well as building up skills in these levels. This measure serves to improve processes and increase customer satisfaction.

Entrepreneuring
Defines classical entrepreneurship characterized by independence and innovation. In a broader sense a term that covers all varieties of entrepreneurial concepts (e.g. intrapreneuring, interpreneuring, self employment etc.).

Exopreneurs
Entrepreneurs cooperating with large organizations to establish new businesses.

Extrapreneurs
Individuals who leave their employment at an enterprise with the purpose of establishing a separate firm that complements the previous employer.

Functional units
Organizational units that perform a specifically defined function in the value-added activities of an enterprise. Functional areas such as purchasing, manufacturing, marketing and research &development are regarded as functional units. In the broader sense, functional units also include so-called organizational units for cross-sectional tasks such as logistics, quality assurance or environmental protection.

Halo effect
Error in the appraisal of persons when a positive (or negative) assessment of one aspect has the effect that all other aspects of the person are seen positive (or negative) (e.g. intelligent persons are also reliable, friendly and innovative).

Heterarchy
Overlay of several contrary hierarchical (asymmetrical) relationships between two organizational units resulting in an overall symmetrical relationship (e.g. positional hierarchy and expert hierarchy between staff units and line units).

Integration
Integration or coordination describes the orientation of several organizational units towards the whole, mostly towards a common goal.

Internal Customer-Supplier Relationships
The application of customer-supplier type business relationships to intra-organizational units along the value chain, e.g. between service and business units.

Interpreneuring
Entrepreneuring within networks: interpreneurs cooperate to run a business (e.g. multimedia, facility management).

Interprise
Short for "extended enterprise", i.e. a boundary spanning or boundaryless ("virtual") network company.

Intrapreneuring
"Intracorporate entrepreneuring" in terms of entrepreneurship within corporations with employed managers as intrapreneurs.

Job enlargement
Measures of extending the scope of activity of an organizational unit, through the inclusion of additional operational activities.

Job enrichment
Measures of extending the scope of decision-making of an organizational unit through the inclusion of additional managerial and decision-making powers.

Kaizen
Continuous improvement of product, processes, management and organization. The change (Kai) for the better (Zen) must be the driving force of every employee. Continuous improvement processes (CIP) are implemented quickly and directly by those affected and include all activities in direct and indirect sectors.

Leadership
Managerial concept, which ascribes a manager the role of visionary, promoter and coach in strategically relevant processes.

Lean Management
Japanese management concept, which has spread in the USA and in Europe as a reaction to comparative studies conducted by the Massachusetts Institute of Technology (USA) about the Japanese, American and European automotive industry. The approach is founded on the basic principles of decentralisation and simultanisation linked with cooperative organizational forms, eg team work. The approach also serves to reduce costs with the simultaneous improvement in customer orientation.

Learning Organization
An organization which learns primarily on the basis of learning in groups and implementing what has been learnt directly into practice. The learning process of the employees is a necessary but not sufficient condition of the learning organization.

Individual learning has to be adopted in the structures and processes of the organization. This goal is achieved above all by learning in groups and archiving knowledge.

Line units
The „tougher" responsibilities of decision-making, authorisation, vetoes, and management by direction are incumbent upon lines.

Line-staff organization
Form of division of authority based on the delegation principle. The responsibilities of preparation for decisions are outsourced to staff units, whereas the decision-making responsibilities remain with the line units.

Macro-organization
Organizational structures, whose components are organizational aggregate units (groups, sectors, divisions, areas, enterprises etc).

Management by exception
Management model based on delegation, in which decision-making by the superior unit is the exception. As a rule, the subordinate unit is delegated the responsibility of taking decisions.

Management by objectives
Management model based on participation. The agreement on targets between superiors and subordinates is at the core of the model.

Matrix organization
Two-dimensional organizational form with a two-line system, comprised of the levels of overall matrix management (1st level), the second level of the matrix positions (matrix managers) of both matrix dimensions and, the third level, the matrix interfaces. The area of responsibility of each unit on this third level is defined by a combination of two job features, eg „marketing/product line B".

Matrix organization, symmetrical andasymmetrical
With the symmetrical ("balanced") matrix organization, both matrix dimensions have the same amount of authority. With the asymmetrical ("unbalanced") matrix organization, one matrix dimension has more authority than the other.

Micro-organization
Organizational structures, whose components are the smallest organizational units (positions).

Moderation
A method of interaction for working groups. When decisions have to be made, a neutral moderator is appointed to control group processes, activate the potential of experience and ideas of the participants, and deal constructively with conflicts.

Motivation
A tendency to behave in a specific way determined by motives, rewards and expectancies.

Motivation, extrinsic
Being rewarded by the context of a job (e.g. by pay, feedback, recognition).

Motivation, intrinsic
Being rewarded by the content and the execution of a job (e.g. by variety of tasks, learning on the job).

Multi rating system
Performance appraisal by several raters (e.g. superiors, peers). Most popular multi rating system is the 360-degree rating/ feedback.

Network Organization
Organization form between and within enterprises. A network organization is characterised by a heterarchy and not a hierarchy; a high level of independence of the individual organizational units (nodes); independence in building up interaction and relationships within and between the units, and great variety in organizational forms.

Object units
Organizational units, whose activities are focused on a product, a segment of customers, a key account, a region or resource. Object units are, for example, product divisions, customer divisions, international divisions, the personnel department, materials and information management.

Offshoring
The practice of basing business processes or services overseas, e.g. to take advantage of lower costs.

Organization as institution
Equates „organization" with "enterprise" or institution (eg non governmental organizations, non profit organization). Aide-mémoire: „The enterprise is an organization."

Organization as structure
Organization is understood as the structure of an enterprise resulting from differentiation and integration. Aide-mémoire: „The enterprise has an organizational structure."

Organization chart
Graphic diagram of the hierarchically structured primary organization of an enterprise with the aid of nodal points (organizational units) and branches (lines as symbols of communication links within the hierarchy).

Organization, divisional
Exists, when the essential decisions are taken at the sub-corporate management level in business units (divisions).Also called "M-form".

Organization, functional
Exists, when the essential decisions are taken at sub-corporate management level in functional units. Also called "F- or U-form" (u =unitary).

Organization, functionalised
The entire complex of managerial functions is distributed amongst several superiors. Such a division of managerial responsibility leads, for example, to the simultaneous existence of professional and disciplinary superiors, or of technical managers and commercial managers. This division is accompanied by a multiple-line system.

Organizational Development
The procedure of planning, initiating and executing organizational changes and adjustments. This process begins with the conduct of the members of the organization. Organizational development is based on a high degree of participation by those affected, and is seen as a long-term learning and development process.

Outsourcing
Fielding out operational value-adding processes and their delegation to a third party (supplier, provider etc).

Participation
Form of the division of authority, in which the rights of several people or positions are commonly exercised. With the transition from centralised decision-making to participation, the persons affected become the persons involved. Prerequisites for the participative exercise of authority are suitable voting rules for coordinated decision-taking, eg via majority votes or unanimity (principle of consensus).

Participation, direct
Personal participation in the decision-making processes, eg within the framework of management by objectives.

Path dependency
dynamic process (trend, …) exhibiting sensitive dependence on initial conditions

Participation, indirect
The exercise of individual interests via lobbyists, eg the workers' council (co-determination), spokesman for the executive employees or spokesman from team work units.

Primary organization
Permanent positions and departments set up to cope with day-to-day processes.

Project base
Organizational units with a major function in the project. These units are completely available for the project work. Level of the project organization that includes the project manager and the core project team.

Project infrastructure
Organizational units which are at times included in a project. These units support the project by means of specialist services.

Project organization
Special structures designed to cope with new tasks by installing assignments of limited duration.

Project organization, line-integrated-type
Project managers and project co-workers are not wholly available for project work but collaborate in projects alongside their line activity.

Project organization, matrix-type
The project managers for the individual projects form the secondary organizational matrix dimension "projects".

Project organization, pure type
In the primary organization of an enterprise, project units have the same position as business and functional units. As much capacity and authority required for the project management is assigned to the project. Thus, one also talks about a "self-sufficient" project organization.

Project organization, staff-type
Project managers are set up as staff units (eg of the corporate management) and can focus entirely on their project activities.

Project super-structure
Coordinative supra-structure of a project-type organization which decides when a project is to be started or stopped, the project budget, authorisation or extension of a project. It also resolves conflicts between project and line and sets priorities between several projects within the framework of multi-project management. The steering committee is at the centre of the project superstructure.

Promoters
Persons, who, on the basis of their power of disposal and position (power promoters), their professional expertise (professional promoters) or moderation skills (process promoters), drive forward projects of change and innovation.

Promoters in project organization
In order for a project to win through against the line and other projects, three categories of promoter potential are required: experts (promoters who are specialists in the given field), sponsors (power promoters) and champions (project-process promoters, more often than not the project manager).

Prosumer
Hybrid role concept comprising the role of a consumer and a producer (also: co-producer).

Scenarios
Projections of possible environmental constellations in the future which are determined on the basis of specific macro-economical, social, technological and scientific assumptions.

Secondary organization
Organizational units such as project teams, councils, committees, advisory boards, circles, communities, which overlay as temporary special purpose organizations for new types of tasks and coordination jobs.

Self-coordination
Is effected via direct communication between the organizational units to be coordinated.

Service center
Organizational unit within a corporation providing services for other units in the corporation as internal customers (e.g. procurement, HR, IT, law/ contracting, logistics, quality assurance).

Slack, organizational
Reserves in the form of privileges, deliberate slackening and buffering in the flow of materials (eg inventories).

Span, horizontal
Number of direct subordinate organizational units (span of control, management or coordination).

Span, vertical
Number of hierarchy levels in an enterprise.

Spin-off
Organizational center carved out of a parent company representing a separate legal unit.

Staff units
The „softer" responsibilities of preparation for a decision are incumbent upon staff units. This includes collecting data, forecasting, making proposals and planning. Staff units are usually made up of experts, eg legal or technical experts.

Team Life Cycle
The development of a team via the stages of forming (establishing), storming (dealing with conflicts), norming (finding norms and roles) and performing (fulfilling jobs).

Teams, self-managing
The team itself decides the assignment of activities, operating procedures as well as the attendance times and holiday periods.

Third-party coordination
Execution of the coordination task by a third party, eg superior organizational units, coordination units, mediators, liaison units or network brokers.

Total Quality Management (TQM)
Complete comprehension of quality assurance in which, quality is not only monitored during or after manufacturing, but is also planned and produced by all the employees involved during the whole value-adding process. Formal organizational

instruments (eg quality assurance system, manuals) and participative instruments (quality cycle, project team etc.) are used to this aim.

Two-line system
Organizational units have two superior units. These two management units can wield the same or different levels of influence.

Virtual Organization
Form of collaboration, which is project-oriented and supported by information technology, between legally independent enterprises and individuals. This form of collaboration does not have the features of conventional enterprises, eg legal form, headquarters or joint offices.

Virtual size
Size of a company determined by access to resources via all kinds of contracts with/ relationships to partners (not only based upon property status or regular employment contracts)

Sources

Abrahamson, E. (2004), Change Without Pain: How Managers Can Overcome Initiative Overload, Organizational Chaos, and Employee Burnout, San Francisco 2004

Achilles, A.; Bedeian, A. (1999), Organizational Change: A Review of Theory and Research in the 1990s, in: Journal of Management, 25 (1999) 3, pp. 293–315

Ackoff, R. (1990), The management of change and the changes it requires of management, in: Systems Practice, 3 (1990) 5, pp. 428-440

Aguirre, A.; Finn, L.; Harshak, A. (2007), Ready, willing, and engaged, Booz Allen Hamilton, 2007

Aiken, C.; Keller, S. (2009), The irrational side of change management, in: The McKinsey Quarterly, 18 (2009), 2, pp. 101-109

Albach, H. (1995), Management of structural change. Contributions to modern management, in: Zeitschrift für Betriebswirtschaft, supplement issue, No. 4 (1995)

Allen, J.; Jimmieson, N.L.; Bordia, P.; Irmer, B.E. (2007), Uncertainty during Organizational Change: Managing Perceptions through Communication, in: Journal of Change Management, 7 (2007) 2, pp. 187-210

Almeida Costa, L.; De Matos, J. A.; Cunha, M. P. E. (2003), The Manager as ChangeAgent, in: International Studies of Management & Organization, 33 (2003) 4, pp. 65-93

Anderson, D.; Ackerman Anderson, L. (2001), Beyond Change Management: Advanced Strategies for Today's Transformational Leaders, San Francisco 2001

Andler, N. (2011), Tools for Coaching, Leadership and Change Management: A Most Complete Compendium of Tools and Techniques for Working Smarter with People, Erlangen 2011

Arend, R.J.; Bromiley, P. (2009), Assessing the dynamic capabilities view: spare change, everyone?, in: Strategic Organization, 7 (2009) 1, pp.75-90

Armenakis, A. A.; Bedeian, A. G. (1999), Organizational Change: A Review of Theory and Research in the 1990s, in: Journal of Management, 25 (1999) 3, pp. 293-315

Armenakis, A.A.; Harris, S.; Cole, M.; Fillmer, J.; Self, D. (2007), A top management team's reactions to organizational transformation: The diagnostic benefits of five key change sentiments, in: Journal of Change Management, 7 (2007) 3-4, pp. 273–290

Armenakis, A. A.; Harris, S. G. (2009), Reflections: our Journey in Organizational Change Research and Practice, in: Journal of Change Management, 9 (2009) 2, pp. 127–142

Arnold, N. (2002), Outside the Square: Pentagonal and Hexagonal Models of Leadership, in: Journal of Change Management, 3 (2002) 2, pp. 110–133

Aubry, M.; Hobbs, B.; Thuillier, D. (2007), A new framework for understanding organizational project management through the PMO, in: International Journal of Project Management, 25 (2007), pp. 328-336

Aubry, M.; Hobbs, B.; Thuillier, D. (2008), Organizational project management: An historical approach to the study of PMOs, in: International Journal of Project Management, 26 (2008) pp. 38–43

Axelrod, R. H. (2000), Terms of Engagement: Changing the Way We Change Organizations, San Francisco 2000

Baden-Fuller, C.; Volberda, H.W. (1996), Strategic Renewal in Large Complex Organizations: A Competence-Based View, Rotterdam 1996

Bahner, R.R.; Stroh, L.K. (2004), TheTransformation Management Model: A Total Evaluation Route to Business Change Success, in: Problems and Perspectives in Management, 4 (2004) pp. 180-191

Bain & Co. (2010),
http://www.bain.com/management_tools/BainTopTenTools/default.asp

Baines, T.S. et al. (2009), The servitization of manufacturing, in: Journal of Manufacturing Technology Management, 20 (2009) 3, pp. 347-567

Baitsch, C.; Heideloff, F. (1997), Collective construction changes organizational reality. An illustration of the relative influence of both consultants and organizations, in: Journal of Organizational Change, 10 (1997) 3, pp. 217–234

Balling, R. (2008), Change-Portfolio,
http://www.webermanagement.ch/download/88dext0KnOhD.pdf, access date: 03/03/2008

Balogun, J.; Gleadle, P.; Hailey, V. H.; Willmott, H. (2005), Managing Change Across Boundaries: Boundary-Shaking Practices, in: British Journal of Management, 16 (2005) 4, pp. 261-278

Barett, F. (2004), Coaching for Resilience, in: Organization Management Journal, 22 (2004) 1, pp. 93-96

Bartunek, J. M.; Moch, K. M. (1987), First-Order, Second-Order, and Third-Order Change and Organization Development, in: Journal of Applied Behavioral Science, 23 (1987), pp. 483–500

Bartunek, J. M. (2003), Organizational and Educational Change: The Life and Role of a Change Agent Group, Mahwah/New Jersey, London 2003

Becerra-Fernandez, I.; Sabherwal, R. (2010), Knowledge management: systems and processes, Armonk, NY 2010

Beck, N.; Brüderl, J. (2008), Momentum or deceleration? Theoretical and methodological reflections on the analysis of organizational change, in: Academy of Management Journal, 51 (2008) 3, pp. 413-435

Beech, N.; MacPhail, S.; Coupland, C. (2009), Anti-dialogic Positioning in Change Stories: Bank Robbers, Sviours and Peons, in: Organization, 16 (2009) 3, pp. 335-352

Beer, M.; Eistenstat, R.A.; Spector, B. (1990), The Critical Path to Corporate Renewal, Boston 1990

Beer, M.; Nohria, N. (2000), Cracking the Code of Change, in: Harvard Business Review, May-June (2000), pp. 133-141

Ben Mahmoud-Jouini, S.; Charue-Duboc, F.; Fourcade, F. (2007), Multilevel integration of exploration units: beyond the ambidextrous organization, in: Academy of Management Proceedings, 2007, pp. 1-6

Bennis, W. G.; Benne, D. D.; Chin, R. (1994), The Planning of Change, New York 1969

Berger, L.; Sikora, M. (1994), The Change Management Handbook, New York 1994

Biedenbach, T.; Söderholm, A. (2008), The Challenge of Organizing Change in Hypercompetitive Industries: A Literature Review, in: Journal of Change Management, 8 (2008) 2, pp. 123–145

Billinghurst, M.; Kato, H. (2002): Collaborative augmented reality. In: Communications of the ACM 45 (2002) 7, pp. 64-70

Blom, H.A.; Lygeros, J. (Eds., 2006), Stochastic Hybrid Systems. Theory and Safety Critical Applications, Berlin 2006

Bloodgood, J.M.; Morrow Jr, J.L. (2003), Strategic Organizational Change: Exploring the Roles of Environmental Structure, Internal Conscious Awareness and Knowledge, in: Journal of Management Studies, 40 (2003) 8, pp. 1761-1782

Bloomberg Business Week (2012): http://bx.businessweek.com/change-management/blogs/

Booz Allen Hamilton (2004), Ten Guiding Principles of Change Management, 2004

Booz & Co. (2008): Change Management Graduates to The Boardroom: From Afterthought To Prerequisite, http://www.booz.com/media/uploads/ChangeManagementGraduatesToTheBoardroom.pdf

Bowman, E.; Kogut, B. (1995), Redesigning the Firm, New York 1995

Braganza, A. (2001), Radical Process Change: A Best Practice Blueprint, Chichester 2001

Bridges, W. (1991), Managing Transitions: Making the Most of Change, Cambridge 1991

Brill, P.L.; Worth R. (1997), The Four Levers of Corporate Change, New York 1997

Brown, A.; Gabriel, Y.; Gherardi, S. (2009), Storytelling and Change: An Unfolding Story, in: Organization, 16 (2009) 3, pp. 323-333

Brown, D.; Scott, W. (2006), The black book of outsourcing. How to manage the changes, challenges and opportunities, Hoboken, New Jersey 2006

Brown, S.; Eisenhardt, K. (1997), The Art of Continuous Change: Linking Complexity Theory and Time-paced Evolution in Relentlessly Shifting Organizations, in: Administrative Science Quarterly, 42 (1997), pp. 1-34

Brown, W.J.; Malveau, R.C./ McCormick, H. W./ Mowbray, T.J. (1998): Anti-patterns. Refactoring Software, Architecture and Projects in Crisis, New York 1998

Bruce, R.R.; Wyman S. (1998), Changing Organizations: Practicing Action Training and Research, Thousand Oaks 1998

Bruch, H.; Gerber, P.; Maier, V. (2005), Strategic Change Decisions: Doing the Right Change Right, in: Journal of Change Management, 5 (2005) 1, pp. 97-107

Brynjolfsson, E.; Renshaw, A.; van Alstyne, M. (1996), The Matrix of Change: A Tool for Business Process Reengineering, in: MIT Sloan Management Review, 38 (1996) 2, pp. 37-54

Buchanan, D.; Dawson, P. (2007), Discourse and Audience: Organizational Change as Multi-Story Process, in: Journal of Management Studies, 44 (2007) 5, pp. 669-686

Burnes, B. (2009), Managing Change, 5. ed., Harlow 2009

Burns, J.; Nielsen, K. (2006), How Do Embedded Agents Engage in Institutional Change?, in: Journal of Economic Issues, 40 (2006) 2, pp. 449-456

By, T.R. (2005), Organizational Change Management: A critical review, in: Journal of Change Management, 5 (2005) 4, pp. 369–380

Caldwell, R. (2003), Change leaders and change managers: different or complementary?, in: Leadership & Organization Development Journal, 24 (2003) 5, pp. 285–293

Caldwell, R. (2003), Models of Change Agency: a Fourfold Classification, in: British Journal of Management, 14 (2003) 14, pp. 131-142

Caldwell, R. (2006), Agency and Change: Rethinking change agency in organizations, London 2006

Caldwell, R. (2007), Agency and Change: Re-evaluating Foucault's Legacy, in: Organization, 14 (2007) 6, pp. 769-791

Caluwé, L.; de Vermaak H. (2003), Learning to Change. A guide for Organizational Change Agents, Thousand Oaks 2003

Cameron, E.; Green, M. (2011), Making sense of change management - A complete guide to the models, tools & techniques of organizational change, 2. ed., London, Philadelphia 2011

Campbell, C. (1989), Change Agents in the New Economy: Business Incubators and Economic Development, in: Economic Development Review, 7 (1989) 2, pp. 56-59

Capgemini (2008): Change management 2003/2008. Significance, strategies, trends. URL: http://www.cz.capgemini.com/m/cz/tl/Change_Management_2003_2008_-_Significance__strategies__trends.pdf [Retrieved: 13.02.2012]

Cappelli, P. et al. (1997), Change at Work, New York 1997

Carnall, C.A. (2003), Managing change in organizations, 4. ed., Harlow, Munich 2003

Carr, A. (2000), Critical theory and the psychodynamics of change: A note about organizations as therapeutic settings, in: Journal of Organizational Change Management, 13 (2000) 3, pp. 289-299

Carroll, J. S., Hatakenaka, S. (2001), Driving Organizational Change in the Midst of Crisis, in: MIT Sloan Management Review, Spring 2001, pp. 70-79

Carter, L. et al. (2001), Best Practices in Organization Development and Change Handbook: Culture, Leadership, Retention, Performance, Coaching, San Francisco 2001

Carter, M. (2005), Book Review: DEC Is Dead, Long Live DEC Culture, Consulting, Change: The Story of DEC, in: Organization Development Journal, 23 (2005) 2, pp.86-90

Cawsey, T.; Deszca, G. (2008), Toolkit for Organizational Change, London 2008

Champy, J. (2002), X-Engineering the corporation: reinvent your business in the digital age, London 2002

Change Source (2012), http://www.change-management-toolbook.com/

ChangingMinds. (2012). How we change what others think, feel, believe and do, retrieved from http://changingminds.org

Chow, W.S.; Chan, L.S. (2008), Social network, social trust and shared goals in organizational knowledge sharing, in: Information & Management, 45 (2008), pp.458-465

Christ, W. (1999), Leadership in Times of Change: A Handbook for Communication and Media Administrators, Annandale 1999

Christensen, C. M.; Overdorf, M. (2000), Meeting the Challenge of Disruptive Change, in: Harvard Business Review, (2000) 3-4, pp. 66–67

Chui, M.; Miller, A.; Roberts, R. (2009), Six ways to make Web 2.0 work, The McKinsey Quarterly, 18 (2009) 2, pp. 64-73

Clardy, A. (2003), Learning to change: A guide for organization change agents, bookreview in: Personnel Psychology, Oct. 2003, pp. 785-788

Clark, E.; Soulsby, A. (2007), Understanding Top Management and Organizational Change Through Demographic and Processual Analysis, in: Journal of Management Studies, 44 (2007), pp. 932-954

Clark, S.; Gioia, D.; Ketchen, D.; Thomas, J. (2010), Transitional Identity as a Facilitator of Organizational Identity Change during a Merger, in: Administrative Science Quarterly, 55 (2010) 3, pp. 397–438

Clark, T. R. (2008), EPIC Change: How to Lead Change in the Global Age, San Francisco 2008.

Clark, T.; Salaman, G. (1996), The Management Guru as Organizational Witchdoctor, in: Organization, 3 (1996) 1, pp. 85-107

Clarke, M.; Meldrum, M. (2003), Creating change from below: early lessons for agents of change, in: The Leadership & Organization Development Journal, 20 (1999) 2, pp. 70-80

Coetsee, L. (1999), From Resistance to Commitment, in: Public Administration Quarterly, Summer 1999, pp. 204-222

Conger, J.A.; Spreitzer, G.M.; Lawler, E.E. III. (1999), The Leader's Change Handbook: An Essential Guide to Setting Direction and Taking Action, San Francisco 1999

Conner, D. (2005), Managing at the speed of change. How resilient managers succeed and prosper where others fail, Chichester 2005

Connor, D.; Horney, N.L.; Harrington, H.J. (1999), Project Change Management, Boston 1999

Connor, R. (2004), Institutional change for sustainable development, Cheltenham 2004

Cook, J.; Wharrad, H.; Windle, R.J.; Leeder, D.; Morales, R.; Boyle, T.; Alton, R. (2007), Implementations, change management and evaluation: A case study of the centre for excellence in teaching and learning in reusable learning objects, in: Journal of Organizational Transformation and Social Change, 4 (2007) 1, pp. 57-73

Cook, S.; Macaulay, S.; Coldicott, H. (2004), Change management excellence: using the four intelligences for successful organizational change, London 2004

Cooper, D.; Hinings, C.R.; Greenwood, R.; Brown, J.L. (1996), Sedimentation and Transformation in Organizational Change: The Case of Canadian Law Firms, in: Organization Studies. 17 (1996) 4, pp. 623-648.

Cornelissen, J. (2004), What are we playing at? Theatre, organization, and the use of metaphor, in: Organization Studies, 25 (2004) 5, pp. 705-726

Cosack, S.; Guthridge, M.; Lawson, E. (2010), Retaining key employees in times of change in: McKinsey Quarterly, 19 (2010) 3, pp. 135-139

Covin, T.; Kilmann, R. (1990), Participant Perceptions of Positive and Negative Influences on Large-Scale Change, in: Group & Organization Management, 15 (1990) 2, S. 233–248

Craine, K. (2007), Managing the Cycle of Change, in: The Information Management Journal, Sept. 2007, pp. 44-50

Crosby, L.A.; Johnson, S.L. (2005), Change Agents – Chief marketing officers are positioned to create customer-loyalty centered enterprises, in: Marketing Management, Nov. 2005, pp. 12-13

Crucini, C.; Kipping, M. (2001), Management consultancies as global change agents?, in: Journal of Organizational Change Management, 14 (2001) 6, pp. 570-589

Cummings, T.G.; Worley, C.G. (2009), Organization development & change, 9th ed., Mason 2009

Davidow, W.H.; Malone, M.S., The Virtual Corporation: Structuring and Revitalizing the Corporation For the 21st Century, New York (NY) 1992

Deeg, J. (2009), Organizational Discontinuity: Integrating Evolutionary and Revolutionary Change Theories, in: management revue, 20 (2009) 2, pp. 190-208

Deering, A.; Cook, A.; Jonk, G.; van Hall, A. (2008), Internet tools enable organizational transformation from the inside out: the Nokia Siemens Networks case, in: Strategy & Leadership, 36 (2008) 5, pp. 34-37

Denison, D. R.; Hooijberg, R.; Quinn, R.E. (1995), Paradox and Performance: Toward a Theory of Behavioral Complexity in Managerial Leadership, in: Organization Science 6 (1995) 5, pp. 524-540

Devos, G.; Buelens, M.; Bouckenooghe, D. (2007), Contribution of Content, Context, and Process to Understanding Openness to Organizational Change: Two Experimental Simulation Studies, in: The Journal of Social Psychology, 147 (2007) 6, pp. 607–629

Dibella, A. (2007), Critical Perceptions of organizational change, in: Journal of Change Management, 7 (2007) 3-4, pp. 231-242

Dittrich, K.; Dusters, G. (2007), Networking as a Means to Strategy Change: The Case of Open Innovation in Mobile Telephony, in: The Journal of Product Innovation Management, 24 (2007), pp. 510-521

Donaldson, G. (1994), Corporate Restructuring: Managing the Change Process from Within, Boston, 1994

Doppler, K.; Lauterburg, C. (2001), Managing Corporate Change, Berlin, Heidelberg 2001

Dosi, G. (2007), Understanding industrial and corporate change, Oxford u.a. 2007

Dotlich, D.L.; Cairo, P. C.; Rhinesmith, S. H. (2009), Leading in times of crisis: navigating through complexity, diversity, and uncertainty to save your business, San Francisco 2009

Dover, P. (2003), Change agents at work: Lessons from Siemens Nixdorf, in: Journal of Change Management, 3 (2003) 3, pp. 243-257

Dover, P.; Lawler, W.; Hilse, H. (2008), Creating an Entrepreneurial Mindset at Infincon Technologies: The Infineon-Babson Global Manager Development Programme, in: Journal of Change Management, 8 (2008), 3-4, pp. 265-277

Doyle, M. (2001), Dispersing change agency in high velocity change organizations: issues and implications, in: Leadership & Organization Development Journal, 22 (2001) 7, pp. 321-329

Driver, M. (2009), From Loss to Lack: Stories of Organizational Change as Encounters with Failed Fantasies of Self, Work and Organization, in: Organization, 16 (2009) 3, pp. 353-369

Drucker, P. (1999), Management Challenges for the 21st Century, New York 1999

Drucker, P. (2001), Leading In a Time of Change: What It Will Take to Lead Tomorrow, New York 2001

Duck, J. D. (1993), Managing Change: The Art of Balancing, in: Harvard Business Review, 71 (1993) 6, pp. 109-118

Dunphy, D. und Stace, D. (1988), Transformational and Coercive Strategies for Planned Organizational Change: Beyond the O.D. Model, in: Organization Studies, 9 (1988) 3, pp. 317-334

Dunphy, D.; Griffiths, A.; Benn, S. (2007), Organizational change for corporate sustainability: a guide for leaders and change agents of the future, London 2007

Ebersbach, A.; Glaser, M.; Heigl, R. (2006), Wiki: web collaboration, Berlin 2006

Edosomwan, J.A. (1996), Organizational Transformation and Process Reengineering, London 1996

Edwards, M.G. (2005), The integral holon - A holonomic approach to organizational change and transformation, in: Journal of Organizational Change Management, 18 (2005) 3, pp. 269-288

Eisenbach, R.; Watson, K.; Pillai, R. (1999), Transformational Leadership in the Context of Organizational Change, in: Journal of Organizational Change Management, 12 (1999) 2, pp. 80-88

Emerald ManagementFirst (2012), http://strategic-change-management.com/change-management-53/

Farjoun, M. (2010), Beyond Dualism: Stability and Change as a Duality, Academy of Management Review, 35 (2010) 2, pp. 202-225

Farmer, N. (2008), The invisible organization: how informal networks can lead organizational change, Burlington 2008

Ferdig, M. A. (2007), Sustainability Leadership: Co-creating a ASustainable Future, in: Journal of Change Management, 7 (2007) 1, pp. 25-35

Fields, D. (2007), Governance in Permanent Whitewater: the board's role in planning and implementing organizational change, in: Corporate Govermamce, 15 (2007) 2, pp. 334-344

Fincham, R. (1999), The consultant-client relationship: critical perspectives on the management of organizational change, in: Journal of Management Studies, 36 (1999) 3, pp. 335-351

Flamholtz, E.; Randle, Y. (2008), Leading strategic change: bridging theory and practice, 3. ed., Cambridge 2008

Fombrun, C. J. (1992), Turning points: creating strategic change in corporations, New York 1992

Ford, J.; Ford, L. (2009), Decoding Resistance to Change, in: Harvard Business Review, 87 (2009) 4, pp. 99-103

Ford, J.D.; Ford, L.W.; D'Amelio, A. (2008), Resistance to change: The rest of the story, in: Academy of Management Review, 33 (2008) 2, pp. 362-377

Ford, R. (2006), Open-processional Change: three principles of reciprocal-relational power, in: Journal of Change Management, 6 (2006) 2, pp. 193–216

Foster, R.N.; Kaplan, S. (2001), Creative Destruction: Why Companies that are Built to Last Underperform the Market – and How to Successfully Transform Them, New York 2001

Frappaolo, C.(2002),Knowledge Management,Oxford 2002

Furnham, A. (2002), Managers as change agents, in: Journal of Change Management, 3 (2002) 1, pp. 21-29

Galavan, R.; Murray, J.; Markides, C. (2008), Strategy, innovation, and change: Challenges for management, Oxford 2008

Gallos, J.V. (eds., 2006), Organization Development, San Francisco 2006

Gao, J. et al. (2011), Service-oriented manufacturing: a new product pattern and manufacturing paradigm, in: Journal of Intelligent Manufacturing, 22 (2011) 3, pp. 435-446

Garatt, B. (2005), Organizational change, learning and metrics: hard and soft ways to effective organizational change, in: Development and Learning in Organizations, 19 (2005) 6, pp. 4-6

Garnsey, E.; McGlade, J. (eds., 2006), Complexity and co-evolution. Continuity and change in socio-economic systems, Cheltenham 2006

Gartner Group (2012): Interpreting Technology Hype,
http://www.gartner.com/technology/research/methodologies/hype-cycle.jsp
[Retrieved: 13.02.2012]

Gersick, C. J. G. (1991), Revolutionary Change Theories: A multilevel Exploration, in: Academy of Management Review, 16 (1991) 1, pp.10-36

Gibson, C.; Birkinshaw, J. (2004), The antecedents, consequences, and mediating role of organizational ambidexterity, in: Academy of Management Journal, 47 (2004) 2, pp. 209–226

Gill, R. (2003), Change Management - or Change Leadership?, in: Journal of Change Management, 3 (2003) 4, pp. 307-318

Ginsberg, A.; Abrahamson, E. (1991), Champions of Change and Strategic Shifts: The Role of Internal and External Change Agents, in: Journal of Management Studies, 28 (1991) 2, pp. 173–190

Golembiewski, R.T. (2004), Twenty Questions for our Future: Challenges facing OD and ODers, or whatever it is labelled, in: Organization Development Journal, 22 (2004) 2, pp. 6-20

Goncalves, M. (2007), Change management: concepts and practice, New York 2007

Goodman, J.; Truss, C. (2004), The medium and the message: communicating effectively during a major change initiative, in: Journal of Change Management, 4 (2004) 3, pp. 217-228

Goodman, P.S.; Rousseau, D.M. (2004), Organizational change that produces results: The linkage approach, in: Academy of Management Executive, 18 (2004) 3, pp. 7-19

Graetz, F.; Smith, A. (2005), Organizing Forms in Change Management: The Role of Structures, Processes and Boundaries in a Longitudinal Case Analysis, in: Journal of Change Management, 5 (2005) 3, pp. 311–328

Greenwood, R.; Hinings, C. (1988), Underestimated strategic change: The contribution of archetypes, in: Academy of Management Journal, 36 (1993) 5, pp. 1052-1081

Griffith, J. (2002), Why change management fails, in: Journal of Change Management, 2 (2002) 4, pp. 297–305

Grundei, J. (2008), Are managers agents or stewards of their principals? Logic, critique, and reconciliation of two conflicting theories of corporate governance, in: Journal fuer Betriebswirtschaft, 58 (2008), pp. 141-166

Guy, G.R.; Beaman, K.V.; Weinstein, C.: Effecting Change in Business Enterprises. Current Trends in Change Management. URL:

http://www.corprenewal.co.za/pdf/effecting%20change%20in%20business%20enterprises.pdf
[Retrieved: 13.02.2012].

Hackman, J. R.; Edmondson, A.E. (2008), Groups as agents of change, In: T. Cummings (Ed.) Handbook of Organization Development, Thousand Oaks 2008, pp. 167-186

Hagel, J.; Brown, J. S.; Davison, L. (2009), The Big Shift. Measuring the Forces of Change, in: Harvard Business Review, 87 (2009) 7/8, pp. 86-89

Hagel, J.; Brown, J.S.; Davison, L. (2008), Shaping strategy in a world of constant disruption, in: Harvard Business Review, Oct. 2008, pp. 81-89

Halé, J.A.G. (1995), From concepts to capabilities. Understanding and exploiting change as a competitive advantage, Chichester 1995

Hambrick, D.; Nadler, D.A.; Tushman, M.L. (1998), Navigating Change: How CEO's, Top Teams, and Boards Steer Transformation, Boston 1998

Hamel, G.; Välikangas, L. (2003), The Quest for Resilience, in: Harvard Business Review, 81 (2003), 9, pp. 52 – 63

Hammer, M.; Champy, J. (1993), Reengineering the Corporation: A Manifesto for Business Revolution, New York 1993

Hannan, M. T.; Freeman, J. (1984), Structural Inertia and Organizational Change, in: American Sociological Review, 49 (1984) 2, pp. 149-164

Harrington, H. J.; Conner, D. R.; Horney, N. L. (2000), Project Change Management: Applying Change Management to Improvement Projects, New York 2000

Harris, J. (2001), The Learning Paradox: Gaining Success and Security in a World of Change, Chichester 2001

Harris, J. (2002), Blindsided: How to Spot the Next Breakthrough that Will Change Your Business Forever, Oxford 2002

Hartley, J.; Benington, J.; Binns, P. (1997), Researching the Roles of Internal-Change Agents in the Management of Organization Change, in: British Journal of Management, 8 (1997) 1, pp. 61–73

Harvard Business School (2006), Harvard Business Review on Leading Through Change, Boston 2006

Hayes, J. (2010), The theory and practice of change management, Basingstoke 2010

Heath, C. (2010), Making the emotional case for change, in: McKinsey Quarterly, 19 (2010) 2, pp. 88-97

Heifetz, R.; Grashow, A.; Linsky, M. (2009), Leadership in a (Permanent) Crisis-Harvard Business Review, 87 (2009) 7/8, pp. 62-69

Helfat, C.E. (2007), Dynamic capabilities: understanding strategic change in organizations, Malden, MA. 2007

Helfat, C.E.; Peteraf, M.A. (2009), Understanding dynamic capabilities: progress along a development path, in: Strategic Organization, 7 (2009) 1, pp. 91-102

Henry, J.; Mayle, D. (eds., 2002), Managing Innovation and Change, 2. ed., London, Thousand Oaks, New Delhi 2002

Heracleous, L. (2002), The contribution of a discursive view to understanding and managing organizational change, in: Strategic Change, 11 (2002) 5, pp. 253-261

Higgins, J.M.; McAllaster, C. (2004), If you want strategic change, don't forget to change your cultural artefacts, in: Journal of Change Management, 4 (2004) 1, pp. 63-73

Higgs, M.; Rowland D. (2000), Building change leadership capability: "The quest for change competence", in: Journal of Change Management, 1 (2000) 2, pp. 116-130

Higgs, M.; Rowland, D. (2001), Developing Change Leaders: Assessing the Impact of a Development Programme, in: Journal of Change Management, 2 (2001) 1, pp. 47–64

Higgs, M.; Rowland D. (2005), All Changes Great and Small: Approaches to Change and its Leadership, in: Journal of Change Management, 5 (2005) 2, pp. 121-151

Hobbs, B.; Aubry, M.; Thuillier, D. (2008), The project management office as an organizational innovation, in: International Journal of Project Management, 26 (2008), pp. 547–555

Holman, P.; Devane, T.; Cady, S. (2007), The change handbook: the definitive resource on today's best methods for engaging whole systems, San Francisco 2007

Hornstein, H. (2001), Organizational Development and Change Management: Don't Throw the Baby out with the Bath Water, in: Journal of Applied Behavioral Science, 37 (2001) 2, pp. 223–226

Hoverstadt, P. (2004), Mosaic transformation in organizations, in: Journal of Organizational Transformation and Social Change, 1 (2004) 2–3, pp. 163-177

Huff, A.S.; Huff, J.O.; Barr, P.S. (2000), When Firms Change Direction, Oxford 2000

Hughes, M. (2007), The Tools and Techniques of Change Management, in: Journal of Change Management, 7 (2007) 1, pp. 37-49

IBM Global Business Services (2008), Making Change Work, 2008

Isaksen, S.G. (2007), The climate for transformation: Lessons for leaders, in: Creativity and Innovation Management, 16 (2007) 1, pp. 3-15

Jack, S.; Drakopoulou Dodd, S.; Anderson, A.R. (2008), Change and the development of entrepreneurial networks over time: a processual perspective, in: Entrepreneurship & Regional Development, 20 (2008), pp. 125-159

Jackson; P.: Changing how you change,
http://www.ravenbrook.com/doc/2003/03/06/changing-how-you-change/
[Retrieved: 13.02.2012]

Jarrett, M. (2004), Tuning into the emotional drama of change: extending the consultant's bandwidth, in: Journal of Change Management, 4 (2004) 3, pp. 247-258.

Jarrett, M. (2003), The seven myths of change management, in: Business Strategy Review, 14 (2003) 4, pp. 22–29

Jellison, J.M. (2007), Managing the dynamics of change, New York 2007

Johnson, J. R. (1998), Embracing change: a leadership model for the learning organization, in: International Journal of Training and Development, 2 (1998) 2, pp. 141–150

Jones, J; Aguirre, D.A.; Calderone, M. (2004), 10 Principles of Change Management, in: Resilience Report strategy and business, Booz Allen Hamilton, April 2004

Joyce, W. (1999), Mega-Change: How Today's Leading Companies Have Transformed Their Workforces, New York 1999

Kaarst-Brown, M.L. (1999), Five symbolic roles of the external consultant, in: Journal of Organizational Change Management, 12 (1999) 6, pp. 540-561

Kane, G.; Fichman, R.; Gallaugher, J.; Glaser, J. (2009), Community Relations 2.0, in: Harvard Business Review, 87 (2009) 11, pp. 45–50

Kanter, E.M. (1983), The Change Masters: Innovation for Productivity in the American Corporation, New York 1983

Kanter, R. M. (1988), The Change Masters: Corporate Entrepreneurs at Work, Sydney 1988

Karp, T. (2006), Transforming Organizations for Organic Growth. The DNA of Change Leadership, Journal of Change Management, 6 (2006) 1, pp. 3-20

Karp, T. (2005), Unpacking the Mysteries of Change: Mental Modelling, in: Journal of Change Management, 5 (2005) 1, pp. 87–96

Katzenbach, J. (1996), Real Change Leaders: How You Can Create Growth and High Performance at Your Company, New York 1996

Kavanagh, M. H.; Ashkanasy, N. M. (2006), The Impact of Leadership and Change Management Strategy on Organizational Culture and Individual Acceptance of Change during a Merger, in: British Journal of Management, 17 (2006), pp. 81-103

Kerber, K.; Buono, A.F. (2005), Rethinking organizational change: Reframing the challenge of change management, in: Organizational Development Journal, 23 (2005) 3, pp. 23-38

Kerzner, H. (2009), Project Management, 10th ed., New York 2009

Kim, T.; Rhee, M. (2009), Exploration and exploitation: internal variety and environmental dynamism, in: Strategic Organization, 7 (2009) 1, pp. 11-41

Kim, T.-Y.; Oh, H.; Swaminathan, A. (2006), Framing Interorganizational Network Change: A Network Inertia Perspective, in: Academy of Management Review, 31 (2006) 3, pp. 704-720

Kinnie, N.; Hutchinson, S.; Purcell, J. (1998), Downsizing: Is it always lean and mean?, in: Personnel Review, 24 (1998) 4, pp. 296-311

Kirsch, C.; Chelliah, J.; Parry, W. (2011), Drivers of change: a contemporary model, in: Journal of Business Strategy, 32 (2011) 2, pp.13-20

Klein, S. (1996), A management communication strategy for change, in: Journal of Change Management, 9 (1996) 2, pp. 32-46

Kock, N.; D'Arcy, J. (2002), Resolving the E-collaboration Paradox: The Competing Influences of Media Naturalness and Compensatory Adaptation, in: Information Management and Consulting (Special Issue on Electronic Collaboration), 17 (2002) 4, pp. 72-78

Kotter, J. (1990), A Force For Change: How Leadership Differs From Management. New York, London 1990

Kotter, J. P. (1995), Leading Change: Why Transformation Efforts Fail, in: Harvard Business Review, 73 (1995) 3, pp. 59–65

Kotter, J.P. (1996), Leading Change, Cambridge 1996

Kotter, J.P.; Cohen, D.S. (2002), The Heart of Change. Real Life Stories of How People Change Their Organizations, Boston 2002

Koza, M. P.; Lewin, A.Y.(1998), The co-evolution of strategic alliances, in: Organization Science, 9 (1998) 3, pp. 255–264.

Kwahk, K.-Y.; Lee, J.-N. (2008), The role of readiness for change in ERP implementation: Theoretical bases and empirical validation in: Information & Management, 45 (2008), pp. 474–481

Lacey, M. (1995), Internal consulting: perspectives on the process of planned change, in: Journal of Organizational Change Management, 8 (1995) 3, pp. 75–84

LaClaire, J.A.; Rao, R.P. (2002), Helping employees embrace change, in: The McKinsey Quarterly, 11 (2002) 4, pp. 17-20

Lawler, E. E. III; Worley, C.P. (2006), Built to Change: How to Achieve Sustained Organizational Effectiveness, San Francisco 2006

Lawrence, T.; Dyck, B.; Maitlis, S.; Mauws, M. (2006), The Underlying Structure of Continuous Change, in: MIT Sloan Management Review, 47 (2006) 4, pp. 58–66

Lee, S.; Ahn, H. (2008), Assessment of process improvement from organizational change, in: Information & Management, 45 (2008), pp. 270–280

Lengnick-Hall, C.A.; Beck, T.E. (2005), Adaptive fit versus robust transformation: How organizations respond to environmental change, in: Journal of Management, 31 (2005) 5, pp. 738-757

Leppitt, N. (2006), Challenging the Code of Change: Part 1. Praxis does not make Perfect, in: Journal of Change Management, 6 (2006) 2, pp. 121-142

Leppitt, N. (2006), Challenging the Code of Change: Part 2. Crossing the Rubicon: Extending the Integration of Change, in: Journal of Change Management, 6 (2006) 3, pp. 235-256

Lévi-Strauss, C. (1966): The Savage Mind, Chicago 1966

Lewin, A.Y.; Volberda, H.W. (1999), Prolegomena on co-evolution: a framework for research on strategy and new organizational forms, Organization Science. 10 (1999) 5, pp. 519-534.

Lewis, M.; Maylor, H. (2007), Game playing and operations management education, in: International Journal of Production Economics 105 (2007), pp.134–149

Lientz, B. P.; Rea, K. P. (2004), Breakthrough IT change management - How to get enduring change results, Amsterdam 2004

Lines, R.; Selart, M.; Espedal, B.; Johansen, S.T. (2005), The Production of Trust During Organizational Change, in: Journal of Change Management, 5 (2005) 2, pp. 221-245

Lippitt, G. L.; Langseth, P.; Mossop, J. (1985), Implementing Organizational Change, San Francisco 1985

Lovas, B.; Ghoshal, S. (2000), Strategy as guided evolution, in: Strategic Management Journal, 21 (2000), pp. 875-896

Luscher, L.S.; Lewis, M.W. (2008), Organizational change and managerial sensemaking: Working through paradox, in: Academy of Management Journal, 51 (2008) 2, pp.221-240

March, J. G. (1981), Footnotes to Organizational Change, in: Administrative Science Quarterly, 26 (1981) 4, pp. 563-577

Marek, S.A.; Sibbald, A.M.; Bagher, M. (2006), Implementing web-assisted learning and engaging academic staff in the change process, in: Journal of Organizational Transformation and Social Change, 3 (2006) 3, pp. 269-284

Marshak, R.J. (2004), Morphing: The leading edge of organizational change in the twenty-first century, in: Organization Development Journal, 22 (2004) 3, pp. 8-21

Marshak, R.J.; Grant, D. (2008), Organizational Discourse and New Organization Development Practices, in: British Journal of Management, 19 (2008), pp. 7-19

Massey, C.; Walker, R. (1999), Aiming organizational learning: consultants as agents of change, in: The Learning Organization, 6 (1999) 1, pp. 38–44

McAfee, A. (2006), Enterprise 2.0 – The Dawn of Emergent Collaboration, in: MIT Sloan Management Review, 47 (2006) 3, pp. 20-28.

McDonald, N. (2006), Organizational Resilience and Industrial Risk. In: Hollnagel, E.; Woods, D.; Leveson, N. (eds.), Resilience Engineering: Concepts and precepts, Aldershot 2006, pp. 155-180

McManus, S.; Seville, E.; Brunsdon, D.; Vargo, J. (2007): Resilience Management: A Framework for Assessing and Improving the Resilience of Organizations, Resilient Organizations Research Report 2007/01, http://www.resorgs.org.nz/pubs/Resilience%20Management%20Research%20Repor t%20ResOrgs%2007-01.pdf [Retrieved: 13.02.2012]

McKinsey (2006), Organizing for successful change management - A McKinsey Global Survey, in: The McKinsey Quarterly, 15 (2006) 2, pp. 1–8

McKinsey (2009): How companies are benefiting from Web 2.0: A McKinsey global Survey. URL: https://www.mckinseyquarterly.com/How_companies_are_benefiting_from_Web_2 0_McKinsey_Global_Survey_Results_2432 [Retrieved: 13.02.2012]

McKinsey (2010), What successful transformations share, http://www.ihrim.org/Pubonline/Wire/April2010/Transformations.pdf [Retrieved: 13.02.2012]

Mento, A. J.; Jones, R. M.; Dirndorfer, W. (2002), A Change Management Process: Grounded in Both Theory and Practice, in: Journal of Change Management, 3 (2002) 1, pp. 45-59

Meyer, C.B.; Stensaker, I.G. (2006), Developing Capacity for Change, in: Journal of Change Management, 6 (2006) 2, pp. 217–231

Miles, R. (2010), Accelerating Corporate Transformations (Don't Lose Your Nerve!), in: Harvard Business Review, 88 (2010) 1, pp. 68–75

Miller, D. (1982), Evolution and Revolution: A Quantum View of Structural Change in Organizations, in: Journal of Management Studies, 19 (1982) 2, pp. 131-151

Mills, J.H.; Dye, K.; Mills, A.J. (2007), Understanding organizational change, London 2007

Miller, D. (2002), Sucessful Change Leaders: What makes them? What do they do that is different?, in: Journal of Change Management, 2 (2002) 4, pp. 359–368

MindTools (2012). Change Management - Making organization change happen effectively, retrieved from http://www.mindtools.com/pages/article/newPPM_87.htm

Mintzberg, H. (1979),TheStructuring of Organizations, Englewood Cliffs, NJ 1979

Mintzberg, H. (2009), Rebuilding Companies as Communities, in: Harvard Business Review, 87 (2009) 7/8, pp. 140 143

Mishra, A.K.; Mishra, K.E.; Spreitzer, G.M. (2009), Downsizing the company without downsizing morale, in: MIT Sloan Management Review, 50 (2009) 3, pp. 39-44

Moore, J.S.: SPA©E: A New Synthesis of Ideas for Organizational Turnaround, in: Journal of Change Management, 7 (2007) 1, pp. 51–68

More, E. (1998), Managing Changes: Exploring State of the Art, Greenwich 1998

Morgan, D.E.; Zeffane, R. (2003), Employee involvement, organizational change and trust in management, in: Int. J. of Human Resource Management, 14 (2003) 2, pp. 55 75

Nadler, D. A. (1988), Concepts for the Management or Organizational Change, in: Tushman, M. L.; Moore, W. L. (eds.), Readings in Management of Innovation, New York 1988, pp. 718-731

Nadler, D.A.; Tushman, M.L. (1990), Beyond charismatic leader: Leadership and organizational change, in: California Management Review, Winter 1990, pp.77-97

Nadler, D. A.; Tushman, M. L. (1995), Types of Organizational Change: From Incremental Improvement to Discontinuous Transformation, in: Nadler, D. A.; Shaw, R. B.; Walton A. E. (eds.), Discontinuous Change: Leading Organizational Transformation, San Francisco 1995, pp. 15-34

Nadler, D. (1998), Champions of Change: How CEOs and Their Companies are Mastering the Skills of Radical Change, San Francisco 1998

Nag, R.; Corley, K.G.; Gioia, D.A. (2007), The intersection of organizational identity, knowledge, and practice: Attempting strategic change via knowledge grafting, in: Academy of Management Journal, 50 (2007) 4, pp. 821–847

Nalebuff, B. J.; Brandenburger, A. M. (1996),Co-opetition: A revolutionary mindset that combines competition and cooperation in the marketplace, London 1996

Neus, A.; Scherf, P. (2005), Opening minds: Cultural change with the introduction of open-source collaboration methods, in: IBM Systems Journal, 44 (2005) 2, pp. 215-225

Neves, P.; Caetano, A. (2006), Social Exchange Processes in Organizational Change: The Roles of Trust and Control, in: Journal of Change Management, 6 (2006) 4, pp. 351–364

Nikolaou, I.; Gouras, A.; Vakola, M.; Bourantas, D. (2007), Selecting change agents: Exploring traits and skills in a simulated environment, in: Journal of Change Management, 7 (2007) 3-4, pp. 291-313

Nonaka, I. (1994), A Dynamic Theory of Organizational Knowledge Creation, in: Organization Science, 5 (1994) 1, pp. 14-37

Nonaka, I.; von Krogh, G. (2009), Tacit Knowledge and Knowledge Conversion, in: Organization Science 20 (2009), pp. 635-652

North, D.C. (2009), Institutions, institutional change and economic performance, 27. ed., Cambridge 2009

O'Toole, J.; Galbraith, J.; Lawler, E. (2002), When two (or more) heads are better than one: The promise and pitfalls of shared leadership, in: California Management Review, 44 (2002) 4, pp. 65-83

Olson, E.E. et al. (2001), Facilitating Organizational Change: Lessons from Complexity Science, New York 2001

Piotrowski, C; Armstrong, T.R. (2004), Organization Development: Recent Trends and Current Directions, in: Organization Development Journal, 22 (2004) 2, pp. 48-54

Ottaway, R.; Cooper, C. (1978), Moving Toward a Taxonomy of Change Agents, in: International Studies of Management & Organization, 8 (1978) 1-2, pp. 7–21

Palmer, I.; Dunford, R. (2008), Organizational Change and the Importance of Embedded Assumptions, in: British Journal of Management, 19 (2008), pp. 20-32

Palmer, I.; Dunford, R.; Akin, G. (2009), Managing organizational change - A multiple perspectives approach, 2. ed., Boston, Mass. 2009

Pasmore, W. A. (1994), Creating Strategic Change: Designing the Flexible, High-Performing Organization, Toronto 1994

Pasmore, W.; Fagans, M. (1992), Participation, Individual Development, and Organizational Change: A Review and Synthesis, in: Journal of Management, 18 (1992) 2, pp. 375–397

Pasternak, B.A.; Viscio, A.J. (1999), The Centerless Corporation. London 1999

Paton, S.; Boddy, D. (1999), Stuck in the middle: a case study investigating the gap between top-down and bottom-up change, in: Journal of General Management, 32 (2007) 4, pp. 39-51

Pellegrinelli, S.; Garagna, L. (2009), Towards a conceptualisation of PMOs as agents and subjects of change and renewal, in: International Journal of Project Management, 27 (2009) 1, pp. 19–30

Pendelbury, J.; Grouard, B.; Meston, F. (1998), The Ten Keys to Successful Change Management, Chichester 1998

Peón-Escalante, I.; Oliva-López, E.; Badillo-Piña, I. (2008), Methodology for an organizational development process: An integral and sustainable qualitative transformation of complex inter-institutional networks, working on social and environmental problem situations, in: Journal of Organizational Transformation and Social Change, 5 (2008) 1, pp. 31-44

Pettigrew, A. M. (1988), The Management of strategic change, 1988

Pettigrew, A. M.; Whipp, R. (1993), Managing change for competitive success, Oxford 1993

Pettigrew, A. M.; Woodman, R. W.; Cameron, K. S. (2001), Studying Organizational Change and Development: Challenges for Future Research, in: Academy of Management Journal, 44 (2001) 4, pp. 697-713

Peus, C.; Frey, D.; Gerkhardt, M.; Fischer, P. (2009), Leading and Managing Organizational Change Initiatives, in: management revue, 20 (2009) 2, pp. 158–175

Pinchot, G.; Pellman, R. (1985), Intrapreneuring. Why You Don't Have to Leave the Corporation to Become as Entrepreneur. New York 1995

Piotrowski,C.; Armstrong, T.R. (2004), The Research Literature in Organization Development: Recent Trends and Current Directions, in: Organization Development Journal, 22 (2004) 2, pp. 48-54

Pitt, L.; Murgolo-Poore, M.; Dix, S. (2001), Changing change management: The intranet as catalyst, in: Journal of Change Management, 2 (2001) 2, pp. 106-114

Pitt, M; Sims, D.; McAulay, L. (2002), Promoting strategic change: 'playmaker' roles in organizational agenda formation, in: Strategic Change, 11 (2002) 3, pp. 155–172

PMI (2008), A Guide to the Project Management Body of Knowledge, 4th ed., Newtown Square, PA 2008

Previde, P.G.; Rotondi, P. (2008), Leading and Managing Change through Adaptors and Innovators, in: Journal of Leadership Studies, 3 (1996) 3, pp. 120-134

Probst, G.; Raisch, S. (2005), Organizational crisis: The logic of failure, in: Academy of Management Executive, 19 (2005) 1, pp. 90-105

Prokesch, S. (2009), How GE teaches teams to lead change, in: Harvard Business Review, (2009) 1, pp. 99-106

Pugh, L. (2000), Change Management in Information Services, Aldershot 2000

Quinn, J. B. (1978), Strategic Change: "Logical Incrementalism", in: MIT Sloan Management Review, 20 (1978) 1, pp. 7-21

Quinn, J. B. (1980), Strategies for Change: Logical Incrementalism, Homewood, Ill. 1980

Rademacher, M.; Kaufmann, L. (2008), Successful benchmarking: From Imitation to the Blue Ocean approach, in: io new management, Nov. 2008

Rafferty, A.E.; Griffin, M.A. (2004), Dimensions of transformational leadership: Conceptual and empirical extensions, in: The Leadership Quarterly, 15 (2004), 6, pp. 329-354

Ragsdell, G. (2000), Engineering a paradigm shift? A holistic approach to organizational change management, in: Journal of Organizational Change Management, 13 (2000) 2, pp. 104-120

Raja, J. Z.; Green, S. D.; Leiringer, R. (2010), Concurrent and disconnected change programmes: strategies in support of servitization and the implementation of business partnering, in: Human Resource Management Journal, 20 (2010) 3, pp. 258–276

Rajagopalan, N.; Spreitzer, G. M. (1996), Toward a Theory of Strategic Change: A Multi-lens Perspective and Integrative Framework, in: Academy of Management Review, 22 (1996) 1, pp. 48-79

Rampersad, H.K. (2004), Learning and unclearing in accordance with organizational change, in: Organization Development Journal, 22 (2004) 4, pp. 43-60

Reiss, M. (2001), Interprise: Leading virtual companies, in: Grabner-Kraeuter, S.; Wuehrer, G.A. (eds.): Trends in International Management, Linz 2001, pp. 133-159

Reiss, M. (2004), A Complexity-Based Approach to Production Management in the New Economy, in: Fandel, G. et al. (eds.): Modern Concepts of the Theory of the Firm, Berlin, Heidelberg 2004, pp. 264-284

Reiss, M. (2009), Blended Change Management: Conceptual and Empirical Investigation of Blending Patterns, in: iBusiness, 1 (2009) 1, pp. 47-56

Reiss, M.; Koser, M.: From Mass Customization to Mass Personalization. A New Competitive Strategy in E-Business, in: Bensberg, F.; vom Brocke, J.; Schultz, M.B. (eds.): Trendberichte zum Controlling, Heidelberg 2004, pp. 285-310

Resilience in Change (2012), http://resilienceinchange.com/

Rickards, T. (1999), Creativity and the Management of Change, Oxford 1999

Rising (2012), http://strategic-change-management.com/change-management-53/

Robertson, B. J. (2006), Holacracy: A Complete System for Agile Organizational Governance and Steering, in: Agile Project Management, Vol. 7, 2006, No. 7, pp. 1-21

Roland Berger Strategy Consultants (2003), Restructuring in Germany – earlier, faster and stronger, Düsseldorf 2003

Rooney, M.J. (2005), Toyota System Production Meets Large Scale Change: A Synergy for Sustainable Improvements, in: Organization Development Journal, 23 (2005) 2, pp. 21-28

Rouse, W. B. (eds., 2006), Enterprise transformation: understanding and enabling fundamental change, Hoboken, N.J. 2006

Rüegg-Stürm, J. (2005), The New St.Gallen Management Model - Basic Categories of an Approach to Integrated Management, Basingstoke 2005

Russ, T. (2008), Communicating Change: A Review and Critical Analysis of Programmatic and Participatory Implementation Approaches, in: Journal of Change Management, 8 (2008) 3-4, pp. 199–211

Saka, A. (2003), Internal change agents' view of the management of change problem, in: Journal of Change Management, 16 (2003) 5, pp. 480-496

Samples-help (2012), http://www.samples-help.org.uk/mission-statements/corporate-vision-statements.htm

Sanchez, R.; Heene, A. (2002), Managing Strategic Change: A Systems View of Strategic Organizational Change and Strategic Flexibility, in: Morecroft, J.; Sanchez, R.; Heene, A. (eds.), Systems Perspective on Resources, Capabilities, and Management Processes, Amsterdam, 2002, pp. 71-91

Santos, V.; Garcia, T. (2006), Organizational change: the role of managers' mental models, in: Journal of Change Management, 6 (2006) 3, pp. 305–320

Schein, E. (1994), The concept of "client" from a process consultation perspective: A guide for change agents, in: Journal of Organizational Change Management, 10 (1994) 3, pp. 202–216

Schreyögg, G. (2001), Organizational theatre and organizational change, in: Diskussionsbeiträge Folge 13 des Instituts für Management der Freien Universität Berlin, Berlin 2001

Schwarz, G.M.; Huber, G.P. (2008), Challenging organizational change research, in: British Journal of Management, 19 (2008), pp. 1-6

Scott, B. (2007), Facilitating organizational change: Some sociocybernetic principles, in: Journal of Organizational Transformation and Social Change, 4 (2007) 1, pp.13-24

Self, D.R.; Armenakis, A.A.; Schraeder, M. (2007), Organizational Change Content, Process, and Context: A Simultaneous Analysis of Employee Reactions, in: Journal of Change Management, 7 (2007) 2, pp. 211–229

Senge, P. (2000), The Dance of Change, New York 2000

Shaw, P. (1997), Intervening in the shadow systems of organizations. Consulting from a complexity perspective, in: Journal of Organizational Change, 10 (1997) 3, pp. 235–250

Sirkin, H. L.; Keenman, P.; Jackson, A. (2005), The Hard Side of Change Management, in: Harvard Business Review, 83 (2005) 10, pp. 108–118

Smid, G.; van Hout, E.; Burger, Y. (2006), Leadership in Organizational Change: Rules for Successful Hiring in Interim Management, in: Journal of Change Management, 6 (2006) 1, pp. 35–51

Smollan, R. K. (2006), Minds, Hearts and Deeds: Cognitive, Affective and Behavioural Responses to Change, in: Journal of Change Management, 6 (2006) 2, pp. 143–158

Spector, B. (2007), Implementing Organizational Change. Theory and Practice, Upper Saddle River, N.J. 2007

Speight, R. (1999), Changing the way we change: Managing the soft strands of change at British Airways World Cargo, in: Journal of Change Management, 1 (1999) 1, pp. 91–99

Stacey, R.D. (2011), Strategic Management and Organizational Dynamics, 6. ed., London et al. 2011

Stalinski, S. (2004), Organizational intelligence: A systems perspective, in: Organization Development Journal, 22 (2004) 2, pp. 55-67

Strategies for Managing Change (2012), http://www.strategies-for-managing-change.com/change-management-tools.html

Styhre, A. (2004), Becoming empowered: organization change in a telecom company, in: Int. J. of Human Resource Management, No. 15 (2004), pp.1445-1462

Sull, D. (2009), Competing through organizational agility, in: The McKinsey Quarterly, 19 (2010) 1, pp. 1-9

Sullivan, W. (2002), Aligning individual and organizational values to support change, in: Journal of Change Management, 2 (2002) 3, pp. 247-254

Swailes, S. (2004), Commitment to change: Profiles of commitment and in-role performance, in: Personnel Review, 33 (2004) 2, pp. 187–204

Sweet, T.; Heritage, V. (2000), How managers gain commitment to change: Using a simple cultural questionnaire to involve people, in: Journal of Change Management, 1 (2000) 2, pp. 164–178

Swierczek, F. (1980), Collaborative Intervention and Participation in Organizational Change, in: Group & Organization Management, 5 (1980) 4, pp. 438–452

Sydow, J.; Schreyögg, G.; Koch, J. (2009), Organizational path dependence: Opening the black box, in: Academy of Management Review, 34(2009) 4, pp. 689-709.

Taffinder, P. (1998), Big Change: A Route-Map for Corporate Transformation, Chichester 1998

Tanner, R.; Sternin, J. (2005), You're company's secret change agents, in: Harvard Business Review, 83 (2005) 5, pp. 72–81

Teece, D. J.; Pisano, G. (1994), The Dynamic Capabilities of Firms: An Introduction, in: Industrial and Corporate Change, 3 (1994) 3, pp. 537-556

Teece, D. (2007), Explicating dynamic capabilities: the nature and microfoundations of (sustainable) enterprise performance, in: Strategic Management Journal, 28 (2007) 13, pp 1319-1350

Thiry, M.; Deguire, M. (2007), Recent developments in project-based organizations, in: International Journal of Project Management, 25 (2007), pp. 649–658

Thorne, K. (2003), Blended learning: how to integrate online & traditional learning, London 2003

Tiberius, V. (2011), Towards a "Planned Path Emergence" View on Future Genesis, in: Journal of Future Studies 15 (2011) 4, pp. 9-24

Tichy, N. (1974), Current Trends in Organizational Change, in: Columbia Journal of World Business, 9 (1974) 1, pp. 98-111

Tichy, N. (1978), Current and future trends for change agentry, in: Group Organization Management, 3 (1978), pp. 467-482

Tushman, M.L.; Anderson, P. (2002), Managing Strategic Innovation and Change: A Collection of Readings, New York 2002

Välikangas, L.(2010), The Resilient Organization: how adaptive cultures thrive even when strategy fails, New York 2010

Van Buren, M.; Safferstone, T. (2009), Quick wins paradox, in: Harvard Business Review, Jan. 2009, pp. 55-61

Van de Ven, A. H.; Huber, G. P. (1990), Longitudinal Field Research Methods for Studying Processes of Organizational Change, in: Organization Science, 1 (1990) 3, pp. 213-219

Van de Ven, A. H.; Poole, M. S. (1995), Explaining Development and Change in Organizations, in: Academy of Management Review, 20 (1995) 3, pp. 510-540

Van de Ven, A. H.; Poole, M. S. (2005), Alternative Approaches for Studying Organizational Change, in: Organization Studies, 26 (2005) 9, pp. 1377-1404

Varney, G. (2006), Challenges facing the field of organization development: An academic perspective, in: Organization Development Journal, 24 (2006) 1, pp. 101-105

Venkatraman, M. P. (1989), Opinion Leaders, Adopters, and Communicative Adopters: A Role Analysis, in: Psychology & Marketing, 6 (1989) 1, pp. 51-68

Vithessonthi, C.; Schwaninger, M. (2008), Job motivation and self-confidence for learning and development as predictors of support for change, in: Journal of Organizational Transformation and Social Change, 5 (2008) 2, pp. 141-157

Vrakking, W. (1995), The implementation game, in: Journal of Organizational Change Management, 8 (1995) 3, pp. 31-46

Watkins, M.D. (2009), Picking the right transition strategy, in: Harvard Business Review, Jan. 2009, pp. 47-53

Weick, K.E. (1979), Social psychology of organizing, 2nd ed., Reading, MA 1979

Whitmore, J. (2004), Something really has to change: change management as an imperative rather than a topic, in: Journal of Change Management, 4 (2004) 1, pp. 5–14

Whittle, A.; Mueller, F.; Mangan, A. (2009), Storytelling and ‚Character‘: Victims, Villains and Heroes in a Case of Technological Change, in: Organization, 16 (2009) 3, pp. 425-442

Wilson, J; Hynes, N. (2009), Co-evolution of firms and strategic alliances: Theory and empirical evidence, in: Technological Forecasting & Social Change 76 (2009) 5, pp. 620–628

Wissema, J.G. (2001), Offensive change management with the step-by-step method, in: Journal of Change Management, Vol. 1, No. 4, 2001, pp. 332–343

Woodman, R.W. (2008), Discourse, Metaphor and Organizational Change: the Wine is New, but the Bottle is Old, in: British Journal of Management, 19 (2008), pp. 33-37

Woodward, S.; Hendry, C. (2004), Leading and Coping with Change, in: Journal of Change Management, 4 (2004) 2, pp. 155-183

Wooten, K.; White, L. (1989), Toward a Theory of Change Role Efficacy, in: Human Relations, 42 (1989) 8, pp. 651–669

Worren, N.; Ruddle, K.; Moore, K. (1999), From Organizational Development to Change Management: The Emergence of a New Profession, in: The Journal of Applied Behavioral Science, 35 (1999) 3, pp. 273–286

Zell, D. (2003), Organizational Change as a Process of Death, Dying, and Rebirth, in: Journal of Applied Behavioral Science, 39 (2003) 1, pp. 73-96